Media, Gender and Identity

An introduction

David Gauntlett

London and New York

First published 2002
by Routledge
11 New Fetter Lane, London EC4P 4EE

Simultaneously published in the USA and Canada
by Routledge
29 West 35th Street, New York, NY 10001

Routledge is an imprint of the Taylor & Francis Group

Typeset in Galliard by
Wearset Ltd, Boldon, Tyne and Wear
Printed and bound by
The Cromwell Press, Trowbridge, Wiltshire

British Library Cataloguing in Publication Data
A catalogue record for this book is available from the British Library

Library of Congress Cataloging in Publication Data
A catalog record for this book has been requested

ISBN 0–415–18959–4 (hbk)
ISBN 0–415–18960–8 (pbk)

To my students

(for the discussions about existing texts,
and for telling me to do a new one)

and for Susan

CONTENTS

Acknowledgements   ix

1. **Introduction**   **1**
2. **Some background debates**   **19**
3. **Representations of gender in the past**   **42**
4. **Representations of gender today**   **57**
5. **Giddens, modernity and self-identity**   **91**
6. **Michel Foucault: discourses and lifestyles**   **115**
7. **Queer theory and fluid identities**   **134**
8. **Men's magazines and modern male identities**   **152**
9. **Women's magazines and female identities today**   **181**
10. **Directions for living: role models, pop music and self-help discourses**   **211**
11. **Conclusions**   **247**

References   257
Index   271

ACKNOWLEDGEMENTS

This is the book that I have been wanting to write for many years. Many people, therefore, have helped me form my ideas on media, gender and identity.

First of all I would like to thank those people who were kind enough to read parts of the text and provide their perceptive comments: Susan Giblin, Ross Horsley, Clare O'Farrell, Nick Stevenson and Kirsten Pullen. Ross also gave me generous access to the outstanding movie database stored in his brain. I am also very grateful to the people who very kindly gave their time to be interviewed by email about lifestyle magazines, pop stars and other matters.

Marsha Jones, Beverley Skeggs, Mike Mulkay, and the late Arthur Brittan, all helped to enthuse me with the study of media and/or gender and/or identity, through their teaching and support. At Routledge, Christopher Cudmore, Rebecca Barden and Kate Ahl were always patient and helpful. At Wearset, Carl Gillingham was a careful and perceptive copy editor.

My ideas about media, gender and identity have been most thoroughly challenged by several cohorts of ruthlessly intelligent students at the Institute of Communications Studies, University of Leeds, since the mid-1990s, so big and broad thanks to all of them. Thank you to my ICS colleagues too, especially Graham Roberts, Phil Taylor, Robin Brown, Jayne Rodgers and Isobel Rich. I am also very grateful to Annette Hill and David Buckingham for academic encouragement.

Visitors to the theory.org.uk website ('Social theory for fans of popular culture — Popular culture for fans of social theory') regularly send me thought-provoking responses, so I am grateful to them. Thanks also to Layla Heyes, Emma McDevitt, Hayley Jones, Jenny Wood, Aled Prosser, Leela Cottey, Jawad Malik, Derrick Cameron, David Silver, Carolina Repiso Toquero and Angela Martini. Finally, loving thanks to Susan Giblin, for all of the discussion, inspiration and support.

PICTURE CREDITS

Photographs and images created or compiled by David Gauntlett, except:

Page 11, photograph of Claire by Vanessa Bridge, reproduced by kind permission. Page 224, drawing of Britney Spears by Carolina Repiso Toquero, reproduced by kind permission.

Chapter 1

INTRODUCTION

WHY EXPLORE THE relationship between media, gender and identity? Media and communications are a central element of modern life, whilst gender and sexuality remain at the core of how we think about our identities. With the media containing so many images of women and men, and messages about men, women and sexuality today, it is highly unlikely that these ideas would have no impact on our own sense of identity. At the same time, though, it's just as unlikely that the media has a direct and straightforward effect on its audiences. It's unsatisfactory to just assume that people somehow copy or borrow their identities from the media. To complicate things further, we live in changing times. What we learned in the 1960s, 1970s or 1980s about media and gender might not be so relevant today, because the media has changed, and people's attitudes have changed. The 'role models' of times gone by might be rather laughable and embarrassing now.

This book sets out to establish what messages the media sends to contemporary audiences about gender, and what the impact of those messages might be. We will consider some of the previous writings on media and identity, but rather than dwell on the same set of works that textbooks have covered in the past – a set of concepts and ideas which I will suggest are not always so helpful today – this book seeks to introduce the reader to particular social theorists (such as Anthony Giddens, Michel Foucault and Judith Butler) whose ideas about identity give us more to work with when considering the role of the media in the formation and negotiation of gender and sexual identities.

WHY MEDIA INFLUENCES ARE IMPORTANT

In modern societies, people typically consume many hours of television each week, look at magazines and other publications, surf the Internet, pass billboards, go to the movies, and are generally unable to avoid popular culture and advertising. In the most obvious example, people in Europe and the USA typically spend three or four hours per day watching TV. That's a lot of information going into people's heads – even if they don't see it as 'information', and even if they say they're not really paying much attention to it. (For statistics on leisure activities and media consumption, see www.worldopinion.com, www.statistics.gov.uk.)

It seems obvious and inevitable, then, that we will be affected by these experiences somehow. The media shows us situations and relationships from other people's points of view – indeed, it is part of the eternal fascination of drama that we can see 'how the world works' in lives other than our own. This could hardly fail to affect our own way of conducting ourselves, and our expectations of other people's behaviour. For example:

- domestic or romantic dramas (including soap operas) show us how neighbours, friends and lovers interact. When a person has a lover for the first time in their lives, how do they know how to behave? And where do we learn the typical shape and content of friendships? Our main reference points are surely films and TV.
- magazines aimed at women, and increasingly those for men, contain all kinds of advice on how to live, look and interact. Even if we only read these items in an ironic state of mind, it must all sink in somewhere.
- movie heroes, female or male, are almost uniformly assertive and single-minded. The attractive toughness of these stars, whilst not necessarily a problem, is 'advertised' to us continuously, and therefore should have *some* impact on our own style and preferences.
- images of 'attractive people' abound. This may have absolutely no influence on how we rate our own appearance, and that of others – but that's improbable.

So it is imperative that, as students of contemporary culture, we try to investigate the ways in which everyday popular media material affects people's lives. Researchers have tried to do this before, of course – not always with great success, as we will see in the next chapter.

MEN AND WOMEN TODAY

Before we consider the media's role further, it is worth establishing the relative positions of women and men in modern Western democracies. If there is a 'battle of the sexes', who is winning nowadays? Women and men generally have equal rights – with a few exceptions within various laws, which we see being campaigned against and changed. The sexes today are generally thought to be 'equal', to the extent that the cover of *Time* magazine wondered if feminism was 'dead' in June 1998. There is even a noisy minority who argue that feminism has 'gone too far' and that it is now men who have the worst deal in society (Farrell, 2001).

Equality and inequality

The modern Western world is an odd mix of equal and unequal. Women and men may 'feel' equal, but at the same time are aware that this is not entirely accurate. Women have the formal *right* to do most things that a man can do, and vice versa; situations where this is not the case can become well-publicised courtroom battles. More informally, women and men generally believe themselves to be equals within the sphere of personal relationships. The sociologist Anthony Giddens (of whom more in Chapter 5) asserts that intimate relationships have become 'democratised', so that the bond between partners – even within a marriage – has little to do with external laws, regulations or social expectations, but is based on the internal understanding between two people – a trusting bond based on emotional communication. Where such a bond ceases to exist, modern society is generally happy for the relationship to be dissolved. Thus we have 'a democracy of the emotions in everyday life' (Giddens, 1999).

A 1999 study based on longitudinal data from the US General Social Survey, run by the National Opinion Research Center at the University of Chicago, concluded that over the previous 27 years:

> Marriage has declined as the central institution under which households are organized and children are raised. People marry later and divorce and cohabitate more. A growing proportion of children has been born outside of marriage. Even within marriage the changes have been profound as more and more women have entered the labor force and gender roles have become more homogenous between husbands and wives.
>
> (Smith, 1999)

Compared to the findings of similar studies in 24 other advanced industrial countries, Americans were found to be 'on the middle range of many of the attitude scales' and could be expected to further 'evolve in their attitudes towards acceptance of more non-traditional attitudes', the study found (ibid.). In other words, the new 'democracy of the emotions' which is beginning to take hold means that adults are less willing to stay in unhappy relationships or dysfunctional households, and are increasingly likely to 'vote with their feet' and go in search of happiness elsewhere.

Women increasingly reject dated ideas regarding their gender role, and men are changing too. The UK's National Centre for Social Research (2000) reported that their annual survey of social attitudes had found that:

> The traditional view of women as dedicated 'housewives' seems to be all but extinct. Only around one in six women, and one in five men [mostly older people], think women should remain at home while men go out to work.

It should be pointed out that despite this change in *attitudes*, women still do more housework then men (UK: Social Trends, 2001; USA: Bureau of Labor Statistics, 2001). On the other hand, it can be noted that men do more paid work outside the home (ibid.), and that for many men this is more of an obligation than an enjoyable privilege. Others would retort that women still need more opportunities to gain access to the more rewarding kinds of paid work. All of these things are true, and reflect the broader reality that things are changing and shaking down, on the individual level.

At the same time, we are aware of obvious inequalities on the West's 'macro' level – most visibly, those people we see on TV running governments and businesses are more often men than women. For example, the proportion of women in Western European parliaments was just 21 per cent on average in 2000 (UN, 2000). Only the Nordic countries and the Netherlands have a proportion of at least one-third women in their parliaments (ibid.). Only 23 per cent of businesses in the European Union are owned by women (EU Commission, 2001), and according to a United Nations study:

> In 1999, women accounted for 11 to 12 per cent of corporate officers in the 500 largest corporations in the United States. While women accounted for 12 per cent of the corporate officers of the 560 largest corporations in Canada in 1999, they occupied only 3 per cent of the highest positions of those corporations.
>
> (UN, 2000)

The principal jobs in businesses and organisations are no doubt protected by a 'culture of men' at the top. For example, when Cambridge University – a supposedly 'enlightened' institution – commissioned a report from external consultants to find out why women were not well represented in its top jobs, the researchers identified 'an insular and secretive "macho" culture, dominated by white males' (BBC Online, 2001a) – revealing how everyday attitudes at the 'micro' level can have an impact upon the 'macro' level employment statistics.

Traditional attitudes can have an impact on other people's lives at all levels. At school, for example, studies have suggested that British girls with non-traditional career aspirations are let down by their teachers and careers advisors, who still shuttle girls 'into "feminine" jobs such as super-market sales for work experience' (Apter, 2000). Masculine stereotypes meanwhile mean that young men still tend to avoid careers which are seen as traditionally 'female' (Woodward, 2000). In July 2001, Julie Mellor, chair of the UK's Equal Opportunities Commission, warned that society would have to change to match the expectations of confident female school leavers:

> Britain still has to address the glaring inequalities that so many women and men face. Otherwise we risk disappointing the high hopes of the 'girl power' generation, some of whom will be entering the job market before very long. Despite all their achievements, young women still enter a far narrower range of jobs than young men, they are already earning 10 per cent less than their male colleagues by the age of 20, and they are less likely ever to reach the top of their field of work.
>
> (UN, 2000)

Furthermore, bell hooks reminds us that, although people say that 'the [feminist] movement is no longer needed, as "all women have improved their lives"', there is still violence against women, single mothers are 'pathologized' by politicians and the media, and female poverty is increasing (2000: xiv).

All bad news?

In spite of the depressing facts and figures above, there is still a lot of on-going transformation for us to be optimistic about. Society clearly changed a great deal in the second half of the twentieth century, and sexual equality is something that almost everybody in power at least *says* they are in favour of. On the everyday level, as noted above, women and men expect to be treated equally, and are frustrated if this does not happen. As we will see in later chapters, magazines for women encourage their readers to be assertive and independent. Pop stars like Destiny's Child, and other media icons such as Oprah Winfrey, convey the same message. Magazines for men, whilst sometimes going overboard with macho excess, encourage men to understand women, and face up to modern realities. Women and men are usually equals in today's movies and TV shows; we raise an eyebrow when this isn't so. Things have changed quite quickly, and there is still some way to go, but equality within everyday life is now quite well established. This needs to be carried forward into the formal world of work and government where a disproportionate number of men are running the show. Other changes are needed in the world of work too – amazingly in the 'modern' world, working fathers are allowed few concessions to spend time with their children, and paternity leave, which is typically minimal or non-existent, is viewed as a luxury. (Tony Blair set a poor example by refusing to take paternity leave upon the birth of his son in 2000; instead he said he would work less for a short period so that he would be able to 'help out', but insisted 'I have to run the country', as if no Prime Minister had ever taken a break (BBC Online, 2000a).) Mothers are still seen as the natural carers of children, but attitudes and regulations are changing, albeit very slowly, in this area too.

Masculinity

There's quite a lot of talk about 'masculinity in crisis' these days. It brewed up again in Britain with the publication of Anthony Clare's book *On Men: Masculinity in Crisis* in 2000 – which gained coverage and publicity since Clare is a well-known broadcaster – and, separately, London's Royal Festival Hall ran a series of public discussions on 'Masculinity in Crisis' in spring 2001. Similar discussions were prompted in the USA by the publication of Susan Faludi's *Stiffed: The Betrayal of the Modern Man* (1999), in which Faludi, well-known as the bestselling feminist author of *Backlash: The Undeclared War Against Women* (1991), appeared to come out in sympathy for the modern man. Anthony Clare sets out the 'masculinity in crisis' idea at the start of his book:

> Now, the whole issue of men – the point of them, their purpose, their value, their justification – is a matter for public debate. Serious commentators declare that men are redundant, that women do not need them and children would be better off

without them. At the beginning of the twenty-first century it is difficult to avoid the conclusion that men are in serious trouble. Throughout the world, developed and developing, antisocial behaviour is essentially male. [. . .] And yet, for all their behaving badly, they do not seem any the happier. Throughout North America, Europe and Australia, male suicides outnumber female by a factor of between 3 and 4 to 1. [. . .] Men renowned for their ability and inclination to be stoned, drunk or sexually daring, appear terrified by the prospect of revealing that they can be – and often are – depressed, dependent, in need of help.

(2001: 3)

Men used to know their place, as provider for their family, says Clare, and this was a role to be proud of. But today, as women show that they can do everything that men can, this provider role becomes diminished. Women are also finding that they can bring up families perfectly well without the father being present at all, and scientific advances seem to be making men unnecessary to reproduction itself (ibid.: 7).

All this adds up to the modern men's 'crisis' although, of course, it's a bit over-excitable to call it a crisis. It's a set of changing circumstances, and men, most certainly, need to renegotiate their place within this new culture. But – without wanting to sound too masculine and rational about it – it's surely nothing to have a crisis about. Men may not be able to fit into their *traditional* role, but that's no reason to conclude that life is over for men. Men just have to find a new, modern, useful place for themselves in the world – just as women have to. And this is where the mass media and popular culture come in, because they offer important tools to help men – and women – adjust to contemporary life. Many of the academic books on 'masculinity' are disappointing, as they dwell on archetypes from the past, and have little to say about the real lives of modern men; whereas top-selling magazines and popular self-help books – and, to a lesser but signific-ant extent, TV shows and movies – are full of information about being a man in the here-and-now. These are discussed later in this book.

To be fair, Anthony Clare doesn't think that men need to have a crisis, either, but they do need to change. Emotional communication, and the expression of love and vulnerability, are important. Men don't need to become 'like women' but can develop a new form of masculinity which places 'a greater value on love, family and personal relationships and less on power, possessions and achievement', he suggests (ibid.: 221). He carefully sifts through scientific evidence in order to reject the idea that men cannot help themselves for biological reasons. As one reviewer noted,

> Clare does a thorough job of demolishing the 'unrecon-
> structable caveman' that pop science peddles to the media. It's
> easy (but false) to say that testosterone causes aggression; the
> truth – that [testosterone]-levels and aggressive behaviour are
> linked in a circular relationship dependent on a multitude of
> environmental factors – is hard to fit into a tabloid headline.
>
> (Kane, 2000)

Clare is particularly good on the masculine drive to 'prove' oneself through work – perhaps because, as he admits in the book, he has suffered from this himself. He marshals evidence from major studies, though, to support his point that the quality of personal relationships has a much greater impact on a person's levels of life satisfaction than their success in work. Indeed, 'once a person moves beyond the poverty level, a larger income contributes almost nothing to happiness' (2001: 100). Therefore he recommends social changes to allow men and women to spend less time in work, and more time experiencing their relationships with each other, with children, and with the world in general – which, the evidence shows, makes for happier people and – lest employers be worried by all this talk of leisure – better workers.

In Susan Faludi's *Stiffed* (1999), as mentioned above, the well-known feminist surprised readers by arguing that contemporary culture damages men just as much as women, albeit in different ways. (This, of course, is not actually inconsistent with the basic idea of feminism, which originally sought to free both women and men from constricting gender stereotypes). Explaining the book's title in a 1999 interview, Faludi said:

> To me it has three meanings: working stiff; the way guys have
> been cheated by this society; and the fact that men are supposed
> to be stiff – that they have to show their armoured self to the
> world all the time. Having to do that hurts them as much as it
> hurts everyone else.
>
> (Halpern 1999)

Like Clare, Faludi notes that men who spend their lives in work miss out on a proper engagement with their partners, children and friends, and don't get anything for it except an early death. Faludi finds that the traditional male 'provider' role also bitterly hurts men who cannot find employment. In this sense, Faludi feels that men have been 'betrayed' by a society which had seemed to promise them that the traditional masculine role would deliver some ultimate happiness. She also implies that feminism was mistaken to see men's traditional role as being one of 'power', and wrong to think that men had kept the best lifestyle for themselves and only given women the boring responsibilities. A role which turns men into bread-winning robots, subject to the whims of the employment market and disconnected from quality relationships and parenthood, is not particularly powerful or desirable, she observes. It is important to note that Faludi does not renounce feminism, or suggest that women now have a better deal in society than men; her point is more that contemporary society is just as depressing and constricting for the average man as it is for the average woman, and that men deserve to be heard.

Faludi further argues that both sexes have now become victims of the culture of consumerism, appearances, and glamour:

> Truly, men and women have arrived at their ornamental imprisonment by different routes. Women were relegated there as a sop for their exclusion from the realm of power-striving men. Men arrived there as a result of their power-striving, which led to a society drained of context, saturated with a competitive individualism that has been robbed of craft and utility, and ruled by commercial values that revolve around who has the most, the best, the biggest, the fastest. The destination of both roads was an enslavement to glamour.
>
> (1999: 599)

It is our media-saturated consumer culture which now has men as well as women 'by the throat' (ibid.: 602), she suggests, and she urges men to overthrow the overly competitive, uncommunicative and ultimately unrewarding world they have created for themselves.

There is general agreement, then, that this is not a particularly stable time for the 'male identity', if such a singular thing exists. Some parts of popular culture are said to be 'reasserting' the traditional forms of masculinity, whilst others are challenging them – and as we will see later in the book, it's even debatable which media products are conveying which messages. So, more of that later; now we'll turn to masculinity's opposite – or counterpart – femininity.

Femininity

The ideas of 'masculinity' and 'femininity' have been pulled through the social changes of the past few decades in quite different ways. Masculinity is seen as the state of 'being a man', which is currently somewhat in flux.

Femininity, on the other hand, is not necessarily seen as the state of 'being a woman'; instead, it's perceived more as a stereotype of a woman's role from the past. Men like their identities to fit within 'masculinity', even if we have to revise that term as attitudes change. Modern women are not generally bothered about fitting their identity within the idea of 'femininity', perhaps because feminists never really sought to *revise* femininity, preferring to dispose of the fluffy, passive concept altogether. Femininity is not a core value for women today. Instead, being 'feminine' is just one of the performances that women can choose to employ in everyday life – perhaps for pleasure, or to achieve a particular goal.

There's plenty of evidence that traditional femininity is no longer popular. Virtually everybody wants young women to be successful, so the traditional characteristics of femininity – passivity, reticence, assuming that men and authority figures are probably right and that you are probably wrong – are therefore redundant. Schoolgirls today have shaken off 'feminine' docility and are out-performing boys at all levels of school education in both the UK and USA (Bailey and Campbell, 2000; Cassidy, 2001; and see for UK: www.statistics.gov.uk, for USA: www.nces.ed.gov). Sales of the Barbie doll are reported to be falling because only the youngest girls will accept such a 'girly' toy nowadays (Moorhead, 2001), whilst young women have a range of assertive 'girl power' role models to choose from in magazines, movies and pop music – all of which will be discussed in the following chapters.

Traditional ways of thinking are still present in modern society, of course, so we can think of occasions when a woman may be criticised for her 'lack of femininity'. And elements of fashion, say, might be commended for adding 'a dash of femininity' to a woman's appearance. Even these examples of the term in use, however, incorporate a recognition of the broadly 'optional' role which femininity has today. Whole books have been written about how Madonna showed that femininity is a 'masquerade' or a 'performance' in her videos from the early 1990s such as *Express Yourself* and *Justify My Love* (Frank and Smith, 1993; Lloyd, 1993; Schwichtenberg, 1993). For example, E. Ann Kaplan wrote that '[Madonna's] image usefully adopts one mask after another to expose the fact that there is no "essential" self and therefore no essential feminine but only cultural constructions' (1993: 160). Madonna was seen to be playing with 'the given gender sign system' where 'femininity' was just one of the available guises. And indeed, the idea of a woman being seductively 'feminine' in order to get her own way is a dramatic cliché appearing in various movies from throughout the last century, so the idea of femininity as a mere performance, to be used by wily women, is not new.

*Figure 1.1   Girls today (such as eight-year-old Claire) have adopted
the idea of 'girl power'*

Today, magazines such as *Cosmopolitan* suggest ways in which cunning
women might use 'feminine' tricks to get certain things from gullible men,
but traditional femininity is far from being essential to the modern female
reader – instead, it is just one technique amongst many, and an amusing,
lightweight one at that. In a fascinating in-depth study of a group of British
working-class women, Beverley Skeggs (1997) found that her subjects had a
complex relationship with 'femininity', since they sought the 'respectability'
which was associated with the 'feminine' role, but had no interest in being
associated with its connotations of passivity or weakness. The women

rejected the historical idea of women's 'divine composure' in favour of their modern 'having a laugh'. As Skeggs explains, 'They had knowledge and competencies to construct feminine performances, but this was far removed from *being* feminine. They usually "did" femininity when they thought it was necessary' (ibid.: 116). The women found that they were compelled to invest in femininity in order to succeed economically – such as when applying for a job – and that femininity was also a kind of 'cultural capital' which brought both pleasures and problems.

> Their forays into femininity were immensely contradictory. Femininity offered a space for hedonism, autonomy, camaraderie, pleasure and fun whilst simultaneously regulating and generating insecurities. The women simulated and dissimulated but did not regard themselves as feminine. [. . .] Aspects of femininity are, however, something which they have learnt to perform and from which they can sometimes take pleasure.
>
> (ibid.)

Femininity, then, whilst seen as a 'nice' thing for women traditionally, is increasingly irrelevant today. Whilst 'masculinity' always included a number of positive attributes which men are keen to hang on to – assertiveness and independence, for example, are clearly good things when not taken to extremes – 'femininity' was traditionally loaded, by the unsubtle patriarchs of yesteryear, with weak qualities like subservience and timidity. The sensible woman of today has little enthusiasm for these traits, and so the meaning of 'femininity' now is just a swishy kind of glamour – and ideally is just a masquerade, utilised by a confident woman who knows *exactly* what she's doing.

SEXUAL IDENTITIES TODAY

Although lesbians, gays and bisexuals continue to face prejudice and discrimination, from older generations in particular (but not exclusively), there is a growing amount of evidence that society is becoming more accepting of sexual diversity. In 2001, a study by Britain's largest market research group, Mintel, found that gay and straight lifestyles were increasingly convergent, and that an atmosphere of tolerance and social mixing dominated in cities (Arlidge, 2001). A MORI poll in the same year also found a blossoming of tolerance: just 17 per cent of people in England said that they felt 'less positive' towards lesbians and gays, and three-quarters of people with children in their household said that they would be comfortable if the child had a gay or lesbian teacher (MORI, 2001).

In the USA, the population appears to be rather less open-minded. Regular surveys conducted by Gallup show that the number of people willing to agree that 'homosexuality should be considered an acceptable alternative lifestyle' has risen from 38 per cent in 1992 to 52 per cent in 2001 (Newport, 2001). However, disagreement was high at 43 per cent. Almost the same number (42 per cent) felt that 'homosexual relations between consenting adults' should *not be* legal. The strength of this intolerance gives little cause for optimism, but the long-term trends show a clear decline in homophobia, and young people are more sympathetic to gay liberties than older generations. Indeed, a decent proportion of US citizens are willing to join pro-gay campaigns: one recent survey found that 42 per cent of heterosexual consumers (as well as 74 per cent of gay consumers) said that they would be less likely to buy a product from a company which advertised on a TV programme that expressed negative views of lesbians or gays (Harris Interactive, 2000).

It is not possible to measure the relative influence of the mass media upon these changing attitudes, of course (although when questioned, MORI respondents said that the media was an important source of information about minorities (MORI, 2001)). In his book, *Striptease Culture*, Brian McNair (2002) shows how sex and sexuality have come to be represented in a diverse range of ways in popular culture, and makes a strong case for the central role of popular culture in the rejection of tradition and the transformation of society. It seems likely that as the media introduces the general audience to more everyday gay and lesbian (and bisexual, and transgendered) characters, tolerance should grow. Discussions of the representations of sexual minorities in television and film appear in Chapter 4.

OTHER AXES OF IDENTITY

Identities, of course, are complex constructions, and gender is only one part of an individual's sense of self. Ethnicity is obviously an important aspect of identity, and, like gender, may be felt to be more or less central to self-identity by each individual, or might be *made* significant by external social circumstances (such as a racist regime or community). Other much-discussed axes of identity include class, age, disability and sexuality. In addition, a range of other factors may contribute to a sense of identity, such as education, urban or rural residency, cultural background, access to transportation and communications, criminal record, persecution or refugee status. Furthermore, whilst usually less significant in terms of overall 'life chances', any aspects of the physical body can be relevant to self-identity: for example, whether one is seen as overweight or underweight, tall or short, hairy or shaven or bald, or wearing spectacles, unusual clothes, or piercings. Researchers have studied all of these aspects of identity. This book generally confines itself to discussing gender, though, as one particular *part* of identity which all individuals, in whatever way, have to integrate and express within their personalities.

MEDIA, *ETHNICITY* AND IDENTITY

Valuable books have been written on representations of 'race' and their implications. See, for example, *Say It Loud!: African–American Audiences, Media, and Identity* edited by Robin Means Coleman (2002), *Representing Black Britain: Black and Asian Images on Television* by Sarita Malik (2002), *Representing 'Race'* by Robert Ferguson (1998), *Black and White Media* by Karen Ross (1995) and *Watching Race: Television and the Struggle for 'Blackness'* by Herman Gray (1995). For a thought-provoking black feminist perspective, see the work of bell hooks, in particular *Black Looks: Race and Representation* (1992) and *Reel to Real: Race, Sex, and Class at the Movies* (1996).

OUTLINE OF THIS BOOK

In Chapter 2, we catch up on previous debates about the power of the media within cultural theory and psychological research. Then we consider representations of gender in the media, both in the past (Chapter 3) and today (Chapter 4). In Chapters 5–7, we look at some theoretical approaches which we can employ to help us understand how people form their sense of self and identity in relation to the media: Chapter 5 takes up the work of Anthony Giddens, Chapter 6 employs Michel Foucault, and Chapter 7 makes use of queer theory. (No previous knowledge of these approaches is assumed.) In Chapters 8–10, we turn back to actual contemporary media, and seek to relate some of these theoretical ideas to popular culture. In Chapter 8 we consider popular lifestyle magazines aimed at men, such as *FHM* and *Maxim*, and Chapter 9 looks at those for women, such as *Cosmopolitan* and *Glamour*: do these glossy publications play a role in shaping gender identities, or are they pure entertainment? Chapter 10 looks at some aspects of popular culture which provide ideas about 'ways of living', from the notion of 'role models', via case studies from the world of pop music, to self-help books and their more explicit advice about self-fulfilment. Finally, the conclusion brings together a number of key themes which emerge through the course of the book.

A note on methodology

The book mixes an analysis of previous theories and research with some new material. Email interviews are particularly central to the chapters on men's magazines, women's magazines, and role models, providing qualitative information about how people relate to media texts. Email interviews are very similar to any other kind of interview, except that the researcher is able to contact people from different parts of the world quite easily. As a means of surveying the general population, this is a bad method (the most obvious problem is that only people with internet access are even *potentially* reachable). For interviewing *fans* or users of a particular media artist or artefact, though, the internet is extremely valuable – fans can be found via websites and message boards dedicated to the performer or thing in question, and are often happy to share their thoughts about the object of their interest. It's also not too hard to find people willing to be interviewed about their other media habits and interests.

Some people say, 'You don't know who you're talking to on the internet – they might be lying to you', but this is often a weak reservation; people are no more likely to waste their time lying in an email interview than in a face-to-face interview. Where in-depth interviews about magazine reading or pop music idols are concerned, in particular, it seems unlikely that anyone would bother making fictional submissions. Of course, respondents may leave out or 'modify' parts of their account, but that is the case in any interview situation.

Elsewhere I have sometimes taken the responses of consumers (of a movie, or a self-help book, say) from websites where everyday people are requested to post their views – such as The Internet Movie Database (www.imdb.com) for movies, and Amazon (www.amazon.com) for books and music. Whilst comments from these sites could not be used as the basis for a whole thesis – because their authors are a self-selected group interested in reviewing things on websites (who may not, therefore, represent the 'general audience') – quotes from these sites are useful for fleshing out an idea or illustrating a point, and they do represent the spontaneously-offered views of people who are actually interested in the media product in question.

A funny way of talking

This book is not intended to be written in pointlessly complex language, but a few specific terms from the worlds of sociology and cultural studies will spring up here and there. Most students will probably be familiar with them already, but for clarification, here's what I mean by the following terms:

Text – in media studies, 'text' can refer to any kind of media material, such as a television programme, a film, a magazine, or a website, as well as a more conventional *written* text such as a book or newspaper.

Discourse – broadly means 'a way of talking about things' within a particular group, culture or society; or a set of ideas within a culture which shapes how we perceive the world. So when I talk about 'the discourse of women's magazines', for example, I am referring to the ways in which women's magazines typically talk about women and men and social life, and the assumptions that they commonly deploy.

Biological determinism – the view that people's behaviour patterns are the result of their genes and their biological inheritance. Biological determinists typically argue that women and men are fundamentally different, and that they cannot help it – they were born that way.

Social constructionism – the view that people's personality and behaviour are *not* pre-determined by biology, but are shaped by society and culture. People are not fixed from birth, then, and can adapt and change.

Modern life and *modernity* – the present time in developed Western countries. Although postmodernists have correctly observed a range of cultural features of developed societies (such as scepticism towards science, religion and other 'macro' explanations; consumerism; superficiality, and the importance of appearance and media image), I agree with Giddens that it's not really worth calling these features 'post'-modern, because we do not really live in a wholly new era. The term 'post-traditional' is certainly useful, however. More on these terms appears in Chapter 5.

Other terminology will be explained as it appears.

WHAT'S WRONG WITH THIS BOOK

Like all books, this one spends time discussing things that the author considers to be relevant and interesting, at the expense of other matters which are judged to be less pertinent, or which there simply wasn't room for. This section offers brief explanations for some of its limitations.

The emphasis tends to be more on the choices of individuals, and less on the social constraints which they may face

There is a growing social perception, which is certainly encouraged by popular media, that people can make what they want of their own lives. This book explores this idea of personal autonomy – and therefore might occasionally appear to be assuming that we all live in a 'middle class' world where people are free to do what they like and not be inhibited by lack of money, or fear of social rejection or violence. Needless to say, however, most people do face social, cultural and financial constraints, which have been well documented by social scientists for many decades. These constraints can be very powerful. At the same time, though, individuals do have *choices*, and we are surrounded by media which celebrates a range of possible lifestyles (whilst also selecting and channelling what seems to be available). Rather than simply rehash the sociological pessimism which assumes that any sense of individual autonomy is more-or-less irrelevant because of the poverty and sexism imposed by capitalism and patriarchy, this book takes individual identities – and their relationship with popular media – more seriously, because changes in people's consciousness will ultimately lead to changes in the wider society (an idea developed further in Chapter 5). We should also note that the notion that you can choose a way of living, as suggested by some of the theorists and media which are discussed in this book, is not actually limited to the middle classes, even if it sounds, to some people, like a 'middle class' discourse.

The book doesn't spend much time criticising media texts themselves

A number of previous books on media and gender have consisted of detailed criticism of particular representations of women (e.g. MacDonald, 1995; Tasker, 1998; Gateward and Pomerance, 2002), or representations of men (e.g. Cohan and Hark, 1993; Lehman, 2001; Spicer, 2001). Even Liesbet van Zoonen's excellent introduction to *Feminist Media Studies* (1994) spends more time on critical approaches to texts than on the more significant question of how audiences relate to them. Although these text-based approaches may reveal 'hidden' aspects of media messages, they often do not help us to understand why such texts are appealing or popular, or how they are consumed by actual audiences. (They may also suggest interpretations of texts which are not apparent to most viewers, and it is difficult to assert that a particular academic reading of a text is superior to that made by any other person.) In this book I will discuss the changing representations of gender in Chapters 3 and 4, and elsewhere, but rather than describing worrying aspects of texts *in themselves*, I will be considering – in later chapters in particular – how we can understand the ways in which popular media are connected to the gendered identities of real people. In other words, how do mass-produced items (from the 'outside' world) become significant in how we think of ourselves (in our 'inner' world)?

The book only focuses on popular, mainstream media

Although many delightful challenges to the status quo are made by small-scale or minority media producers and artists, this book is concerned with the messages about identity, gender and lifestyle which people most commonly encounter, which means that there is a deliberate focus on the popular and mainstream.

The book doesn't simply spell out the process by which we acquire gender

This book argues that there is not a single, straightforward psychological process through which gender identities are formed; instead, there is a complex interaction of thoughts, evaluations, negotiations, emotions and reactions. We have to forget the desire to draw a flow diagram showing how personalities are 'formed', and try another approach.

The book is focused on Western media and culture

Indeed, this book's remit is the discussion of media and gender identities in developed Western countries, with examples from the USA and UK in particular. Of course, the question of media influences on gender and identities in non-Western countries around the world is also very important (Curran and Park, 1999; Altman, 2000; Stald and Tufte, 2001), but is beyond the scope of the present volume.

THE BOOK'S WEBSITE

A website for this book can be found at www.theoryhead.com/gender. The site contains additional resources, including some extended analyses, extra articles, discussions between the author and other people, and links to related websites. You can also send suggestions and comments via the site.

Chapter 2

SOME BACKGROUND DEBATES

IN THIS CHAPTER we will consider some existing theoretical and empirical approaches to the impact of the mass media. Is the media a powerful force, shaping the consciousness of the modern public? What do we know about the 'effects' of the media? What have psychologists had to say about the development of gender and identity? And what has film studies claimed about media, gender and identity? This chapter considers some of the previous theories – ones which are often, for different reasons, unsatisfactory, and which we might hope to go 'beyond' later in the book.

MEDIA POWER VERSUS PEOPLE POWER

One of the biggest debates about the social impact of the media – perhaps *the* debate – can be boiled down to one question: does the mass media have a significant amount of power over its audience, or does the audience ultimately have more power than the media? It is, perhaps, not very sensible to consider the matter in such extreme, polarised terms, but we shall put that thought to one side temporarily, because it is at least *instructive* to consider both sides of the debate in their most clear-cut form. In one corner, then, we have Theodor Adorno, who felt that the power of mass media over the population was enormous and very damaging, and in the opposite corner we have John Fiske, who argues that it is the audience, not the media, which has the most power. We could have picked other theorists to represent these positions, perhaps, but Adorno and Fiske are probably the most celebrated exponents of each position.

Adorno: media power

Theodor Adorno (1903–1969) was a member of the Frankfurt School for Social Research (established in 1923), a group of largely German, Jewish intellectuals, who fled from Frankfurt to New York and Los Angeles when the Nazis rose to power in the 1930s. Many of them returned to Germany at the end of the 1940s. Their antipathy towards the mass media will likely have been increased by the observation that Hitler had apparently been able to use the media organisations as a tool for widespread propaganda, and also by their sudden encounter with American popular culture, which was clearly not to their 'high art'-centred, bourgeois tastes. Even more crucially, the revolution predicted by Karl Marx in the middle of the nineteenth century – in which the workers were meant to recognise their exploitation, and overthrow the rulers and factory owners – had not come to pass. Instead, the workers of the world seemed to be reasonably happy; the work itself may not have been rewarding, but they had some decent films to watch, and the radio played nice songs to cheer them up.

And so Adorno and his colleague Max Horkheimer (1895–1973) wrote the book *Dialectic of Enlightenment* (1979), first published in 1947, which contains the essay 'The Culture Industry: Enlightenment as Mass Deception', encapsulating their views on the mass media and its impact upon society. The essay alternates between sharp, lucid points about media power, and rather more rambling prose about the nature of mass culture – as if Adorno and Horkheimer were fighting for control of the typewriter, and one of them was drunk. It's well worth reading. Adorno also helpfully revisited these ideas in a shorter essay, 'Culture Industry Reconsidered', published in English after his death.

The mass media was referred to as the 'culture industry' by Adorno and Horkheimer to indicate its nature: a well-oiled machine producing entertainment products in order to make profit. Whilst this comes as no surprise to us today – we are happy to recognise the 'music industry' or the 'movie business' as such – the German intellectuals were clearly devastated by the reduction of culture to a set of manufactured products. They explain that they deliberately avoided referring to this business as 'mass culture', because they wanted to make it clear that this is not a culture produced by the people. Instead, the culture consumed by the masses is imposed from above – churned out by the culture industry. Because of this commercial context, media products (whether films, music, TV dramas or whatever) can never be 'art' which just happens to be a commodity: instead 'they are commodities through and through' (Adorno, 1991: 86).

All products of the culture industry are 'exactly the same' (Horkheimer and Adorno, 1979: 122) – not literally, of course, but in the sense that they all reflect the values of the established system. 'Each product affects an individual air', explains Adorno, but this is an 'illusion' (1991: 87). Unusual talents who emerge are quickly 'absorbed' into the system (1979: 122): think of the 'challenging' rock acts who almost always end up signing big-money deals with the major record labels – themselves part of even bigger media and business conglomerates – and generating fat profits for their masters. Marilyn Manson and Eminem may be scary to middle America, but in Wall Street terms they are embodiments of the American capitalist dream. The teen 'rebels' who are fans of such acts, Adorno would suggest, are just consumers: buying a CD is not rebellion, it's buying a CD. The tough guy who has just bought the latest angry rap CD, takes it home and plays it loud, may be thinking, 'Yeah! Fuck you, consumer society!', but as far as Adorno is concerned, he might as well say, 'Thank you, consumer society, for giving me a new product to buy. This is a good product. I would like to make further purchases of similar products in the near future'.

We might think that the media offer a range of different forms of entertainment, giving different groups what they want, but Horkheimer and Adorno fit this into their account too: 'Something is provided for all so that none may escape' (1979: 123). They remind us that the person seeking entertainment 'has to accept what the culture manufacturers offer him' (ibid.: 124), so choice is an illusion too. We can choose what we like, certainly, but from a limited *range* presented by the culture industry. And our consumption merely fosters 'the circle of manipulation and retroactive need in which the unity of the system grows ever stronger' (ibid.: 121). Because we've never really had anything different, we want more and more of the same. 'The customer is not king, as the culture industry would have us believe, not its subject but its object,' states Adorno (1991: 85).

Horkheimer and Adorno's points can seem worryingly relevant in relation to the Hollywood blockbusters of today. Even back in the 1940s, they observed that new films were usually a set of 'interchangeable' elements borrowed from previous successes, with slight modifications or upgrades in terms of expense, style or technology (1979: 123–125). The authors say: 'As soon as the film begins, it is quite clear how it will end, and who will be rewarded, punished, or forgotten' (ibid.: 125). The fact that John Travolta has a speech saying *exactly* this at the start of the 2001 blockbuster *Swordfish* does not show that movie-makers are stepping outside of the formula; after a brilliantly explosive (but 'blockbusterey') beginning, *Swordfish* is more-or-less as formulaic as every other – just one of the many movies that we rush along to see during the summer, in the hope that this particular one will be surprisingly good, only to emerge from the cinema feeling slightly empty, more often than not, a couple of hours later.

So far we've considered Horkheimer and Adorno's criticisms of the *quality* of popular culture – they think it's all very similar, formulaic and manufactured. Now we'll turn to their view of its *impact* on society. Their concern is, in part, unrelated to the content of any particular TV show, film, or magazine, but is more generally focused on the fact that this 'rubbish' (1979: 121) takes up so much time in people's everyday consciousness – 'occupying [their] senses from the time they leave the factory in the evening to the time they clock in again the next morning' (ibid.: 131), leaving no opportunity for resistance to develop. If your response to this is, 'But I enjoy watching TV – I choose to watch it and I enjoy it!', then you are merely confirming Horkheimer and Adorno's view: they do not deny that people have a 'misplaced love' for popular culture (ibid.: 134). The programmes are well-made and provide enjoyment, and we may well watch an educational or political documentary occasionally, but these things make no difference to the main argument: we are still just people consuming TV. We may feel emotions, or have a conversation about an interesting show with friends, but Adorno would say that we are still drones, manipulated by the system to want the pleasures which it offers, and satisfied (in a rather passive, brainless way) with the daily diet of entertainment which it pours forth.

So it is the *passivity* which media consumption brings to people's lives that is Adorno's main concern. In addition, there is a belief that the media's content encourages conformity:

> The concepts of order which [the culture industry] hammers into human beings are always those of the status quo . . . It proclaims: you shall conform, with no instruction as to what; conform to that which exists anyway, and to that which everyone thinks anyway as a result of its power and omnipresence. The power of the culture industry's ideology is such that conformity has replaced consciousness
>
> (1991: 90)

He further argues that the culture industry 'impedes the development of autonomous, independent individuals who judge and decide consciously for themselves'. (ibid.: 92). Critical thinking is closed off by mass-produced popular culture. All of this explains, of course, why Marx's revolution didn't happen: pacified by pleasant, shallow entertainments offered by the culture industry, people didn't really feel the need. With communities fragmented

into a world of individuals staying in their homes watching TV or listening
to pop music, or isolated in the darkness before a cinema screen, resistance
was unlikely to find a space to develop, and was further discouraged by the
broadly 'conformist' media. Even if you disagree with Horkheimer and
Adorno's snobbish attitude to popular culture and its consumers, their
argument about its role in society still seems to stand up. This is partly
because it's a 'false consciousness' argument – you might be certain that the
mass media hasn't damaged you, but the argument says that you wouldn't
notice this anyway, and so your protestations are in vain; only Horkheimer
and Adorno know better. Even if you think that they are fantastically arro-
gant and elitist for taking that position, you still haven't proven them
wrong. You need a better argument than that. So let's consider the case for
the opposition.

Fiske: audience power

John Fiske is best known for a pair of books, *Understanding Popular
Culture* and *Reading the Popular*. At the time of their simultaneous publication in 1989, Fiske was a fiftysomething professor, and a self-confessed
fan of pop culture, who had taught in Britain, Australia and the USA. The
time-pressed modern consumer may like to note that an article by Fiske
called 'Moments of Television' (1989c) offers a decent introduction to the
views which he discusses in much more depth in the books.

Fiske's work represents a view diametrically opposed to Adorno's. Near
the start of *Understanding Popular Culture*, he tells Adorno fans bluntly:

> Popular culture is made by the people, not produced by the
> culture industry. All the culture industries can do is produce a
> repertoire of texts or cultural resources for the various forma-
> tions of the people to use or reject in the on-going process of
> producing their popular culture.
>
> (1989a: 24)

In other words, the power of the audience to interpret media texts, and
determine their popularity, far outweighs the ability of media institutions to
send a particular message or ideology to audiences within their texts. This
position did not, of course, appear out of the blue. Stuart Hall's 'encoding/
decoding' model (1973) had already suggested, in more modest terms, that
a media message could be 'decoded' by the audience in different and unpredictable ways (see box, pp. 26–27) – a point which, you might think, was
pretty obvious anyway. Fiske, however, offers a radically exaggerated version

of this view, which – no doubt as a reaction to the pessimism of Adorno and his followers – often appears to be a gleeful celebration of the audience's power of interpretation and choice.

We should note that although Fiske was opposed to the cynical stance of left-wing critics like Adorno, Fiske's arguments are not (nor are they intended to be) a 'right-wing' response. Instead, Fiske comes across as an upbeat 'leftie' and a 'man of the people' who wants to show that 'the people' are not foolish dupes. He says, indeed, that we can't even talk about 'the people' or 'the audience' because a singular mass of consumers does not exist: there is only a range of different individuals with their own changing tastes and a 'shifting set of social allegiances' which may or may not relate to their social background, and which are complex and contradictory (Fiske, 1989a.). Fiske does not deny that we live in a capitalist and patriarchal society, but suggests that it is silly to think of popular culture as a manufactured thing imposed by capitalists upon the unsuspecting masses. 'Culture is a living, active process: it can be developed only from within, it cannot be imposed from without or above' (ibid.: 23). Therefore the pop charts are not a set of recordings that people have been somehow duped into liking and purchasing, in a uniform way; instead they reflect what is genuinely popular. Fiske supports this by pointing out that record companies and movie studios put out many products which fail: flops outnumber the hits, showing that the public choose which items they actually want and like. Furthermore, people relate to their current favourite single or film, as they relate to all media texts, in a complex, shifting way, based in their own identity, which is unique to themselves. And rather than the people accepting a stream of similar products, as Adorno would suggest, Fiske says that there is a 'drive for innovation and change [which] comes from the audience activity in the cultural economy' (1989c: 62).

Our media choices are limited, to an extent. Fiske says that 'My argument in favour of difference and a relatively empowered, relatively loosely subjected, subject must not blind us to the determining framework of power relations within which all of this takes place' (1989c: 58). Nevertheless, Fiske says there is an 'overspill' of meanings (ibid.: 70), so that most texts contain the 'preferred' meaning – the one intended by its producers – but also offer possibilities for consumers to create their own alternative or resistant readings. Indeed, Fiske says that people are not merely consumers of texts – the audience rejects this role 'and becomes a producer, a producer of meanings and pleasures' (1989c: 59). Following the French theorist Michel de Certeau (1984), Fiske talks about the 'guerrilla tactics' by which everyday media users snatch aspects of the mass-produced media but then (re-)interpret them to suit their own preferred readings. The text is the source from which the viewer *activates meanings* to make sense of their material existence (1989c: 58).

Let us take, for example, the case of Madonna, who was discussed by Fiske over a decade ago, and remains very popular today. By the end of 2001, Madonna had sold around 140 million albums worldwide. For Adorno, this would well illustrate his thesis that the culture industry can mass-produce one product (or a set of similar products) and successfully flog it to an audience of passive consumers – millions of them – who do not seek out their own preferred entertainments, but settle for the work of a manufactured icon whose image is successfully promoted and marketed around the world. For Fiske, it is quite the reverse. Madonna has sold so many million albums because of her ability to connect with an audience, to be meaningful to individuals. Each album sold may be just another 'unit' to record company executives, but at an individual level, it is a unique item which its purchaser invests with a unique set of meanings. Fiske says that Madonna is

> an exemplary popular text because she is so full of contradictions – she contains the patriarchal meanings of feminine sexuality, and the resisting ones that her sexuality is *hers* to use as she wishes in ways that do not require masculine approval ... Far from being an adequate text in herself, she is a provoker of meanings whose cultural effects can be studied only in her multiple and often contradictory circulations.
>
> (1989a: 124)

By saying that Madonna is not an 'adequate' text, Fiske is not commenting on Madonna per se, but is reminding us of his argument that the meaning of any text is not complete until interpreted by an individual within the context of their lives.

Madonna's image, then, becomes 'a site of semiotic struggle between the forces of patriarchal control and feminine resistance, of capitalism and the subordinate, of the adult and the young' (1989b: 97). In short, Madonna is 'a cultural resource of everyday life' who can be used by each individual fan in a different way to add some meanings or pleasures to their existence. This can be carried through to their whole *way of being* in the world, too. 'Madonna offers her fans access to semiotic and social power; at the basic level this works through fantasy, which, in turn, may empower the fan's sense of self and thus affect [their] behaviour in social situations' (ibid.: 113).

This process is not meant to be unique to Madonna and her audience, of

STUART HALL AND HIS PREDECESSORS

Born in Jamaica in 1932, Stuart Hall came to be the best-known figure in the development of British cultural studies. As a leader, facilitator, theorist and editor, he developed key approaches and strands of theory within the field. In some cases he took up the work of influential European theorists and helped to bring them to the attention of English-speaking audiences. A lot of his work was done in collaboration with colleagues from the Birmingham Centre for Contemporary Cultural Studies and the Open University.

Hall's famous 'encoding/decoding' model (1973) suggested that a media producer may 'encode' a certain meaning into their text, which would be based on a certain social context and understandings, but noted that when another person comes to consume that text, their reading ('decoding') of it – based on their own social context and assumptions – is likely to be somewhat different. This might seem obvious, but one benefit of this model was that it highlighted the importance of understanding the meanings and interpretations of significant actors in both media production (journalists, writers, producers, editors) and media reception (the numerous audiences) – as well as those intermediaries in media distribution (executives, marketers, broadcasters, distributors, regulators).

Hall's writings on ideology were more sophisticated, and sought to understand how particular political positions could become meaningful and popular when articulated in terms which people could identify with. (Such communication would primarily take place, of course, through the mass media.) This approach reflected Hall's interest in the work of Antonio Gramsci (1891–1937), who had noted that leaders could win the assent of the people ('hegemony') if they were able to make their policies appear to be 'common sense'. Hall's studies of Thatcherism were rooted in this idea: Thatcherism became successful because it was able to articulate a right-wing political agenda in terms which addressed the concerns of 'ordinary people' and made the solutions seem sensible and obvious (Hall 1983, 1988). In studying the media and gender, one could use this kind of approach to see how the media might make certain formations of masculinity, femininity and sexuality seem to be natural, inevitable and sexy.

Hall's work on ideology also drew on a critical reading of the French Marxist thinker Louis Althusser (1918–1990), whose concept of 'interpellation' purported to show how an individual's identity or sense of self is absorbed into – and, indeed, produced by – the dominant ideologies within a society (Althusser, 1971). Interpellation is typically explained as a kind of hailing – like when a figure of authority calls out 'hey you!', and the individual turns round to recognise that they are being addressed. In this moment the person is constituted as a subject – which means that they recognise and acquiesce to their position within structures of ideology. Interpellation occurs when a person connects with a media text: when we enjoy a magazine or TV show, for example, this uncritical consumption means that the text has *interpellated* us into a certain set of assumptions, and caused us to tacitly accept a particular approach to the world. This can be a fruitful notion, then: it could be said, for example, that lifestyle magazines use glamour, humour and attractive photography to seduce (interpellate) readers into a particular worldview. However, as Hall and others have noted, the approach is limited by its determinism – it attributes power to grand ideologies, and none to individuals.

Hall's work on the media has focused more on productions and representations than audiences, although he assumes the two are connected: Hall suggests that we can try 'to theorise identity as constituted, not outside but within representation; and hence of cinema [or other media], not as a second-order mirror held up to reflect what already exists, but as that form of representation which is able to constitute us as new kinds of subjects, and thereby enable us to discover places from which to speak' (Hall, 1997: 58). This is a clear rationale for studying media representations – although such work can remain at the level of interesting speculation, unless backed up by some responses from actual audiences.

Further Reading: *Stuart Hall: Critical Dialogues in Cultural Studies* (Morley and Chen (eds), 1996); *Althusser: A Critical Reader* (Elliot (ed.), 1994).

course – Fiske would say that this is just an illustration of a mode of media consumption which happens all the time. Similarly, for example, the *TV Living* study found that people used TV science fiction shows as a way of thinking through their sense of 'otherness' – even though they were not, themselves, eccentric Time Lords like *Doctor Who* or alienated androids like Data in *Star Trek: The Next Generation* – and thereby arrived at a comfortable sense of their own identity (Gauntlett and Hill, 1999). The media is thus an 'enabler' of ideas and meanings, promoting diversity and difference, which might lead to social change (Fiske, 1989c: 73). The obvious criticism of Fiske's work is that it is far too optimistic about the challenging impact of mainstream texts – or, to be precise, the challenging consequences of people's own unique readings of mainstream texts. But it's certainly a thought-provoking response to Adorno's extreme pessimism. At this stage in the book I'll leave it for you to decide who you think is closer to the truth. Now we'll move on to consider the empirical, rather than theoretical, studies of the media's impact.

UNHELPFUL PSYCHOLOGY RESEARCH

In the previous chapter we mentioned several ways in which everyday popular media could be expected to affect people's feelings, responses and actions, both in general terms and in relation to ideas about gender. Those were not wholly new observations. Researchers, in particular psychologists, have been studying these matters for a few decades now. When I tell people that I am studying the relationship between media and gender, I sometimes get a sympathetic, puzzled smile, because people assume (quite reasonably) that psychologists must have 'done that' quite satisfactorily already. But, in fact, whilst many studies have indeed been produced, the level of useful insight remains low.

There are two relevant streams of existing research: the research on media 'effects' in general, and the work within psychology on 'development of gender identity'. In this part of the chapter, then, we will look at the shortcomings of media 'effects' studies, followed by the gender-development studies.

Problems with media 'effects' studies

Media 'effects' studies – by which we mean those studies which seek to identify a particular 'effect' which is the result of exposure to a particular type of media content – have had a most unusual history. The majority of this research has been centred, predictably enough, on the question of whether watching violence on screen will lead individuals to be aggressive in real life. On the one hand these studies have been quite popular, with newspapers and politicians always eager to have more of them, and with several (usually American) academics always eager to build entire careers on producing them. On the other hand they have been entirely useless, showing nothing except the somewhat interesting fact of their own redundancy.

The central problem for these studies is that isolating one particular thing, such as TV viewing or magazine reading, as the cause of a person's behaviour is basically impossible. The idea that a bit of media content 'made' somebody do something will always seem silly, for the perfectly good reason that, as we all know, the influences upon any decision to do something are a complex combination of many elements, including previous experiences, opinions, values and suggestions from various sources.

It might seem overhasty to dismiss these studies out of hand. Instead one could consider each piece of research in some detail, as I tried to do once in a whole book dissecting these studies (*Moving Experiences*, 1995). But to do that is really to take these studies much too seriously. Their individual flaws were often curious, amusing and a bit depressing, but would not usually be worthy of much attention, were it not for the fact that 'media effects' continues to be a subject of much public discussion – and also because some 'experts' like to cheekily claim that the case for negative media effects has been proved. (On a UK television discussion about screen violence in 1994, for example, American psychologist Leonard Eron confidently told the audience that in the USA this was no longer an issue for debate: 'The search for media effects is *over*,' he declared, asserting that 'conclusive proof' had finally persuaded everyone that media content could have a clear and identifiable influence on people's behaviour. This claim was, of course, not true). For this reason it remains important to be able to look at the studies themselves – to show, for what it's worth, that they don't show anything.

Generally, however, it makes more sense to tackle the 'media effects' studies in a broader way, considering the paradigmatic problems which almost always dog such research. These I have grouped together in the following list of overarching flaws (Gauntlett, 1998, 2001).

TEN THINGS WRONG WITH THE MEDIA 'EFFECTS' MODEL

1 The effects model tackles social problems 'backwards'

If researchers are concerned about the causes of problematic behaviour, such as violence, it seems obvious that they should study people who engage in these activities, and try to ascertain the roots of their behaviour. Media effects researchers, however, have typically started at the wrong end of this question: informed only by speculation (and often, it seems, a grimly unsympathetic attitude to youth culture), they start with the idea that the media is to blame, and then try to make links *back to* the world of actual violence. This approach to a social problem is, in a literal sense, backwards. To understand violent people, we should study violent people. But in the uncommon cases where researchers have sought to identify links between screen violence and real-life violence by interviewing actual violent individuals (e.g. Hagell and Newburn, 1994), they have found no such connection.

2 The effects model treats children as inadequate

The media effects studies position children exclusively as potential 'victims' of the mass media, and (rather cruelly) allow young people no opportunity to express their critical abilities, intelligence, or free will. Hundreds of shallow quantitative studies, usually conducted by 'psychologists', have often been little more than traps for the subjects, and ironically allow no scope for developing psychological insights. More generous research methods, which are willing to listen to children, have shown that they can talk intelligently and indeed cynically about the mass media (Buckingham, 1993, 1996), and that children as young as seven can make thoughtful, critical and 'media literate' video productions themselves (Gauntlett, 1997).

3 Assumptions within the effects model are characterised by barely-concealed conservative ideology

Media effects studies support conservative and right-wing ideologies, even if that is not necessarily the conscious intention of the people producing them. The studies typically suggest that social problems are not rooted in the organisation of society, and inequalities, but are actually the evil magic products of popular culture. Their conception of screen violence as a meaningless but measurable 'thing' also helps those who want to blame modern media instead of considering the serious social causes of violence. The researchers' categorisations of 'antisocial' behaviour often reveal that they are worried about challenges to the status quo. The tendency to patronise and devalue children and young people, by assuming that they have no competencies worth considering, also fits with these illiberal trends.

4 The effects model inadequately defines its own objects of study

Media effects studies are usually extremely undiscriminating about how they identify worrying bits of media content, or subsequent behaviour by viewers. An act of 'violence', for example, might be smashing cages to free some trapped animals, or using force to disable a nuclear missile. It might be kicking a chair in frustration, or a horrible murder. In many studies, 'verbal aggression' is included within the categories of aggression, which means that studies which are interpreted by most people as being about physical violence may actually be more about the use of swear words. Once processed by effects research, any of these depictions or actions simply emerge as a 'level of aggression', but without a more selective and discriminating way of compiling these numbers, the results can be deceptive and virtually meaningless.

5 The effects model is often based on artificial studies

Careful sociological studies of media influences require large amounts of time and money, and so they are heavily outnumbered by simpler studies which often put their subjects into artificial, contrived situations. Laboratory and field experiments involve compelling participants to watch a particular programme or set of programmes, and – just as artificially – observing them in a particular setting afterwards. Here, behaviour of the children towards an inanimate object is often taken (artificially) to represent how they would behave towards a real person. Furthermore, this all rests on the artificial belief that children's behaviour will not vary even though they know that they are being manipulated, tested and/or observed. (Studies by researchers such as Borden (1975) have shown that this is quite erroneous – children's behaviour in experiments changes in accordance with what they think the adults would like to see.)

6 The effects model is often based on studies with misapplied methodology

The studies which do not use the experimental method, and so may not be guilty of the flaws described in the previous point, nevertheless often fall down by applying a methodological procedure incorrectly, or by drawing inappropriate conclusions from particular methods. Meaningless comparisons are made, glaring inconsistencies are overlooked, and sometimes methods which are unable to demonstrate any causal links are treated as if they have found them (details in Gauntlett, 1995, 2001). This reckless abuse of research procedures seems to be acceptable when people are pinning blame on 'media effects'.

7 The effects model is selective in its criticisms of media depictions of violence

The ideological motive behind effects studies (see point 3 above) may mean that some media representations are criticised, whilst others are strangely exempt. Violence in news and factual programmes, for example, which is often presented suddenly and without much context, is not seen as a worry, whereas violence in popular drama and movies is of great concern. This again suggests that researchers are more interested in blaming an aspect of popular culture for social problems, than they are in making a coherent and thoughtful argument.

8 The effects model assumes superiority to the masses

Researchers always assume that media effects happen to *other people*. Ironically, surveys show that almost everybody feels this way: whilst varying percentages of the population say they are concerned about media effects, almost nobody ever says that they have been affected *themselves*. Sometimes the researchers excuse their approach by saying that they are mature adults, whereas their concerns lie with *children* (see point 2 above).

9 The effects model makes no attempt to understand meanings of the media

As hinted above, the media effects model rests on simplistic assumptions about media content. Controversial material, such as a scene containing violence, is not treated as part of a relationship between characters, but is seen as a 'thing' cynically inserted by media producers. The meanings of the action, and understandings of character motivation held by the audience, are of no interest in effects research, because media content is just a set of measurable threats. Regardless of the tone and intentions of any piece of media content, the media effects model will always assume that its sole meaning is, 'Hey kids! Here's some stuff that you might like to copy!'. But qualitative studies have unsurprisingly given support to the view that media audiences routinely arrive at their own, often quite varied and unpredictable, interpretations of everyday media texts (e.g. Palmer, 1986; Gray, 1992; Schlesinger, Dobash, Dobash and Weaver, 1992; Buckingham, 1993, 1996; Hill, 1997; Gauntlett and Hill, 1999).

10 The effects model is not grounded in theory

The media effects model would make much more sense if it suggested a coherent theory which could explain *why* people might become motivated to copy actions seen in the media. But no decent explanation is offered. Sometimes the idea that violence is 'glamorised' is mooted and can seem relevant, but effects researchers tend to suggest that children must be protected from the most violent media depictions, which are usually the least 'glamorous' depictions. The violence used by dashing spies in 'family' films, say, usually looks much more attractive, but attracts little criticism. The model just isn't subtle or well-thought-out enough to cope with these things.

This lack of theory has led to the proliferation of the ill-considered ideas outlined above – that the media (rather than people) should be the unproblematic starting-point for research; that children will be unable to 'cope' with the media; that categories such as 'antisocial behaviour' are clear and self-evident; that a veneer of 'science' is more important than developing methods which might actually show us something; that screen fictions are of concern, whilst news pictures are not; that researchers have the unique capacity to observe and classify social behaviour and its meanings, but that those researchers need not attend to the various possible meanings which media content may have for the audience. Each of these substantial problems has been able to develop because there is no one with a decent theory to keep them on the straight and narrow.

So much for that, then

The studies which seek to find a simple causal link between seeing something in the media and subsequent behaviour are, therefore, of little use. That's a disappointment at first, but then you realise it's not a great surprise: we all knew the relationship between media and identity was never going to be that simple, anyway. So we can move on.

PSYCHOLOGISTS ON GENDER IDENTITY

Within the field of psychology, the 'received wisdom' and general level of insight about the development of gender identities remains rather shallow and disappointing. If we look at the contemporary general understanding of the area, such as that passed on in psychology textbooks, we find explanations which are alarmingly simple and mundane (e.g. Malim and Birch, 1998; Phares and Chaplin, 1998; Carver and Scheier, 2000; Huffman,

Vernoy and Vernoy, 2000). This shortcoming is not the fault of the text-book writers, but reflects the lack of valuable theory in the psychology field. There are two main positions on gender role development.

- Some psychologists believe that chromosomal and hormonal differences are the main cause of differences between male and female behaviour. They typically point to evidence from situations where people have grown up with different hormone levels and emerge as more 'masculine' or 'feminine'; but the implications of such findings are rarely clear-cut (see, for example, Malim and Birch, 1998: 516–518).
- Other psychologists argue that socialisation is much more important – gender roles are *learned* during development, and reinforced through-out everyday life. There is a lot of evidence to support this case, and it is often conceded that 'most investigators agree that cultural influences and socialization processes are the main determinants of an individual's gender role identity and roles' (ibid.: 518).

This division of views – the standard 'nature vs. nurture' debate – will be familiar to many people from TV documentaries, magazine articles, and even everyday conversations about how one might bring up children. What is more interesting, perhaps, is the way that the arguments and theories don't get *much* more genuinely varied or complicated than this. Those who assign the most importance to biological factors may come up with further bits of 'evidence', but this will always be viewed with suspicion by those who feel that there is something inherently odd about modern-day scientists trying to 'prove' that sex differences are important.

Meanwhile, social learning theory seems to have surprisingly little flesh on its bones. It includes the idea of *modelling* – that we may imitate and take on behaviour which we observe in same-sex role models (such as a parent, peers, and others); and *reinforcement* – that behaviour which is socially approved-of will be well-received, and so we learn to continue and develop it, whereas socially inappropriate actions will not get a good reception and so will be cut from our repertoire. This seems to ring true to every-day experience, and several studies can be cited which appear to show the theory in action (e.g. Malim and Birch, 1998: 518–519). There's not much *to* it, though, is there?

There is another approach, 'cognitive-developmental theory', which also regards gender roles as learned, but sees the child as more active in the cre-ation of their own gender identity. In this model, the child's own cogni-tions (thought processes) are imperative, as they organise and make sense of the messages about gender which they receive. The child's journey through

GENDER DIFFERENCES ARE FOR OTHER PEOPLE

In one of the more interesting psychology studies, Williams and Best (1977, 1990) produced a 'sex stereotype index' by showing a long list of adjectives to men and women, and asking them to rate each word according to whether it was most associated with women or men. Subsequent studies could then ask people to pick words which described themselves, or others, from this list.

It was found that when participants were asked to pick words which described themselves, there was considerable overlap in the adjectives picked by men and women. Indeed, over 25 per cent of men had self-descriptions that were more stereotypic of women than the average women's stereotype, and over 25 per cent of women had self-descriptions that were more stereotypic of men than the average men's stereotype.

However, when asked to describe *friends*, participants typically gave them somewhat more stereotypical characteristics, and in describing men and women in general, the assessments were clearly divided along stereotyped lines.

These findings suggest that we don't really expect gender stereotypes to apply to ourselves – complicated beings that we know ourselves to be – but that we still apply them to everyone else!

stages of cognitive development is also important. Once a child has acquired 'gender constancy' – the understanding that they are expected to have a continuous gender identity which does not change between different situations – they will then seek to develop their personality within an appropriately 'masculine' or 'feminine' mould (Kohlberg, 1966). This model, then, has the child *actively seeking* information about how to act like a boy or girl, rather than the somewhat more passive modelling described in social learning theory. A development of this approach, called 'gender schematic processing theory' (Martin, 1991), suggests that children initially learn that certain activities and interests are appropriate for one sex or the other – that's the *gender schema* of the title; and then they learn about and interpret the world in terms of this schema, paying most attention to material which will reinforce their own gendered identity.

Like a lot of social psychology, these theories are blandly descriptive on the one hand, whilst also being rather deterministic (or fatalistic) in tone on the other – as if relating a process which will *always* occur. In other words, they make it sound like a natural and necessary part of child development, that a young boy has to recognise the importance of cultivating a masculine identity, or that a girl has to reach a point where she realises the need to develop feminine traits. To be fair, the theories could also be read as critiques of a society which compels children to see these things as important (but the flatly 'scientific', descriptive tone of most child development writing is unlikely to suggest this).

Furthermore, there is the fear that these theories could be used in ways which would reinforce the traditional status quo. People who did not want to conform to gender conventions could be seen to have 'failed' to have acquired 'gender constancy', whilst children interested in non-stereotypical activities could be said to have an incomplete gender schema. This has certainly been an acceptable part of 'psychology' work to date, where people who don't fit within a traditional cultural norm end up being told that they have a medical disorder. For example, whilst the official diagnostic manual of American psychiatrists ceased to define homosexuality as pathological in 1973, in 1980 it introduced a new illness called 'gender identity disorder', which explains that girls or boys who are interested in non-stereotypical activities may have fallen prey to this psychological malady. This 'disorder' is still officially recognised today (see Rekers, 1995; Bartlett *et al.*, 2000; Miller, 2000; Wilson, 2001).

We should acknowledge that there is one more complex section of the 'nurture' camp: the theories based on Freud's psychoanalytic approach. Gender identity is here seen as an outcome of the Oedipus/Electra complex; ideally, the developing child will achieve stability by identifying with their same-sex parent at the end of this stage. Like most Freudian theory, however, this is unproven and speculative – indeed, it's not even clear whether we are meant to take it literally. It might be of value as a metaphor which can be used in some psychiatric situations, but otherwise seems to have little authority. Nevertheless, psychoanalytic theory played a key role in some feminist film theories, which we turn to now.

LAURA MULVEY AND THE 'MALE GAZE'

The publication of Laura Mulvey's article 'Visual pleasure and narrative cinema' in 1975 (reproduced in Hollows *et al.*, 2000, and elsewhere), had a huge impact on feminist film studies in particular, and the study of film, gender and representation more generally. Mulvey's argument rested on a number of psychoanalytic (Freudian) concepts and assumptions, combined with a rather fatalistic form of feminism (and heterosexuality), all of which were clearly popular at the time.

PSYCHOLOGY LOVES THE STATUS QUO

The academic field of psychology often seems to reinforce the status quo, by offering 'explanations' for why things are the way they are. In terms of gender, the field has a subdivision for considering 'the psychology of women', as if women are an entirely different species from men and need to be studied separately. The American Psychological Association has a large 'Psychology of Women' division; there is a successful textbook with associated university classes, *The Psychology of Women* by Margaret Matlin (fourth edition, 2000); a journal, *Psychology of Women Quarterly*; and other books and teaching materials which refer to 'the psychology of women'. Whilst some women will have experiences which men are less likely to have – sexist discrimination, and particularly pregnancy and childbirth – these will not necessarily happen, and to encourage the idea that it makes sense to talk about 'women's psychology' as a coherent and unique entity plays directly into the hands of sexist ideology.

A more critical problem in the discipline of psychology lies in its façade of scientific certainty. The desire to present psychology as a *science* which is using reliable methods to gather *empirical data* means that psychologists typically suppress the fact that all of this knowledge is based on debatable methods deployed by humans who usually have a point to make. (This is the case across the humanities, of course, but elsewhere scholars are more willing to be explicit about their assumptions and uncertainties.) Psychology textbooks, which train the psychologists of the future, are perhaps most guilty of this – they often report the conclusions of research studies as if they are universal fact, rather than the possibly-contentious claims made by researchers on the basis of a localised study which used particular methods (all of which we need to know the details of in order to assess a study's claims.) The insecurity of psychologists about the 'scientific' status of their work can be seen in their embarrassing use of ultra-scientific discourses in a bid to 'paper over the cracks'. The idea seems to be that if psychology is only ever spoken of as a body of scientific fact, then it will somehow become one.

(For more on this, with examples, see the longer version of this section in the 'Extra features' for this book at www.theoryhead.com.)

Mulvey argued that one of the pleasures of cinema is 'scopophilia', a voyeuristic gaze directed at other people. This kind of viewing is encouraged in the cinema, Mulvey suggests, because the conventions of mainstream film 'portray a hermetically sealed world which unwinds magically, indifferent to the presence of the audience', and the darkness of the theatre contrasts with the light of the screen, again helping to promote the 'voyeuristic separation' (1975: 9). Mulvey asserts that a second form of pleasure offered by cinema is a *narcissistic* voyeurism – seeing oneself in a primary character and identifying with them (or, in Mulvey's terms, *him*). At this point in the argument, Mulvey's clear-cut sense of imposed sex roles becomes apparent:

> In a world ordered by sexual imbalance, pleasure in looking has been split between active/male and passive/female. The determining male gaze projects its phantasy onto the female figure, which is styled accordingly. In their traditional exhibitionist role women are simultaneously looked at and displayed, with their appearance coded for strong visual and erotic impact so that they can be said to connote *to-be-looked-at-ness.*
>
> (ibid.: 10)

Male viewers identify with the (male) protagonist, and the female characters are the subject of their desiring gaze. Female viewers, Mulvey says, are also compelled to take the viewpoint of the central (male) character, so that women are denied a viewpoint of their own and instead participate in the pleasure of men looking at women. ('Men look at women; women watch themselves being looked at', as John Berger had put it (1972: 47).) The female character has no importance in a film, Mulvey says, except as a 'spectacle', the erotic object of both the male characters and the cinema spectators; her role is to drive the hero to act the way he does. (This can certainly be seen in many films – think of *Die Hard* (1988) and *Die Hard II* (1990), say, where Bonnie Bedelia is in peril and does very little, whilst her husband Bruce Willis is thereby motivated to go to extremes to save her – and a lot of other people, of course, to underline his heroism). Male viewers would not want to view the male hero as a sexual object, Mulvey says, 'according to the principles of the ruling ideology' (1975: 14), but since he drives the story and makes things happen, identification means he can be admired *narcissistically*, as an ideal version of the self.

Mulvey's article is well-written, thoughtful and interesting – unlike the pseudo-scientific 'psychology' studies discussed above. She is also able to illustrate her thesis with some examples from classic cinema – Hitchcock's films in particular. However, the argument is based on some premises which make it (arguably?) untenable. Mulvey says that the heroes that drive the story are always male, whilst female characters are passive erotic objects. Although it is not difficult to think of films where this occurs, particularly ones made in the time prior to Mulvey's mid-1970s text, today we can list many films with heroic females, and only note a few recent films where women are passive; Chapter 4 of this book gives many examples. (Of course, there is still a troublesome imbalance, and room for many more female heroes and leaders in mainstream movies.)

Perhaps a bigger problem with Mulvey's argument is that it denies the heterosexual female gaze altogether. Within her model, the audience, both male and female, is positioned so that they admire the male lead for his actions, and adopt his romantic/erotic view of the women. There is value in the idea that women come to learn to view themselves and other women through the 'male gaze', given the dominance of male-produced media; but to deny the 'female gaze' altogether does little service to women (although Mulvey's point is not that women are *inadequate* in this respect; rather, she is making a critique of *the position that patriarchy puts women into*). But since their earliest days, movies have included and often *celebrated* physically attractive men, whose sexual allure has surely drawn women into cinemas. Today, women's magazine *More!* rates films with a 'Totty factor' which ranks the desirability of the male stars ('We'd happily tuck into Jonathan Tucker', they note about a star of *The Deep End* (12 December 2001), for example, and note that 'Brad [Pitt] will have you drooling' in *Spy Game* (14 November 2001)).

Mulvey's argument cannot be too strong if a mainstream film like *Lara Croft: Tomb Raider* (2001) can bounce it off the rails altogether. (Note that the artistic merits of this crowd-pulling, if perhaps not very well-written film are not significant here.) Mulvey would be right to note that Angelina Jolie as the titular character is 'coded for strong visual and erotic impact [which] can be said to connote *to-be-looked-at-ness*' (although you could say just the same of, say, Russell Crowe in *Gladiator* (2000)). But rather than being the object of desire who inspires the hero to action, Lara Croft *is* the hero, driving the story forward on her own, and reserving the right to eye certain men with desire – none of which can fit into the Mulvey model at all.

FILM STUDIES BEYOND MULVEY

Ultimately, then, Mulvey's argument may help to illuminate certain films, and some male spectator positions, but simply *does not work* as a comprehensive account of gendered viewings of film today. (The idea that women learn to absorb the 'male gaze' is provocative, though, and will appear again in this book.) Mulvey's article is still discussed and reprinted in film studies textbooks, but feminist film studies has advanced in the meantime. As Liesbet Van Zoonen put it in 1994, 'Mulvey's dark and suffocating analysis of patriarchal cinema has lost ground to a more confident and empowering approach which foregrounds the possibilities of "subversive", that is, non-patriarchal modes of female spectatorship' (1994: 97). Here, the 1970s idea that inevitably-sexist cinema could offer no pleasures to women, was replaced by the 1980s idea that women could find their *own* pleasures in inevitably-sexist cinema (Arbuthnot and Seneca, 1982; Stacey, 1987). Whilst rightfully assigning more agency to women, this approach seems almost as tragically resigned to the patriarchal nature of movies as its predecessor: instead of seeking social change, or even just change in the movies, viewers resign themselves to making 'subversive' readings, or highlighting unusually subversive texts.

By the late 1990s, film studies had begun to change again. Yvonne Tasker's book *Working Girls: Gender and Sexuality in Popular Cinema* (1998) offered a thoughtful, intelligent discussion of newer Hollywood representations of women. Although the roles and images of women in popular movies were generally far from feminist ideals, Tasker does not dwell on the easy-to-find examples of embarrassing sexism in Hollywood product, but provides a thoughtful analysis of the newer roles played by women: as action heroes, detectives, cowgirls, and empowered music stars. She also notes the growing number of equal male/female partnerships (e.g. *Speed, Strange Days, Broken Arrow*). Some baggage from the history of film studies remains: for example, the clothing of the female heroes in *Aliens*, *Terminator 2* and *The Long Kiss Goodnight* is observed to be 'masculine' (Tasker, 1998: 68), which is a silly concern to raise about their sensible apparel (the critic would presumably be no happier to see these women in impractical long dresses . . . or short skirts). The discipline of film studies has a long-standing interest in masculine and feminine archetypes, though – even though these terms are beginning to shed meaning. Overall, Tasker's study is a welcome return to a well-observed engagement with texts. Audience studies are needed too, of course, but these should engage with *actual* viewers. Mulvey's work – which doesn't warrant a single mention in Tasker's book – only considered the viewer as a theoretical psychoanalytic construct in any case.

SUMMARY

At the start of this chapter we considered two rather polarised approaches to the potential power of the media. One view, represented by Adorno, suggested that the mass media has considerable power over the population. The 'culture industry' churns out products which keep the audience blandly entertained, but passive, helping to maintain the status quo by encouraging conformity and diminishing the scope for resistance. Representing the opposite view, Fiske argued that popular culture is created by the people. Rather than being turned into submissive zombies, media audiences have an active and creative engagement with popular culture, using 'guerrilla' tactics to reinterpret media texts to suit their own purposes. Meaning is not sent from 'above' by the culture industry, but is generated 'on the ground' by media users. Neither one of these views can be seen as the 'correct' one – although it's partly a matter of opinion and ideology. (We might like to consider whether a more useful account, matching neither extreme in this polarized debate, can be found. Stuart Hall's ideas, for example, suggest just one kind of 'third way' approach, and others are available.)

The chapter then took a more pessimistic turn as we considered previous empirical studies of media power. The 'media effects' research tradition, which had gone to great lengths to identify the effects of exposure to particular instances of popular media, was seen to have failed for a variety of reasons. The attempts of psychologists to account for the development of gender identities were also found to be rather lacking in depth. Furthermore, the whole approach of the psychology discipline was attacked for its tendency to reinforce the status quo, instead of helping to generate more progressive, challenging or optimistic approaches.

Some classic 'cultural studies' approaches to media, gender and identity developed from Mulvey's feminist film studies thesis, but as we saw, this rested on a monolithic view of male and female roles (in both film and reality). These arguments have fallen from grace more recently, but in the absence of other big ideas, they are still discussed in film classes. This, then, is the historical background to the study of media, gender and identity, and it is not short of some rather disappointing, simplistic and/or sexist ideas. Having set out this series of disappointments, we'd better get on with the rest of the book.

Chapter 3

REPRESENTATIONS OF GENDER IN THE PAST

THIS CHAPTER AND the next one provide an overview of representations of gender in the media. Attempting to talk about such a broad topic, the images of women and men – that's all people – within such a broad field – 'the media' – is a very tall order. Each week a new set of movies is released. Every day, television broadcasters put out dramas, news, current affairs programmes, documentaries, children's entertainment, game shows, chat shows, lifestyle programmes, films, soap operas, music videos and more. Magazines, newspapers and adverts all contain images of women and men, and even songs on the radio (or played in shops and cafes) might feed into, or challenge, our ideas about gender. The internet and World Wide Web bring even more information and ideas into our lives; the material we see online is more likely to be material we have requested quite specifically, but as online magazines and general entertainment sites become increasingly popular, and these merge with digital television, electronic media becomes yet another source of gender information.

So there are many sources of images and ideas about gender, and each one contains a colossal amount of information. This chapter will, then, be a radically simplified overview of general trends in the representations of genders from around the middle of the previous century up to the start of the 1990s. The subsequent chapter covers representations of gender from the 1990s to the present.

WOMEN AND MEN ON TV

Gunter (1995) and Elasmar *et al.* (1999) provide useful summaries of the findings of various content analysis studies, which have counted the prevalence of women and men in significant speaking roles in TV shows. In the 1950s, 1960s and 1970s, only 20 to 35 per cent of characters were female. By the mid-1980s, there were more women in leading roles, but still there were twice as many men on screen. (These figures are generally based on reliable studies of US television; there is no evidence that in Europe the proportions were much different).

Gender disparities varied between programme types, of course. In the mid-1970s, Miles (1975) found that there were nearly equal proportions of men and women in situation comedies – although, of course, the gender roles and the humour could still be traditional and sexist, despite this statistical parity – whereas in action-adventure shows, only 15 per cent of the leading characters were women. A decade later, a 1987 study found female characters to be most common in comedy programmes (43 per cent), but outnumbered two to one in dramas, and in action-adventure shows women had almost doubled their showing to a still-low 29 per cent of characters (Davis, 1990).

Gunter goes on to show how studies in the 1970s consistently found that marriage, parenthood and domesticity were shown on television to be more important for women than men (1995: 13–14). A study by McNeil (1975) concluded that the women's movement had been largely ignored by television, with married housewives being the main female role shown. Women's interactions were very often concerned with romance or family problems (in 74 per cent of cases) whereas men's interactions were not frequently concerned with these matters (only 18 per cent of cases). Female characters were unlikely to work, especially not if they were wives or mothers, and even when they did, this work was typically not seen on screen, McNeil found. Furthermore, various other studies in the 1970s found men to be the dominant characters and the decision-makers on TV; for example, men were twice as likely to make decisions or to give orders, whilst women who were successful at work – where they were to be found – did not get on well with men, or have happy relationships (ibid.: 16–17).

Overall, men were more likely to be assertive (or aggressive), whilst women were more likely to be passive. Men were much more likely to be adventurous, active and victorious, whereas women were more frequently shown as weak, ineffectual, victimised, supportive, laughable, or 'merely token females' (Gunter, 1995).

The potential consequences of this were highlighted by Gaye Tuchman in her well-known article with the striking title, 'The Symbolic Annihilation of Women by the Mass Media' (1978):

> From children's shows to commercials to prime-time adventures and situation comedies, television proclaims that women don't count for much. They are underrepresented in television's fictional life – they are 'symbolically annihilated.' . . . The paucity of women on American television tells viewers that women don't matter much in American society.
>
> (1978: 10–11)

It wasn't just a problem of numbers, either. Tuchman asserts that those women who *were* shown to be working were portayed as 'incompetents and inferiors', as victims, or having 'trivial' interests. Even in women's traditional domain of the home, men were shown solving both emotional and practical problems – leaving women with little value in the TV world (ibid.: 13–14).

A decade later, the book *Boxed In: Women and Television* (Baehr and Dyer (eds), 1987) reported a mixture of the sexist legacy described above, and changing times:

> Television [in the mid-1980s] is increasingly taking women seriously, and there are a number of programmes, or types of programme, that feature women in a more central way . . . Women's issues have arrived on the media agenda – documentaries, discussion programmes and dramas on female topics such as infertility, cervical and breast cancer, rape, etc.
>
> (Dyer, 1987: 7)

From today's perspective it seems sad that women would have been particularly *grateful* for the addition of a few worthy programmes on these serious subjects. The idea that they are 'female topics' is not ideal either (surely men *and* women are affected by these issues?). Elsewhere, TV remained stubborn, with game shows not bothering to change their 'degrading and trivialising views of women', sports programming remaining 'the preserve of men', and news programmes accused of tokenism or 'window dressing' by including some women in key positions whilst retaining a male-dominated culture (Dyer, 1987: 7–8).

The situation in 1980s TV drama was more complex. Gillian Dyer observed that the number of women in central roles in police and crime series had increased, but found a new reason for discomfort:

This development, although in many ways refreshing, raises new contradictions in the portrayal of power and gender for, ironically, 'strong' women policewomen, lawyers, etc. are invariably shown enforcing the patriarchal laws which oppress them.

(1987: 10)

This criticism seems a little unfair. Female TV cops would, like their male counterparts, usually be seen investigating murders or robberies, the laws they were applying are not notably 'patriarchal' or oppressive to women. The other kinds of serious crime which TV detectives might investigate are, of course, rape and sexual abuse, and the introduction of female characters into these investigations clearly *did* make a difference (see *Cagney and Lacey*, *The Bill*, *Juliet Bravo* and other police series at the time, and parallel stories in *LA Law*). Although perhaps it could be called 'tokenism', the rape storyline was typically an opportunity for programme makers to build drama around the feminist critique of police attitudes, and for female characters to clash with the 'old guard' who might not treat rape very sensitively.

WOMEN AND MEN IN MOVIES

Unsurprisingly, the roles of women and men in the movies were generally very similar to their TV counterparts. Here we'll look briefly through recent decades, mentioning films which were amongst the most prominent and successful at the time (see box office and other information at www.imdb.com). This broad-sweep approach, taking in movies that the largest number of people will have seen, is a deliberate alternative to the method typically seen in film studies, where single films – often selected for their uniqueness – are studied in depth. Books such as *Women and Film* (Kaplan, 1983), *Screening the Male* (Cohan and Rae Hark, 1993), *You Tarzan: Masculinity, Movies and Men* (Kirkham and Thumim, 1993), *Me Jane: Masculinity, Movies and Women* (Kirkham and Thumim, 1995), *Feminism and Film* (Humm, 1997) and *Working Girls: Gender and Sexuality in Popular Cinema* (Tasker, 1998, as noted in the previous chapter) offer detailed analyses of gender representations in particular films. These pieces are often intriguing and insightful – although the reader is haunted by concern that each film discussed may be atypical, telling us little about gender in the *majority* of popular films. Here I will assume that you have seen a few films from the past and will have your own idea of how gender was typically shown; this is just an attempt to summarise, and jog the memory.

In the 1950s, the most popular films included *High Noon* (1952), *12 Angry Men* (1957), *Bridge on the River Kwai* (1957), *Touch of Evil* (1959), as well as Hitchcock classics such as *Strangers on a Train* (1951), *Rear Window* (1954) and *North by Northwest* (1959). The films almost always focused on male heroes. These men typically made the decisions which led the story, and were assertive, confident and dominant. Women had important roles in many films but were far more likely than men to be shown as frightened, in need of protection and direction, and offering love and support to the male lead character(s). The stylishness of the gentlemen at the heart of Hitchcock's thrillers, say, can seem more 'feminine' than the grunting macho heroes of 1980s action films, but it was tied to a buttoned-down, statesmanlike, quick-thinking masculinity which contrasted with the feminine beauty and lack of assertiveness of key women characters. *Some Like it Hot* (1959) played with the performance of gender, but only hinted at a challenge to masculine and feminine roles.

The 1960s gave us hits like *Lawrence of Arabia* (1962), *The Manchurian Candidate* (1962), *Dr Strangelove* (1964), *The Sound of Music* (1965), *Doctor Zhivago* (1965) and *2001: A Space Odyssey* (1968). Gender roles, on average, did not differ greatly from the previous decade. The sixties may have been 'swinging', to some extent, but the impact on film scripts, in terms of gender roles, seems quite minimal. As before, it would be wrong to suggest that all women characters were shown as inept, or were always cast as housewives, but male characters were consistently more intelligent, more assertive – and much more prevalent.

In the 1970s, Leia in the decade's top hit *Star Wars* (1977) was pretty good at shooting stormtroopers, but she was also the prized princess that the heroic boys had to rescue, and win the heart of. Ripley in *Alien* (1979), though, was a superior female interplanetary survivor. Other popular films of the seventies such as *The Godfather* (1972), *The Sting* (1973), *The Exorcist* (1973), *Jaws* (1975), *The Deer Hunter* (1978) and *Superman* (1978) fit within the model described for previous decades. Although Lois Lane in *Superman* is a successful reporter, for example, it is still the (super-)heroic man who leads the story and saves the world. Woody Allen found success with films like *Annie Hall* (1977) and *Manhattan* (1979), featuring intelligent women who captured the eye of the famously witty but neurotic and un-macho leading man – which was, at least, somewhat different to the norm.

The 1980s saw Ripley become stronger in *Aliens* (1986), and Sarah Connor was courageous in *The Terminator* (1984), even if patronising future-people did send a man back in time to save her. An executive with an instinct for equal opportunities green-lighted *Supergirl* (1984) but forgot to make it a good film. Meanwhile the reliable heroic male still featured prominently in most films, including the *Indiana Jones* series (1981, 1984, 1989), the *Rambo* series (1982, 1985, 1988), *Crocodile Dundee* (1986), *Die Hard* (1988), and many more. The likeable, funny guys in comedies like *Ghostbusters* (1984) and *Back to the Future* (1985) didn't have any strong female competition. *Three Men and a Baby* (1987) – despite being based on the idea that whilst one woman can readily deal with a baby, even as many as *three* men are going to have trouble – at least gave us something different to contemplate.

This quick skim over films from the 1950s to the 1980s is, it must be admitted, rather simplistic. As the film studies books mentioned at the start of this section show, masculinity and femininity in films is often rather precarious. Characters are made more interesting by being imperfectly masculine, or slightly-different-to-what-you-might-expect feminine, and the nuances of these gender characterisations are often worthy of some examination. The character of Indiana Jones, to take one example, is the typical macho action-adventure hero on the one hand, but we see him being tender with women in each film, acting as a father to Short Round in the second picture, and responding as a son to his dad in the third. We can, no doubt, spot homoerotic elements in the films. We can note that things often go wrong for Indy – his plans are not flawless, and his attractive body may be damaged. *Nevertheless* as with almost all male heroes in almost all films, Indiana Jones is basically reliable and decisive and victorious. We may find some imperfections or quirks, but he's basically *outstanding* as a hero, and unquestionably masculine.

Women's roles, also, have much more complexity and value than my summary suggests. The history of movies is no doubt full of remarkable female characters in supporting roles. Even in a straightforward action hit like *Raiders of the Lost Ark* (1981), to continue the previous example, Karen Allen is not simply a 'love interest' for the hero, but is a spunky, assertive and intelligent character in her own right. *Nevertheless*, she doesn't lead the story, she doesn't make the central decisions, she doesn't repeatedly save her male colleague, and she's not the star of the film. This, we have to note, has typically been the place of women in films.

Feminist critics have put it even more starkly. In 1973, Marjorie Rosen asserted that 'the Cinema Woman is a Popcorn Venus, a delectable but insubstantial hybrid of cultural distortions' (1973: 10). Rosen charted the changing representations of women in Hollywood films, noting backlashes against working women in the 1940s and 1950s, and against female sexual emancipation in the 1960s and 1970s. The representation of women as 'sex objects' varied in *style* but was otherwise constant throughout (Rosen,

1973). The early 1970s also saw the launch of a journal, *Women and Film*, in the first issue of which Sharon Smith declared:

> Women, in any fully human form, have almost completely been left out of film ... The role of a woman in a film almost always revolves around her physical attraction and the mating games she plays with the male characters. On the other hand a man is not shown purely in relation to the female characters, but in a wide variety of roles.
>
> (1972: 13)

A decade later, E. Ann Kaplan felt able to be just as sweeping:

> In Hollywood films, then, women are ultimately refused a voice, a discourse, and their desire is subjected to male desire. They live out silently frustrated lives, or, if they resist their placing, sacrifice their lives for their daring.
>
> (1983: 7–8)

And at the start of the 1990s, Kathi Maio – in a book of her film reviews – observed that Hollywood's ideas about gender were 'often reprehensible' (1991: vii). As a jobbing reviewer, Maio had sat through many popular films of the 1980s (in happy contrast to those film *theorists* who sometimes seemed to have avoided mainstream films altogether). She was not impressed (ibid.: 2):

> Women are not only given less screen time, when we're up there on the screen we are likely to be portrayed as powerless and ineffectual ... Where are the *triumphant* women heroes to match the winner roles men play constantly?

Maio is pleased to find a few exceptions, and notes the roles for resourceful females in *Dead Calm* (1989) and *Heathers* (1989). 'Strong, victorious women [do] exist in film,' she says. 'Just not often enough, and generally not in movies that get much play' (ibid.: 4).

In her best-selling book *Backlash: The Undeclared War Against Women* (1991), Susan Faludi went one step further, arguing that films of the 1980s such as *Fatal Attraction* (1987) and *Baby Boom* (1987) were part of a wider backlash against women's liberation and women's careers. She also noted women being 'reduced to mute and incidental characters or banished altogether' in action movies like *Predator* (1987), *Lethal Weapon* (1987) and *Days of Thunder* (1990) (1991: 169). Even the tough Ripley in *Aliens* is criticised because her motivation to defend the little girl Newt is 'maternal' (ibid.: 145). Faludi marshals an impressive array of evidence to show that the backlash against women stretched throughout popular media and political culture. Some of the examples seem rather exceptional – even the archetypal 'backlash' film, *Fatal Attraction*, was rather unique and not representative of many other movies. Nevertheless, Faludi leaves the reader in no doubt that these 'backlash' tendencies were certainly in circulation.

JAMES BOND AND CHANGING TIMES

The long-running series of James Bond films span the decades, and so give us a chance to see gender roles develop. But in truth, they don't develop much. The charming, tough, self-reliant Bond seen in *Dr No* (1962) had not changed much 19 films later, in *The World is Not Enough* (1999), although the character was at his most patronising to women during the Roger Moore era (1973–1985). His AIDS-aware reincarnation as Timothy Dalton was relatively monogamous in *The Living Daylights* (1987), but this didn't go down so well with audiences. Next time round, in *Licence to Kill* (1989), Dalton's Bond had extinguished all charm and was as romantic as an iceberg. Thankfully recast as Pierce Brosnan in *Goldeneye* (1995), Bond faces his most difficult clash with modernity. His boss, 'M', is now Judi Dench, an authoritative woman who tells him: 'You are a sexist misogynist dinosaur, a relic from the Cold War.' Bond isn't used to this kind of thing. Even the age-old flirtation between Bond and Moneypenny takes a new turn as she mentions – albeit not seriously – that 'this kind of behaviour could qualify as sexual harassment'. Later, in a rare introspective scene, Izabella Scorupco asks Bond, 'How can you be so cold?' He says, 'It's what keeps me alive,' but she tells him: 'No. It's what keeps you alone.' In subsequent films, however, it was business as usual.

Although Bond changes little, the female characters have become more resourceful as the series progressed. For example, not-very-frightening Christopher Walken has superstrong Grace Jones to protect him in *A View to a Kill* (1985), Michelle Yeoh is a martial arts ace in *Tomorrow Never Dies* (1997), and Denise Richards shows that Bond-girl good looks don't stop you being a nuclear scientist in *The World is Not Enough*.

WOMEN'S MAGAZINES IN THE PAST

Today there is a well-known, comical stereotype of the ways in which women's magazines and adverts used to address women as simpering housewives whose dream was to impress their authoritative, working husbands by using the latest kitchen accessory or washing powder. The advice offered to women was not about how to fulfil their own potential, but was instead focused on bringing happiness to their family. Unlike some stereotypes, this one is based on reality: these mags and ads really did exist. (Lifestyle magazines for men, incidentally, did not really take off until the 1990s, and so this book does not contain a parallel *historical* section about magazines for men – but see the discussions of modern men's magazines, pp. 152–180).

Betty Friedan's *The Feminine Mystique* (1963) was the first major assault upon these images of 'the happy housewife heroine'. As a former contributor to women's magazines, Friedan had become troubled by the image of blissful domesticity she was helping to propagate. She considers a typical issue of *McCall's* magazine, from July 1960:

> The image of woman that emerges from this big, pretty magazine is young and frivolous, almost childlike; fluffy and feminine; passive; gaily content in a world of bedroom and kitchen, sex, babies, and home. The magazine surely does not leave out sex; the only goal a woman is permitted is the pursuit of a man. It is crammed full of food, clothing, cosmetics, furniture, and the physical bodies of young women, but where is the world of thought and ideas, the life of the mind and spirit?
>
> (1963: 32)

From the 1940s to Friedan's present (the 1960s), women's magazines had focused on this feminine, home-bound image – but they did not trivialise it; on the contrary, the emphasis was on the great *importance* of this role, in both societal and personal terms. The social value of the housewife was often celebrated and praised. On the other side of the coin, fear of deviance was also fostered. Friedan reports that in the 1940s:

> All the magazines were echoing Farnham and Lundberg's *Modern Woman: The Lost Sex*, which came out in 1942, with its warning that careers and higher education were leading to the 'masculinization of women with enormously dangerous consequences to the home, the children dependent on it and to the

ability of the woman, as well as her husband, to obtain sexual gratification.'

(ibid.: 37)

In the 1950s, concerns that women may have had about their lack of a career were countered with the promotion of 'Occupation: Housewife', one of the most crucial roles in society. The senior staff on women's magazines were mostly men – but these men had a clear idea of what women wanted. As Friedan recalls:

> Writing for these magazines [in the 1950s], I was continually reminded by editors that 'women *have* to identify'. Once I wanted to write an article about an artist. So I wrote about her cooking and [shopping] and falling in love with her husband, and painting a crib for her baby. I had to leave out the hours she spent painting her pictures, her serious work – and the way she felt about it. You could sometimes get away with writing about a woman who was not really a housewife, if you made her *sound* like a housewife, if you left out her commitment to the world outside the home, or the private vision of mind or spirit that she pursued.

(ibid.: 46)

We should note that the 1950s seem to have been a particularly low point for aspirational women; magazines from the 1930s and early 1940s were not afraid to talk about career women – although, ideally, these women's 'feminine' qualities would be emphasised as well (Friedan, 1963). However, it is worth noting that, according to Tuchman, some magazines of the 1950s – *Glamour, Mademoiselle* and *Cosmopolitan* – assumed that women would work *until the birth of their first child*, and accordingly stressed 'the joys of achievement and power' for women in work (1978: 22). However, finding a man to marry and have those children with was still a primary – and seemingly inevitable – goal.

The 1960s saw the seeds of change, sparked in part by the publication of Friedan's book, but the world of magazines was not transformed overnight. Indeed, the traditional titles such as *Family Circle, Ladies' Home Journal, Woman's Own* and *Woman's Weekly*, continued to do well, flourishing *alongside* the less traditional titles which slowly emerged. *Ms*, for example, was launched from New York in 1972, the first US national monthly 'by women, for women' to have been inspired by the women's liberation movement (Phillips, 1978). From the start, the magazine focused on politics, women's achievements outside the home, global current affairs and feminist issues – and was successful (although a circulation of 380,000 by 1975 did not exactly compare with *Family Circle*'s figure of eight million). Barbara Phillips (1978) observed that the 'heroines' featured in *Ms*'s articles were not women who had become millionaires – the traditional model by which American men would be judged a success – but rather were women who had helped to bring important political, social or cultural changes. Therefore it could be argued – as Phillips does – that women were still being praised for their selfless virtue – a 'feminine' trait. This seems unduly picky though, especially as a magazine which simply applied so-called 'male' values to women would be criticised too, for not challenging the accepted models of what makes a person successful or important.

In 1987, Janice Winship's book *Inside Women's Magazines* was published. This was notable because Winship, who felt connected to and sympathetic with the women's movement, dared to break some unwritten feminist rules by admitting that she found women's magazines enjoyable, by suggesting that they could sometimes be engaging and useful, and by noting that magazines were changing in the 1970s and 1980s to take account of women's changing position in society. Winship explains at the start that feminist friends and colleagues had seemed to think that studying women's magazines was unimportant: 'Surely we all know women's magazines demean women and solely benefit capitalist profits. What more is there to say?' (1987: xiii). But Winship was undeterred:

> I continued to believe that it was as important to understand what women's magazines were about as it was, say, to understand how sex discrimination operated in the workplace. I felt that to simply dismiss women's magazines was also to dismiss the lives of millions of women who read and enjoyed them each week.
>
> (ibid.: xiii)

Winship's case studies take in the traditional, such as *Woman's Own*, which in the 1980s was still offering the familiar regular sections on home, fashion, beauty, cookery, knitting and fiction. Winship observed that the magazine was apolitical, casually racist and assumed that its readers were married or would like to be. So far, so predictable. But Winship is willing to admit that in the 1980s, not all women's magazines were the same, and her case study of *Cosmopolitan* is more interesting.

THE *COSMO* FACTOR

Where had the magazine come from? *Cosmopolitan* in its modern form, confident about being sexy and single, had been launched in America in 1964 when Helen Gurley Brown – author of the best-selling *Sex and the Single Girl* – took over the editorship of the 'long-established but moribund' magazine (Winship, 1987: 106). The title was launched in the UK in 1972, and was able to assert a strong sexual identity from the outset. Its readers represented a new generation, and a new kind of reader:

> More of them than ever before had gone away to college, and often on to the pill, and with high expectations of a world at their feet they were set, if nothing else, on ensuring they didn't have to forsake womanly delights, as their spinsterly and not to be envied schoolteachers had, in order to take a public place in the world.
>
> (ibid.: 107)

Cosmo girl might have owed a lot to feminism, but she was unlikely to identify with it; she just wanted to get out there and enjoy her independence. Winship says that the idea of the typical *Cosmo* article being, 'How to get a man into bed,' whilst not completely off the mark, rather misses the point of the magazine's sexual agenda – for *Cosmo* was playing *Playboy* at its own game, seeing sexual pleasure as important, and suggesting that women were entitled to it. *Cosmo*'s assertion of women's right to enjoy sex, and to talk about it, was quite radical, and this new discourse brought other changes – men, for example, were no longer treated with reverence, but could be seen as inadequate, or the butt of jokes.

Examining several issues from the early 1980s, Winship finds that *Cosmo* does not bother being consistent: one article would encourage readers to be happy with their body size, whilst another would encourage slimming; men are given both sympathy and criticism; marriage might be endorsed or condemned; romance and fidelity might be good, or bad, depending on the article; and the style might be serious or silly. This pluralism of contradictions is no accident. *Cosmo*'s editor of the time, Deirdre McSharry, tells Winship that it is her job 'to get the balance right' (ibid.: 100). More challenging articles are countered by more 'reassuring' ones, but 'the clever thing is to always offer a very strong element which will surprise [the readers], and that's really what keeps them going,' McSharry explains. It is not surprising that *Cosmo* woman cannot escape contradiction, as she is expected to be so many things: sexy, successful, glamorous, hard-working;

sharp and relaxed in social settings, powerful and likeable at work. Looking over the magazine's idealised photographs which accompany articles about relationships, as well as fashion, Winship observes:

> [*Cosmopolitan* is aware] firstly, that being a woman involves constantly adjusting one's own image to fit time and place in an ever-changing game of images; and secondly, that 'real life' is constantly thought through '(dream) images'.
>
> (ibid.: 101)

This complex mix of aspirational dreams and multiple realities is a minefield which *Cosmo* celebrates, and tries to help readers with. The possibilities suggested by the magazine are not infinite, of course – *Cosmo*'s dreams are almost always heterosexual, for instance; they don't have much tolerance for the imperfect or the unsexy; and they usually require you to spend a certain amount of money on beauty products. Critics such as Susan Douglas (1995) see this as a triumph of the capitalists, managing to turn feminism into something narcissistic which you have to spend lots of money on, and – in line with L'Oreal's 'Because I'm worth it!' tagline – even feel pleasure and liberation in doing so. *Cosmo*'s selling of arguably rather narrow fantasy lifestyles may certainly be of concern; but we should also not forget Winship's point that *Cosmo* was, at one time at least, a vehicle for liberation and change, giving voice to ideas and perspectives which had not previously been in mass circulation.

Cosmopolitan spawned many imitators and variants, of course, including *Over 21*, *Glamour*, *Working Woman* and *Company*. The late 1980s saw the launch of even more sex-obsessed magazines like the UK's *More!*, which stripped out much of the more 'mature' stuff about lifestyle and work, and gave young readers even more of the glamour, problem pages, handsome hunks and sex – most obviously in the notorious 'position of the fortnight' feature – which they seemed to crave.

GENDER IN ADVERTISING

The stereotypes in advertising have been similar to those in women's magazines, and other media, described earlier, although they have often been slower to change with the times. Friedan's (1963) critique of women's magazines runs alongside a similar assessment of advertising; the stereotypes reproduced by the housewife's journals were the same as those exploited by advertisers. Tuchman's (1978) argument about 'the symbolic annihilation of women' is based on an analysis of advertising as well as other media.

Again, Gunter (1995) provides a useful guide to the many empirical content analysis studies which have been conducted. The studies show that women in magazine adverts prior to the 1970s were rarely shown to be in paid work, and when they were it would usually be a stereotypical role (the smiling secretary or hairdresser). The number of 'housewife' images began to decline slowly after the 1950s, but the image was still common in the 1960s and 1970s (Gunter, 1995: 34). Content analyses of advertising on *television* in the early 1970s found strong evidence of stereotyping: of all ads featuring women, three-quarters were for kitchen and bathroom products. Women were more than twice as likely as men to be seen inside the home, and when seen in a paid work environment, they were more often than not subservient to men. Men were most likely to be seen in authority roles, and were ten times more likely than women to provide the dependable voice-over (ibid.: 35). Studies in the later 1970s and early 1980s saw a continuation of these trends, with men most often shown at work, and women as housewives and mothers at home. Nevertheless, it became somewhat more common for men to be shown at home as well, in the role of husband or father; and the range of women's occupations increased (ibid.: 36–37).

In a study of TV ads, Scheibe (1979) included an assessment of what male and female characters were shown to be *concerned* about – an astute addition to the usual enumeration of role and location. Women in ads were found to be more concerned about beauty, cleanliness, family and pleasing others. Men were only more concerned about achievement and having fun. So even if women and men are shown in more unusual settings, these stereotyped concerns can come shining through. Other studies found strong similarities in gender representations from country to country, and particular sexism in adverts aimed at children (Gunter, 1995: 44–50). In the 1980s, TV advertising did start to take on the idea of the busy working woman – but often by offering solutions to the working woman who, it was assumed, would still have to perform cooking and cleaning chores in the household.

By the start of the 1990s, a study of 500 prime-time TV ads in the UK, by Cumberbatch (reported in Strinati, 1995: 186), found that advertisers had seemingly become wary of showing women doing housework (which was seen in 7 per cent of the ads). For the first time, it was found that men were shown cooking more often than women – but these would be supposedly impressive 'special occasions', in contrast to the more routine cookery duties of women which had traditionally been shown. In other respects, little had changed: women in ads were more likely to be young and attractive; men were twice as likely as women to be shown in paid employment; work was seen as central to men's lives, whereas 'relationships' were shown to be more important to women; and 89 per cent of the ads used a male voice-over.

Unsurprisingly, then, gender representations in ads have been similar to those in other media, usually affirming the same old stereotypes. However, as Macdonald notes (1995: 89–90):

> Advertisers generally lagged behind women's magazines in the cultivation of new modes of address, even when the evidence suggested that commercial advantages could be gained from modernising their approach.

The advertising industry has often been accused of a quiet conservatism, and a fear of challenging certain elements of what it thinks the audience needs and expects. Representation of gender roles seem to have been, for many years at least, one of the areas where advertisers were often reluctant to do anything very different.

Adverts therefore found themselves on the front line of feminist counter-attack. Partly because advertising was seen as a pernicious case of capitalists exploiting gender-related insecurities, and partly because billboards were easier to interfere with than movies and TV broadcasts, feminists in the 1970s and 1980s took their message to the streets – and their spray-paints to the adverts. Ascerbic comments were painted onto billboard ads, such as a Fiat ad with a woman reclining on the vehicle receiving the new tagline, 'When I'm not lying on cars I'm a brain surgeon' (Macdonald, 1995: 87), and the deliciously malicious one where an ad showing a woman carving a lover's message into a tree, with the printed slogan, 'Renew his interest in carpentry', was supplemented by the helpful suggestion, 'Saw his head off' (Posener, 1982).

SUMMARY

We have seen, unsurprisingly, that the mass media used to be very stereo-typed in its representations of gender. As well as showing men being more active, decisive, courageous, intelligent and resourceful, television and movies also showed a much greater *quantity* of men, compared to women. There were exceptions, of course – it's not hard to think of the odd clever, brave, or challenging female character from the past – but these remained exceptions to the norm. Magazines and adverts aimed at women also tended to reinforce the feminine and housewifely stereotypes. The emergence of *Cosmopolitan*, though, with its contradictory but generally forthright, assertive and sexually frank approach, heralded the changes which we would see develop in more recent media – as covered in the next chapter.

Chapter 4

REPRESENTATIONS OF GENDER TODAY

4 / 5

Iɴ ᴛʜᴇ ᴘʀᴇᴠɪᴏᴜꜱ chapter, we established that the media of the past was, pretty much, just as stereotyped as we probably tend to imagine it was. But in the past ten or fifteen years, things have been changing quite considerably. Men and women are seen working side by side, as equals, in the hospitals, schools and police stations of television-land. Movie producers are wary of having women as screaming victims, and have realised that kick-ass heroines do better business. Advertisers have by now realised that audiences will only laugh at images of the pretty housewife, and have reacted by showing women how to be sexy at work instead. Gay characters have slowly started to be more prominent on TV and in the movies, and discussions of the rights of marginalised groups have also surfaced within popular culture. This chapter considers each of these things in turn.

CONTENT ANALYSIS: DO IT YOURSELF

Representations on TV change from year to year. Although a proper content analysis study should ideally take in many hours of broadcast television, and be performed using rigorous measures, you can still do a simple version yourself. Pick a slice of popular, mainstream programming and count up the number of main characters who are female, and those who are male. Note their roles, concerns and leadership. The more shows you include, the more (roughly) reliable your figures will be.

GENDER IN CONTEMPORARY TV PROGRAMMES

During the 1990s and into the new century, gender roles on television became increasingly equal and non-stereotyped – within some limits – although the majority of lead characters were still male. (As throughout this book, our main emphasis here is largely on popular, prime-time programmes from the USA and UK.)

There have been fewer content analysis studies of gender representations published during, and since, the 1990s – although we should also note that academics are often embarrassingly slow to get their findings into print. One key study of the portrayal of women in prime-time TV shows during the 1992–1993 season, by Elasmar, Hasegawa and Brain, was not published until six years later, in 1999. Another major study of women in prime-time series during the 1995–1996 season, by Lauzen and Dozier, was also published in that year. Both studies offer some interesting statistics, although the lack of comparable figures for *men* on TV in some cases makes the findings difficult to interpret – for example, Elasmar *et al.* report the numbers of TV women who are employed, and who care for children, but we cannot really interpret these figures without knowing the parallel figures for male characters in these positions, which they failed to record. Nevertheless, it is worth noting that:

- in prime-time TV shows, 1992–1993, men took 61 per cent of the total number of speaking roles, with women having the other 39 per cent. The 1995–1996 study found that men took 63 per cent of the speaking roles, with women having the other 37 per cent.
- The 1992–1993 study found a startlingly small number of the major characters were female – just 18 per cent – and of this meagre group, more than two-thirds were the stars of domestic situation comedies. However, the 1995–1996 study (which examined a greater range and number of popular programmes) found that 43 per cent of major characters were female – a much greater proportion, although still less than half.
- The 1992–1993 study found that only 3 per cent of women were represented as housewives as their main occupation – a massive decrease from the 1970s. An additional 8 per cent of women were shown as 'homemakers', but without knowing the number of male homemakers it is difficult to interpret this properly.
- The 1995–1996 study examined the roles of women and men in conversations on screen, recording the degree of control they exerted over

dialogue, the power of their language use and the frequency with which they gave direct advice. It was found that on a character-by-character basis, females and males were equal in these respects.
- Overall, the 1992–1993 study found that 'the woman on prime time TV in the early 1990s was young, single, independent, and free from family and work place pressures' (Elasmar, Hasegawa and Brain, 1999: 33).

The studies show a growth in gender equality on screen, although by the mid-1990s there was still some distance to go. However, the researchers note that their findings are part of on-going trends which are seeing women on television becoming (gradually) more emancipated and equal.

It could be said that in the 1990s, to a certain extent, programme makers arrived at comfortable, not-particularly-offensive models of masculinity and femininity, which a majority of the public seemed to think were acceptable. Producers thus seemed to give up on feeling that they might need to challenge gender representations. Take, for example, the internationally popular sit-com *Friends* (1994–). The three men (Ross, Chandler and Joey) fit easily within conventional models of masculinity, but are given some characteristics of sensitivity and gentleness, and male-bonding, to make things slightly refreshing. Similarly, the three women (Rachel, Monica and Phoebe) are clearly feminine, whilst being sufficiently intelligent and non-housewifey to seem like acceptable characters for the 1990s. The six were also, of course, originally all characters with a good set of both male and female friendships – i.e. each other – and the friendship circle was a refreshing modern replacement for the traditional family. (It was not long, of course, before they spoilt that by having Ross and Rachel, then – more implausibly – Monica and Chandler fall in love. The latter relationship and protracted build-up to marriage was particularly destructive of the original, more radical concept, and also quashed the rather more interesting relationship between Chandler and Joey). This model of equal, if somewhat different, genders appears in many other shows from the 1990s onwards, including *ER*, *Dawson's Creek*, *Frasier*, *The West Wing*, and indeed the majority of dramas, reality TV shows and current affairs programmes. Nevertheless we can also note that many series – including most of those named in the previous sentence – may have an ensemble cast of equals but are still often seen to revolve, first and foremost, around one or more male characters.

Some shows put successful professional women at the forefront, and are focused on their quests for sex, pleasure and romantic love. *Ally McBeal* (1997–) and *Sex and the City* (1998–) do this in rather different ways. Ally

Figure 4.1   Fan websites for *Sex and the City*, the hit TV series which shows women
as sexual predators

McBeal is a very good lawyer, but – more stereotypically – is quite desperate
to find a husband. And, as played by Calista Flockhart, she inhabits an alarmingly anorexic-looking body. Oddly, she is probably the weakest main character in the show. Ally's colleagues Ling (Lucy Liu) and Nelle (Portia de Rossi)
are tougher, and both have been out with men from the law firm who are
typically portrayed as rather geeky and lacking self-assurance. The show sides
with the women and often shows them making fun of the men – a character-
istic taken further by *Sex and the City*, in which male sexual performance is
subject to laughter and scathing review. Mulling over the huge popularity of
this show in a British newspaper, Madeleine Bunting (2001) notes:

> [*Sex and the City*'s Carrie, Miranda, Samantha and Charlotte]
> discuss every kind of sex – masturbation, dildos, telephone sex
> and blowjobs – comparing experiences, offering advice and
> encouragement. Nothing is out of bounds, sex is an adventure
> playground which doesn't necessarily have much to do with love
> . . . The sex stuff works because it turns on its head the age-old
> female sexual victimhood. The whole rationale of *Sex and the
> City* is that these women want pleasure, know how to get it and
> are determined to do so. And the kick is in the assumption that
> the women are always great in bed, the men more variable.

Bunting later complains that men will still be able to comfort themselves that they remain 'the sole object of any sensible woman's life', but given these women's very high standards, there is little room for men to be complacent. The character of Samantha, played by Kim Cattrall, has been particularly notable as a portrayal of a sexually assertive woman in her forties. As Cattrall said in an interview, 'I don't think there's ever been a woman who has expressed so much sexual joy [on television] without her being punished. I never tire of women coming up and saying, "You've affected my life"' (Williams, 2002).

A few other female icons? *Buffy the Vampire Slayer* (1997–) made an indelible impact on teen TV, and also broke new ground by becoming hugely popular within the typically male-dominated world of sci-fi fans (*Buffy* has repeatedly won 'Best Television Show' in *SFX* magazine's annual readers poll, for example). It is difficult to think of any contemporary TV character more powerful and heroic than Buffy – even when compared with superheroes. When Superman was relaunched earlier in the 1990s (*Lois and Clark*, a.k.a. *The New Adventures of Superman*, 1993–1997), he was sweet and insecure and always consulting his small-town parents about emotional turmoil, which made a nice change. The newer, younger Clark Kent seen in *Smallville* (2001–) also follows this pattern. But Buffy is more confident and assertive than either incarnation of the Man of Steel – whilst remaining recognisably human. As Polly Vernon has noted (1999):

> Buffy may be styled like Britney Spears on a warm day, but her midriff is very much her own and her whirling intensity, healthy self-irony, and inescapably dark undertones suggests that her main function is not titillation. She's a girl's girl, at once hard as nails and physically confident in a way that's genuinely empowering, and yet warm enough and scared enough not to become some kind of clumsy, shouting, mutated Spice Girl on autopilot . . . Men who fancy Buffy do it with a healthy degree of awe.

Buffy's creator and driving force, Joss Whedon, adds that Buffy 'is a good role model for not just girls but for everybody, because she has to use her

---

WHAT ABOUT POP MUSIC?

Pop music offers a range of images of, and discourses about, women and men. These are considered in Chapter 10, as part of a discussion of 'role models'.

wits and her physical strength to win. Yet, she still has to get high marks in all her courses at school' (www.buffy.com, 2001).

NYPD Blue (1993–) has produced a particularly rich study of modern masculinity over the years, centred around the character of detective Andy Sipowicz (Dennis Franz). When the show began, Sipowicz seemed like a stereotypical stout, sleazy, bigoted, divorced, (recovering) alcoholic cop, but over the years viewers have seen many layers of complexity and vulnerability rise to the surface of his macho mix. His protective love for his younger professional partners – Kelly, then Simone, then Sorenson – has been a constant, and his grief at the death of his grown-up son, and joy at the birth of his young child Theo, have added depth. Numerous other tests (his wife's death, Theo's illness) have made him increasingly tightly-wound, upset and angry. The crime episodes are mere vehicles for character development, and after 174 episodes (by 2001) – that's 130 hours of continuous drama – this adds up to an extremely dense study of a tormented human being, and the division between his gruff exterior and complex emotional core.

Other angles on masculinity have also been offered in *NYPD Blue*. Sipowicz's partners are typically more sensitive but have problems of their own; young Danny Sorenson, for instance, whilst a confident man most of the time, had nervous bursts and a fear of 'getting stirred up'. Their colleague Greg Medavoy – a rather anxious and clumsy figure – has also been presented seriously, rather than as a mere 'joke' character. During one phase of the show (1996–1998), Medavoy seemed to be 'trying for size' the more aggressive masculinity worn by Sipowicz, but he didn't really have the self-assurance to carry it through. Whilst Sipowicz could use violence and threats against suspects in order to gain moral victories, Medavoy's attempts – most notably in an episode when he ridiculously cuffed a suspect with a phone book – never paid off, and this was seen as a kind of crisis of self-image for the detective. Since then, Medavoy's solid relationship with his newer partner, the younger, more confident Baldwin Jones, has helped him to become more self-assured.

On a quite different note, *Queer as Folk* – in both its UK and US versions – offered visions of masculinity (and, to a lesser extent, femininity) which made a break with TV traditions, and the show is discussed in the section 'Emerging alternative sexualities on TV', pp. 82–86. Finally, it must be said that there are so many thousands of TV shows that it would be impossible to consider them all here, so I have merely tried to identify some trends. Representations of gender on TV have changed considerably within the past couple of decades; today, female and male characters are likely to be as intelligent, talented and resourceful – or stupid – as each other, and in this respect – though there may be exceptions – there is 'equality'. Nevertheless, many conventions of masculinity and femininity remain, albeit often in a revised form which takes account of egalitarianism and concern about stereotypes. Nonetheless, male and female roles are often not exactly inter-changeable. It also remains the case that men continue to dominate in certain areas. For example, in the UK, the BBC's coverage of the 2001 general election was led from the studio by authoritative, middle-aged white

CHANGING TIMES, CHANGING *STAR TREK*S

A look at each version of the hugely successful *Star Trek* television franchise allows us to ring the changes. In the original *Star Trek* series (1966–1969), macho Kirk and logical Spock were the masculine leads. The movie series featuring these characters (1979–1991) came to centre upon the friendship between Kirk, Spock and Doctor McCoy and, like the TV series, gave no heroic role to women. (Communications officer Uhura, a kind-of model of success for black women in the 1960s, was regrettably never given much to do.) When the next TV series, *Star Trek: The Next Generation* (1987–1994) was launched, women had stronger roles, including a female doctor and female head of security (who died in the first series). The new captain, Jean-Luc Picard, was a man, but one with a consistent sensitive side. Picard's relationship with non-macho Data, the android who wanted to be human, grew (arguably) to be the core of the series and (more clearly) the subsequent movie series. Female characters were a part of the ensemble, but not at the very front. The next series, *Star Trek: Deep Space Nine* (1993–1999) was comparable to *The Next Generation* in its gender mix, although some female characters were tougher. The captain was again male, but – as these series set in the twenty-fourth century stumbled to keep up with changes in the twentieth – this time was black. A bolder leap in gender terms was made in the next series, *Star Trek: Voyager* (1995–2001), which not only gave viewers a female captain, Kathryn Janeway, but helped her to look good by making her male colleagues a pretty bland bunch. A female chief engineer was also on hand, but the series only really found its feet with the introduction of another strong woman, Seven of Nine, whose powerful, rather loving but often antagonistic relationship with Janeway gave this series its core. So, by the end of the twentieth century, the main *Star Trek* series was built around the friendship and mutual fascination between two women. They were also a tough duo, who regularly had to save the day.

> If we look at Picard and Data in *The Next Generation*, and the movies in particular, they can seem quite a macho double-act, even though both has a sensitive side. But Janeway and Seven behave in just the same ways – indeed, Janeway can be even more ruthless, causing concern to her male colleagues. But they are just being robust and resourceful space people; so perhaps in *Star Trek* – by the time *Voyager* came along, at least – gender really had become irrelevant. (In typically circular fashion, however, *Voyager*'s replacement, *Enterprise* (2001–), set prior to the time of the original series, reverts to having a white, male captain – plus some OK but lower status roles for women.)

men (Dimbleby, Paxman, Snow) who handled the serious politics and statistics, whilst the one main female reporter (Fiona Bruce) had the job of talking to 'ordinary people'. Even the comic take on current affairs in *Have I Got News For You* usually stars either one female face, or none at all, out of five. The same is typical in the other 'comedy quiz' shows, whether about sports, pop music or TV itself. But things are always changing; you can add your own observations to those made here.

GENDER IN CONTEMPORARY MOVIES

In the previous chapter we saw that films in the past had tended to give men all the primary clever and resourceful roles, which made them the lead character(s), whilst women usually got to be love interests and helpers. There were exceptions, of course, but this was the general picture. But what of representations in the 1990s and the new century? Maggie Humm's *Feminism and Film*, published in 1997, didn't seem to think that anything had changed. The book begins with the assertion that:

> Film . . . often and anxiously envisions women stereotypically as 'good' mothers or 'bad', hysterical careerists. [In the past, and] today, every Hollywood woman is someone else's Other.
>
> (1997: 3)

This kind of bold assertion is good for prompting discussion, but doesn't *really* have much connection with today's films. Where are all those 'bad, hysterical careerists'? Humm only mentions one film, *Fatal Attraction*, from back in 1987, though we can probably think of a couple more (such as 1994's *Disclosure*). 'Good mother' icons are pretty thin on the ground too; we've probably got more good fathers these days. Susan Jeffords (1993)

WHAT ABOUT NEW MEDIA?

As noted at the start of Chapter 3, the Internet and World Wide Web do bring us information and images of the social world, and the impact of this should be considered alongside all of the other sources of ideas about gender covered in this chapter and elsewhere.

However, it is more-or-less impossible to provide a meaningful analysis of 'representations of gender on the Internet' because there is no 'mainstream' that a majority of people are looking at – although of course, some websites are much more popular than others. But the most popular sites tend to be ones that people visit on their way to some-where else (search and directory sites), or to get news or information, or because they have a computer-related problem, or because they want to buy something, or because they are collecting their email. Online magazines like Salon.com tend to be text-based and are not exactly comparable to glossy print magazines. Some online magazines offer high-quality images, but at present consumer demand for this remains in the pornography market. For discussion of many of these things, see *Web.Studies* (Gauntlett (ed.), 2000).

As technology improves and converges, new media will become a more influential source of gender information, but we can probably expect it to be, more-or-less, like an interactive version of the kind of TV, movie and magazine material discussed here. In other words, there's no reason to think that gender representations within new media will be any different to the gender representations elsewhere. But having said that, the Web provides opportunities for individuals and groups to provide *alternatives* to the existing set of dominant ideas about women and men, on their own websites.

---

notes how Arnold Schwarzenegger's evil *Terminator* (1984) comes back in *Terminator 2: Judgment Day* (1991) as a protective father-figure to nice little Ed Furlong. Jeffords sees this as part of a 1990s trend of reinventing masculinity as fatherhood and caring (1993: 245):

> What Hollywood culture is offering, in place of the bold specta-
> cle of male muscularity and/as violence, is a self-effacing man,
> one who now, instead of learning to fight, learns to love. We can
> include here such [box office hits] as *Field of Dreams* (1989),
> *Robin Hood* (1991), *The Doctor* (1991), *Regarding Henry*
> (1991), even *Boyz N the Hood* (1991).

The 1990s, of course, did not entirely turn out like that. Looking through the list of hit movies of the past ten years or so, we can find examples of standard male action figures doing pretty much the same old thing: *The Rock* (1996), *Air Force One* (1997), *Gladiator* (2000), *Mission: Impossible II* (2000), *The 6th Day* (2000), *The Fast and the Furious* (2001), for example. But there are many other hit films where the male action hero works alongside a more-or-less equally powerful female action hero: for example, *The Matrix* (1999), *Entrapment* (1999), *Tomorrow Never Dies* (1997), *The Lost World: Jurassic Park* (1997), *Starship Troopers* (1997), *Deep Blue Sea* (1999), *X-Men* (2000), *The Mummy Returns* (2001), and we can even throw in *Speed* (1994), *Titanic* (1997) and *Shrek* (2001). There have also been several films centred around leading female action-hero roles: *Tank Girl* (1995), *The Long Kiss Goodnight* (1996), the *Scream* trilogy (1996–2000), *Alien Resurrection* (1997), *Mimic* (1997), *Mulan* (1998), *Run Lola Run* (1998), *Crouching Tiger, Hidden Dragon* (2000), *Charlie's Angels* (2000), *Hannibal* (2001) and *Tomb Raider* (2001). (Some of the films mentioned here are discussed in a little more depth below, pp. 72–75).

Jeffords's point did not turn out to be wrong, exactly, but a little over-stated. Men in Hollywood films today tend not to be the seamlessly macho heroes which we saw in the 1980s; they more often combine the toughness required of an action hero with a more sensitive, thoughtful or caring side, typically revealed at certain (often quite brief) points in the movie. Mean-while, female roles have definitely become tougher – not least because exec-utives have realised that the audience of movie-going young men, in general, do not insist on the action heroes being male; on the contrary, if the traditional thrills of the action genre can be combined with the sight of Angelina Jolie in shorts and a tight top, for example, then the deal is sealed.

Case study 1: *Charlie's Angels* (2000)

The millennial movie remake of the 1970s TV series *Charlie's Angels* starred Cameron Diaz, Drew Barrymore and Lucy Liu as the detective trio, who are employed by an unseen millionaire, Charlie, to solve mysteries, look good, and kick baddies in the face. The film was directed by McG, making his feature debut after a career in music videos, and Drew Barrymore was one of the producers. *Charlie's Angels* was a big commercial hit, taking over $170 million in its first three months (imdb.com). Just because people went to see it doesn't mean it was necessarily adored, or influential, of course. In fact its reception was split between an 'old guard' who complained that it was an exploitative, stupid movie, and another audience who enjoyed seeing the women 'kick ass'. Those who publicly criticised it were not (necessarily) women and feminists, however – they were the mainstream, mostly male, film critics. Some just didn't like it. Max Messier at *Filmcritic.com* found it 'just plain dumb' in both story and execution. Mick LaSalle of the *San Francisco Chronicle* despaired at this 'utter debacle' (3 November 2000). Richard Schickel at *Time* magazine noticed its cheerfulness but found it 'a waste of time' (3 November 2000). America's celebrated critic Roger Ebert dismissed it as 'eye candy for the blind' (*Chicago Sun-Times*, 3 November 2000), and went on to express concern about its use of women:

> Barrymore, Diaz and Liu represent redhead, blond and brunet respectively (or, as my colleague David Poland has pointed out, T[its], A[ss] and Hair). Sad, isn't it, that three such intelligent, charming and talented actresses could be reduced to their most prominent component parts?

Michael Thomson of *BBC Online* (24 November 2000) was similarly upset by the women's glamour and pouting, saying that the film's message was 'by all means be feisty, but never forget to be feminine'. Many male reviewers (and some women) at the internationally well-known Internet Movie Database (www.imdb.com) made similar complaints, including the occasional note that the women are 'bimbos'.

However, the women are hardly shown as brainless – on the contrary, they are amazingly multi-skilled: they are forensic scientists and electronic engineers, espionage and surveillance specialists, racing-car drivers and superhuman fighting machines. They also defeat their enemies without using guns (at Barrymore's insistence). The film does knowingly showcase the women's physical attractiveness, but their success comes from their use of their brains, and their fighting skills. Nobody ever called Indiana Jones a 'bimbo' just because Harrison Ford took his shirt off, or because he sometimes used his seductive looks and charm to get what he wanted. With *Charlie's Angels* there may be more of a fear that the film will feed existing stereotypes, but we are hardly rolling our eyes at the number of women on screen who can hack into high-security computers, speak several languages, skydive, re-program missiles, *and* beat up a posse of henchmen single-handed.

So I would argue that some of the male reviewers are using this 'concern' about the representation of the *Angels* as a cover for their own disinterest in this happy, fizzy-pop 'post-feminist' celebration of a film. Their other complaints seem to reveal a feeling that pleasure in films comes from suspense and intricate plotting, and not from watching empowered young women get their way in a somewhat camp, jolly entertainment. The film clearly counters a lot of stereotypes about women's abilities. And whilst the film-makers seem to enjoy the women's glamorous looks – in a knowing way which is meant to give pleasure to both women and men in the audience – the characters themselves are confident and independent, only sometimes using their looks to trick stupid, weak men. *Charlie's Angels* has an effervescent 'girl power' zing which had not been seen since the Spice Girls.

Female reviewers seemed more likely to embrace the movie: Susan Stark in the *Detroit News* (3 November 2000) found it to be 'immensely entertaining', and noted approvingly that 'Diaz, Liu and Barrymore obviously get a huge charge from having the chance to play Bond (as opposed to Bond Girl)'. Cindy Fuchs in the *Philadelphia City Paper* found 'excitement' and 'much adorable girl-bonding' (2 November 2000). Kamal Larsuel at *3BlackChicks.com* 'loved it'. And back in the Internet Movie Database, where thousands of filmgoers have rated *Charlie's Angels* from one to ten, we find that in every age group, women consistently rated the film higher than men. The film gets an average score of 6.6 from men and 7.3 from women; amongst females aged under eighteen, the film was rated even higher, at an average of 8.2 (compared to 7.3 from the under-eighteen males).[1]

This is not an attempt to show that *Charlie's Angels* is either good or bad; the point is that although several (not-so-young) male critics claimed that the film was generally poor, but might provide some thrills for adolescent boys, in fact those boys were less keen than their female counterparts, who enjoyed the bubbly 'girl power' exuberance on offer. As one female IMDB reviewer writes, concerning why women enjoy *Charlie's Angels*:

> I think it [is because of] the fact that we so rarely get to see female action heroes, particularly ones we can like. We had Trinity at the beginning of *The Matrix* before the movie quickly found a man to focus on, and we have Max and Buffy on television. It's a sign, though, that even silly movies featuring women kicking butt are so popular among, well, women. We need this. We need strong

---

1 We should note that in the tough world of IMDB voting, 8.2 is a very positive score; and it's also worth pointing out that scores are usually closer between the sexes: for *The Matrix* (1999) and *Hannibal* (2001), for example, both popular films with interesting male and female lead characters, the average score from men and the average score from women is exactly the same (8.6 for *The Matrix* and 6.6 for *Hannibal*). [Ratings quoted were correct at November 2001].

DOES GIRL POWER LEAD TO GIRL VIOLENCE?

A study by psychologists Muncer, Campbell, Jervis and Lewis (2001) responded to growing media concern about 'ladettes' – young women with the assertive/aggressive attitudes usually associated with 'lads'. Their survey asked female students whether acts such as drinking, swearing, fast driving and graffiti-painting were as acceptable in women as in men. The women were also asked to indicate how aggressive they were in their own lives. It was found that women who agreed with the non-sexist view were *not* likely to be more aggressive than other women. In other words, support for 'girl power' ideas does not mean that women will necessarily be more violent themselves. This entirely unsurprising finding is described by the psychologists as 'unexpected'.

females in leading roles, even in silly movies. And this is a very silly movie, make no mistake. I also think it intends to be that way. Each scene has its own cartoon feel, and the movie itself is like a comic book come to life. There are some very nice and admirable touches, added at Drew Barrymore's insistence. We see the Angels eating heartily, we see the Angels use martial arts abilities instead of guns, we see the Angels saving gentlemen in distress.

(1 April 2001)

It may be flawed, but *Charlie's Angels* seemed to be a making some valiant attempts at role-reversal within the blockbuster mainstream. The final complaint from this film's detractors is usually that these supposedly independent women remain *Charlie's* women. But what does Charlie do? Apart from being rich, he is totally impotent. He redistributes his wealth to three women in whom he has absolute trust. In other words, he's a Marxist and a feminist. There can be only one explanation: Charlie's Engels.

Case study 2: *What Women Want* (2000)

With its provocative title alone, the 'romantic comedy' *What Women Want* attracts the attention of those interested in gender representations in the new millennium. The film stars Mel Gibson as an old-school sexist man, whose once-brilliant career as an advertising executive has started to flounder because of his inability to relate to female consumers. But then an electrical accident endows him with the ability to hear women's thoughts. (Not men's thoughts, though, and the film seems happy to support the idea that men and women are wholly different species. Helping Mel adjust to his new-found powers, Bette Midler excitedly tells him that, 'If men are from Mars and women are from Venus – you speak Venutian!'). Helen Hunt co-stars as the advertising whiz who has just been given the top job which Mel had expected to be promoted to. At first Mel cheats and uses his powers to nick Helen's ideas. Later, of course, he learns to be sensitive, and to listen to women, and the two characters fall in love. The film was a big hit, earning $178 million within two months of its release in the USA alone (imdb.com).

With its cheerfully silly premise, and soundtrack stuffed with Sinatra's greatest hits, the film harks back in many ways to the kind of romp that might have starred James Stewart or Cary Grant. At the same time, it is clearly addressing the contemporary question of what insensitive sexist men should do when they find that women don't actually like them very much, and beat them at work too. Its answers are a mixed bag. On the one hand, the film challenges stereotypes by suggesting quite emphatically that men can and should learn to be more like women. But paradoxically, this very idea of what women 'are like' is very stereotypical. Nick is seen joining women in their fascination with manicures, yoga, slushy TV and relation-ship gossip, which is meant to be hilariously incongruous. The film-makers might defend these scenes by saying that the laughs are meant to come from seeing the macho icon *Mel Gibson* engaged in such things, and that's a reasonable explanation, but the stereotypical 'differences between the sexes' are still essential to the humour.

Nevertheless, if the film assumes that women are emotionally articulate, and asserts that men should be too, then it's saying that *people in general* should be sensitive and able to talk about their feelings, and listen to others – and you can't really argue with that. On the other hand, to say that a nice sensitive version of Mel Gibson is a better role model for men than a stupid sexist version, is not that radical. And Helen Hunt's feminine interpretation of clever but somewhat insecure corporate success is a relatively bland role model for women.

Furthermore, like a TV sitcom from three or four decades ago, the film assumes that seeing a man dress up in a bra and try to shave his legs – as Mel does as part of an early quest to understand women – is funny in itself. Then, after a one-night stand with Marisa Tomei, who has become infatu-ated with him due to his great sensitivity, Mel gets out of the relationship by pretending to be gay. Again, the anticipated laughter – at the very idea that a Mel Gibson character could be gay – is very conservative, and Tomei's character rams the stereotype home by saying, 'You talk to me like a woman, you think like a woman. Come on, admit it – you're totally and completely gay!'

⌐ Perhaps the most worrying thing about *What Women Want* was that some viewers seemed to think that they might actually learn 'facts' about 'the needs of women' – as if all women want the same things – from the film. Several of the hundreds of people who have written comments about the film at the Internet Movie Database – a group of people whom we might expect to be at the more thoughtful, critical and literate end of the movie-going public – seem to assume the film may be a carrier of truths:

> Judging from the reactions of the audience I was with, the women certainly can relate to much of what was portrayed . . . If you are after a film with plenty of laughs, some distinct home truths, and an interesting story of what it would be like to read the minds of women, then this is definitely the film for you.
>
> (25 March 2001)

> I thoroughly enjoyed this film. As a woman, I felt that it was about time that the film industry paid attention to a woman's feelings.
>
> (22 January 2001)

> In the end, there is a lot more bite and substance to it than meets the eye . . . extremely insightful.
>
> (17 January 2001)

> [This was] somewhat of a chick flick, but guys should be amused and may pick up something new.
>
> (10 May 2001)

Thankfully, many others were more critical; to give a couple of examples:

> It's hard to believe it was directed by a woman when you look at the awful stereotypes presented here – Tomei's ditzy wannabe actress incomplete without a man [or] sex, Helen Hunt's career girl [who thinks] 'I have to be a bitch to be a success but all I really want is love', a suicidal office girl and two empty-headed assistants. Gibson's daughter is the only one who attains any level of credibility.
>
> (2 January 2001)

Why does this movie include so many women with such inane ways of dealing with real life? . . . You would think this movie was put together by men who hate women – and themselves.

(28 December 2000)

Of course, *What Women Want* is just one film, so we can't use it alone to show 'gender relations in movies today'. Let's run briefly through some other successful and well-known films.

GENDER IN SOME OTHER RECENT FILMS

Interpreting any film is a subjective exercise, of course, but here are some summaries that you can, naturally, assess for yourself.

Action movies

Panic Room (2002) – Jodie Foster's house is invaded by three men, but she subverts the 'damsel in distress' environment by being clever and resourceful instead. One of the male crooks, meanwhile, is frightened and sensitive.

Lara Croft: Tomb Raider (2001) – The 'girl power' icon dreamt up by video-game boys is 100 per cent tough, resourceful and successful.

Final Fantasy: The Spirits Within (2001) – The main character, Dr Aki Ross, is another solid female role model from a video game. Her combination of toughness and intelligence is superior to that of any of the men. As a robust character herself, it is perhaps understandable that she falls for a soldier who is clearly styled on the Action Man doll.

Lord of the Rings: The Fellowship of the Ring (2001) – A group of male heroes go on a quest to save their world. Liv Tyler's character, one of very few females in the picture, was apparently made more feisty than in the book, but is largely absent.

Gladiator (2000) – Russell Crowe is an exceptionally macho warrior. He's upset by the slaughter of his family, but who wouldn't be?

The Patriot (2000) – Mel Gibson is another macho warrior. But at least he's reluctant to fight, he takes being a father very seriously, and cries at various deaths. Joely Richardson dotes on him and doesn't do much.

The Mummy Returns (2001) – Reliably chunky hero Brendan Fraser remains reliable and chunky. But past-life flashbacks reveal Rachel Weisz as the reincarnation of a kick-ass Egyptian warrior. True to form, she ditches her weak librarian image from *The Mummy* (1999) and gets in on all the fights.

Jurassic Park III (2001) – Téa Leoni is the only woman in the dinosaur adventure, but unlike several men, she survives. Not a particularly heroic role, but at least the male and female characters treat each other as equals.

Gone in Sixty Seconds (2000) – Nicholas Cage used to have a stupid macho interest in stealing cars. So did Angelina Jolie. Now Nic would prefer not to, but he's forced into it, so he has to ask Angelina for help. Men still dominate in this film, though, whilst cars are lovingly equated with beautiful women (!).

The Perfect Storm (2000) – Some nice, desperate, overambitious fishermen think that Mother Nature can't hurt them. Clear moral: you can be *too* macho.

X-Men (2000) – The female superheroes are just as cool and useful as the male ones, but it could be said their powers are more 'feminine' (telepathy; absorbing powers of others; directing weather – a force of nature). And they all look up to wise old Patrick Stewart. As noted in a discussion below (pp. 87–90), the nasty senator is equated with anti-gay campaigners.

The Matrix (1999) – Carrie-Anne Moss is a powerful woman who is equal or superior to any man. But then Keanu comes along and turns out to be *actually* superior. Still good though.

Crouching Tiger, Hidden Dragon (2000) – Focused around a woman who can skilfully beat up everybody. In the fights, it is of no consequence whether the people are female or male.

Horror dramas

The *Scream* trilogy (1996–2000) – Neve Campbell is the one constant, resourceful, intelligent core through all three films.

Final Destination (2000) and *Jeepers Creepers* (2001) – As in many other contemporary teen-horror films, the lead male and female characters are equals.

Hollow Man (2000) – Centred initially on Kevin Bacon, but it's Elizabeth Shue who sorts everything out in the end in the now-quite-familiar feisty fashion.

Hannibal (2001) – An intelligent, evil man versus an intelligent, good woman. Fair.

Drama and comedy

Bend It Like Beckham (2002) – Being a female British Asian teenager doesn't stop Jess from becoming a brilliant footballer with a bright future. A film in which weddings, traditions and cooking are stupid, and gay friends, female bonding and sport are great.

Bridget Jones's Diary (2001) – Some successful and interesting men find Bridget Jones to be attractive because she is a bit daft in an endearing way. Good news for endearingly daft women, then, perhaps.

Lucky Break (2001) – Like its predecessor *The Full Monty* (1997), *Lucky Break* is about a group of men who, out of desperation, are led to organise a show, and learn about themselves in the process. Masculinity is tweaked and modified.

Billy Elliot (2000) – Boy wants to do ballet. Dad has crisis but makes moving emotional journey. All good stuff.

Fight Club (1999) – Masculinity in crisis! Sort of.

American Beauty (2000) – Men in crisis, again, but nobody comes out of it that well.

Erin Brockovich (2000) – Based on a true story, Brockovich is sharp, determined and well able to stand up for herself.

The Mexican (2001) – Brad Pitt gets into all sorts of macho scrapes south of the border, while whining hostage Julia Roberts gets trapped in a *Sex and the City*-style subplot with sensitive gay hitman James Gandolfini.

Being John Malkovich (1999) – A riot of gender confusion: Catherine Keener has sex with Cameron Diaz via the body of a portly male character actor. John Cusack locks wife Diaz in a cage, which some found uncomfortable, but it was meant to show his madness.

Shrek (2001) – A princess has to be rescued by the male ogre, Shrek, but turns out to be a *Matrix*-style martial arts expert herself. She worries about not being beautiful, but so does Shrek. Both learn to be happy and equal.

To summarise, women and men tend to have similar skills and abilities in films today. Leading women have to be attractive, within our recognised conventions of what makes women attractive, but leading men also have to be attractive, within the recognised conventions for males. Men can get away with being older though, and there are far more leading men in their forties, fifties and sixties than there are leading women in this age group. (There are too many examples to list here, but look at the careers of Mel Gibson, Harrison Ford, Sean Connery and Michael Douglas.)

GENDER IN CONTEMPORARY ADVERTISING

In advertising today, it seems fair to say that women and men are *usually* equal. Having begun from that premise, we can then consider the ways in which they are sometimes unequally represented. No doubt we can all think of examples of sexist representations in today's adverts, although these are the exception rather than the rule. For example: in autumn 2000, an advert which regularly appeared on UK television showed a man, alone at home, who was unimpressed with the meal which his female partner had left for him in the fridge, but found happiness by eating a tin of Baxter's soup. The man was smart and professional-looking, so this did not appear to be one of the wave of 'laddish' adverts. Perhaps viewers were meant to be impressed that this man had the ability to heat up some soup, but it was always jarring that the man lived in a world where his female partner cooked for him – even when she wasn't there herself! – and even then he didn't want it. The whole ad seemed to make no sense in the modern TV environment. But that's the point – the ad was an exception. Even though we know that in the real world, there *are* many men who depend on their female partners to prepare their food, it's still a bit shocking to see it on TV – which presumably means that advertisers nowadays take their social role relatively seriously, or, to be more precise, have learned that it is not good business to offend any of their customers with sexist stereotypes. There are also a small-ish number of cases where advertisers seem to have decided that it is acceptable to show women as housewives after all; and even in the twenty-first century, rather amazingly, the UK supermarket chain Iceland was still using the slogan, 'That's why mum's gone to Iceland'. Where the modern dad bought his groceries was unclear.

Although the gender *relationships* shown in adverts may usually seem equal, content analyses still find uneven numbers of men and women. A study of over 750 prime-time TV ads from spring 1998 conducted by Bartsch *et al.* (2000) found that, as in earlier studies, women were twice as likely as men to be in commercials for domestic products, and men were twice as likely as women to appear in ads for non-domestic products. Such a basic count-up of men and women does not take into account the story, message or joke within each advert, or the manner of representation of these males and females, but does appear to reflect a basic lack of fundamental change. An analysis of nearly 1,700 TV commercials from 1992–1994 by Coltrane and Messineo (2000) also found that characters in the ads 'enjoy more prominence and exercise more authority if they are white, or men'.

Nevertheless, the woman we *expect* to see in ads these days is the busy, confident, attractive success, in control of her professional and social life, and a kitchen slave to no one. Men do not tell her what to do; instead, she sometimes gets to have a laugh at the expense of a man. Occasionally, 'ironic' adverts patronise female characters in a knowing way which is meant to be funny, though this may not always be successful. Macdonald (1995: 90) summarises the changes from the late 1980s and through the 1990s:

> Believing both that feminism's battles had been won, and that its ideology was now harmless by virtue of being out of date, advertisers invented 'postfeminism' as a utopia where women could do whatever they pleased, provided they had sufficient will and enthusiasm.

Feminist discourses were thus cunningly 'co-opted' by the advertising industry and used to sell things to women. The notions of 'freedom' and 'liberation' had, in the 1970s, been part of a revolutionary slate of changes sought by feminists who wanted to escape the oppression of patriarchy. In the 1990s, 'freedom' and 'liberation' were things offered by the manufacturers of sanitary products, to women who wanted to escape the oppression of periods.

In a similar vein, adverts for the Boots 'No. 7' make-up range showed women assertively *using* their (cosmetically-enhanced) looks to get any man they set their sights on. This novel vision of female empowerment proclaimed, 'It's not make-up. It's ammunition'. The campaign was criticised by people who rolled their eyes and said, 'Oh, it's just the idea of the woman needing a man once again', but by making the lusty gaze a female one, and making men into the helpless prey of the women who desired them, the adverts did challenge some traditions quite radically. One could complain that these women were seeking to entice men by using their *looks* alone, but since the women had power over the helpless men, and since men in contemporary advertising are also seen using their looks to appeal to women, there is less to complain about. Nevertheless, one *could* complain that women are being told that their natural beauty is not enough, and that make-up is required: that *is* an unequal message, since men aren't expected to go to so much trouble.

Selling beauty

Sometimes it is unclear why gendered messages in *advertising* are singled out for particular attention by researchers – there are more publications on women in advertising than there are on women in TV programmes, for example – when TV series take up more of our time and attention than the ads, which fly by every day. But the make-up adverts referred to above remind us of a concern uniquely applicable to advertising – that it is produced by capitalists who want to cultivate insecurities which they can then sell 'solutions' to. Germaine Greer puts the case strongly in *The Whole Woman*:

> Every woman knows that, regardless of her other achievements, she is a failure if she is not beautiful . . . The UK beauty industry takes £8.9 billion a year out of women's pockets. Magazines financed by the beauty industry teach little girls that they need make-up and train them to use it, so establishing their lifelong reliance on beauty products. Not content with showing pre-teens how to use foundations, powders, concealers, blushers, eye-shadows, eye-liners, lip-liners, lipstick and lip gloss, the magazines identify problems of dryness, flakiness, blackheads, shininess, dullness, blemishes, puffiness, oiliness, spots, greasiness, that little girls are meant to treat with moisturisers, fresheners, masks, packs, washes, lotions, cleansers, toners, scrubs, astringents . . . Pre-teen cosmetics are relatively cheap but within a few years more sophisticated marketing will have persuaded the most level-headed woman to throw money away on alchemical preparations containing anything from silk to cashmere, pearls, proteins, royal jelly . . . anything real or phony that might fend off her imminent collapse into hideous decrepitude.
>
> (1999: 19, 23)

Of course, this argument has been an important part of the feminist case for decades, but Greer reminds us that the situation remains unchanged today.

Indeed, she asserts that things have got worse since she wrote *The Female Eunuch* in the late 1960s: 'Women who were unselfconscious and unmade-up thirty years ago', she says, are now 'infected' with the need to conform to certain images of beauty (ibid.: 23–24). Greer also reminds us of the booming cosmetic surgery industry, which promises to make women look more like some mediated ideal, but which appears to be a ridiculous and dangerous business.

The beauty ideal seems to be a substantial pressure on women, then. But it doesn't seem to occur to Greer that this obsession with looks might affect *people*, not just women. For example, she observes:

> Thirty years ago it was enough to *look* beautiful; now a woman has to have a tight, toned body, including her buttocks and thighs, so that she is good to touch, all over.
>
> (ibid.: 22)

This is true, for an 'ideal' woman at least, but it's true for the 'ideal' man as well. Today, men are also expected to spend time in the gym, working to develop 'tight, toned' bodies. Women who have these well-toned bodies are likely to expect – equitably enough – that men will put in a similar effort. Every male film star today has to have a good body, just as women do. So you might say that it's a pressure that our culture puts on *people* these days, but it's not just limited to women. In *The New Feminism*, Natasha Walter (1998) quotes surveys to suggest that today's women are more-or-less happy with how they look, whereas a vast majority of men felt unsatisfied with their own appearance. 'If . . . only 4 per cent of men think they are attractive, we should not be too quick to argue that only women feel cast down by the pressures of beautiful ideals,' she notes 1998: 101).

Greer (1999), nevertheless, reminds us that there is much more pressure on women to impress with their make-up, high heels and wonderbras. And that seems to be true. But Walter (1998) would point out that many women *enjoy* fashion and adornment. Walter is a feminist, but she refuses to see fashion and beauty advertising as a conspiracy to keep women down. She argues that the use of beauty products, fashion and decoration are a source of pleasure which should not be denied – for women *or* men – and which, in any case, do not seem to have a huge impact upon how successful people are in the world. More attractive people *do* earn more than their plain colleagues, a study found in 1993, but the difference was larger for men than for women (Walter, 1998: 101).

Nevertheless, Walter may have been looking at an unusual set of statistics. In 2001 a survey produced by the Social and Public Health Sciences

Unit at the University of Glasgow found that women were up to ten times more likely than men to be unhappy with their body image. This perception persisted even when women were a healthy weight for their height. (The study's main author, Carol Emslie, said that 'Images are still of very thin women as desirable body shapes. There is still an association that beautiful women are thin. For men there is still more of a range of images' (BBC Online, 2001b). This seems to be true, despite the fact that other surveys have shown that men do not find the ultra-skinny look to be especially attractive. (For example, a survey of English adolescents by Dittmar *et al.* (2000) found that teenage boys said that an ideal woman should be 'voluptuous', whereas girls did not. Nevertheless, both sexes felt that ideal women *and* ideal men should be thin.) Correspondingly, magazines for *women* celebrate the very thin look, but magazines for men favour a curvaceous and not-particularly-skinny look. *Loaded* magazine even put it into words: rejecting a female academic's assertion that 'women have the difficulty of living with the male idea of beauty shown on the catwalk', John Perry responds:

> No, men fancy models because they have beautiful faces, not because they look like they've been fed under a door. Sleeping with a supermodel would be about as pleasurable as shagging a bicycle. The truth is, it's women themselves who see these freaks as the epitome of perfection.
>
> (*Loaded*, July 2001: 95)

One could say, though, that the relative levels of skinniness are irrelevant: almost all of the 'beautiful women' in both women's and men's magazines are thin, not fat, and this must have an impact. Men are ideally required to be thin and well-toned too, but can get away with imperfections as long as they can compensate with charm or humour.

Finally, it is worth noting that our media culture is quick to pick out women for the smallest aberrations. Men can get away with being a bit more bald or fat or sweaty than the ideal. But when Julia Roberts was seen to have hairy armpits at the premiere of *Notting Hill* (1999), the world's press went crazy with excitement over this (wholly natural) 'outrage'. Staggered by the amount of coverage this received, Roberts later sardonically responded to a reporter who asked about her $20 million-per-film fees, 'Yeah, I get paid by the armpit hair. For each hair I get an extra dollar' (Helmore, 2001).

Back to some actual ads

At the level of analysis focused on the content of individual adverts, studies still find cause for dissatisfaction. In *Provocateur,* a recent book on representations of gender in advertising, Anthony Cortese asserts that 'Ad deconstruction reveals a pattern of symbolic and institutionalised sexism' (1999: 45), although his argument mixes older and more recent examples, and arguments, without acknowledging that different approaches might be relevant to different decades. Nevertheless, the reader is carried along by Cortese's well-illustrated argument that women are often shown as the 'perfect provocateur' (ibid.: 54):

> The exemplary female prototype in advertising, regardless of product or service, displays youth (no lines or wrinkles), good looks, sexual seductiveness, and perfection (no scars, blemishes, or even pores). The perfect provocateur is not human; rather, she is a form and hollow shell representing a female figure. Accepted attractiveness is her only attribute. She is slender, typically tall and long-legged.

This all seems accurate. It is, of course, silly to complain that a photograph is 'not human' and has no attributes apart from visual ones – that will always be the case with pictures. But nevertheless we get the point. Cortese rightly points out that if women want to look like the ones in the adverts, they will have to spend a lot of time and money on this never-ending quest. So by this point in the argument, we are quite convinced that advertising is oppressive to women and are ready to launch our campaigns against sexism in advertising. But then we get to Cortese's analysis of images of *men* in advertising, where he reveals that men are often shown as . . . the 'perfect provocateur' (ibid.: 58). He's not wrong, of course:

> Baudrillard [in *Seduction,* 1990] states that only women are seducers, but empirical evidence on advertising suggests otherwise. Men, too, are seducers – a male version of the perfect provocateur. The ideal man in ads is young, handsome, clean-cut, perfect, and sexually alluring.
>
> (ibid.: 58)

Cortese doesn't seem to spot the problem with his argument – he's complained that women are told that they must be 'physically perfect' in order to attract the opposite sex (ibid.: 54), but then he (correctly) observes that men are told this too (ibid.: 58–62). So we no longer seem to have a critique of sexism in the media: instead, we are left with a criticism of advertising for telling everybody that they have to look great at all times. Which is a fair point.

But maybe Cortese wasn't doing so badly after all (though he could spell it out more clearly): advertising may not be sexist by virtue of telling only one sex to look great – as we've said, it says this to both sexes – but you *can* say it is sexist because of the different standards set for each sex. Men in today's ads usually have muscular bodies and a rugged look. Cortese says:

> Today's man has pumped his pecs and shoulders and exhibits well-defined abs . . . Not many years ago, the slick and refined look defined fashion's ideal man. Now the muscular guy domi-nates the runways and magazine pages.
>
> (ibid.: 58)

There are certainly exceptions to this – the androgynous, almost waif-like men featured in adverts for the *CK One* fragrance are an obvious example. There may also be international differences – the medley of hunks featured in Cortese's American examples might look out of place in a European pub-lication. And times change. Nevertheless, there is a kind of male body, pro-moted in advertising, which requires a particular kind of body-work from men who want to emulate it; whereas women, to meet the female ideal, have to do more work on the hair, face and cosmetics, as well as maintain-ing fitness of the body.

Overall, today's advertising wants to look modern, and does not want to alienate any possible target audience, so it does not often include the glaring stereotypes we have seen in the past – except, sometimes, in a know-ingly ironic way where we are invited to laugh at the silly and dated assump-tions. Nevertheless, the advertising of the beauty industry does go to a lot of effort to persuade women that they really need the latest skin, hair, nail and leg creams (containing the latest ingredients with complex scientific-sounding names). And advertising regularly reinforces the desirability of particular physical looks, and shows happy heterosexual couples and cheer-ful nuclear families (although there are also humorous adverts which feature unfaithful partners, and other deviations from the harmonious norm).

QUEER TV

An excellent database of gay, lesbian and bisexual characters on television shows in the USA, Canada, Britain, Australia and elsewhere, from the 1960s to the present, appears at http://home.cc.umanitoba.ca/~wyatt /tv-characters.html.

EMERGING ALTERNATIVE SEXUALITIES ON TV

Lesbians, gay men and bisexuals remained hidden from view, in mainstream television shows, for decades. As recently as 1990, even the sight of two men sitting in bed together talking, with no physical contact – in the US drama series *Thirtysomething* – prompted half the advertisers to side with homophobic campaigners and withdraw their support, reportedly losing the ABC network over a million dollars (Brooke, 1997; Miller, 2000). Even in 1997–1998, Ellen DeGeneres's coming out as a lesbian in her sitcom *Ellen* (as well as in real life) caused an even bigger controversy, with advertisers fleeing, and ABC/Disney dropping the popular show after one 'lesbian' season. (Advertisers claim that it is not the content which scares them away, but controversy of any kind; this excuse is supported by the fact that several advertisers have dropped support for the radio and TV broadcasts of 'Dr. Laura' Schlessinger, whose anti-gay views have been widely criticised (Wilke, 2000)). Astonishingly, it was not until May 2000 that teen soap-drama *Dawson's Creek* included 'what is considered to be the first male–male romantic kiss on a prime-time [US] TV program' (Wilke, 2000).

To get an overview of the sluggish emergence of gays into mainstream media, we will have to rewind a few decades. The first serial drama to feature recurring gay characters was probably Australia's *Number 96* (Network Ten, 1972–1977), a deliberately controversial story of life in and around a block of flats in Sydney. Regular characters included Don, a gay man who had several partners during the show's run, Karen, a lesbian, and Robyn, a transsexual. The series was adapted by NBC for America in the early 1980s, but the gay characters were cut. In the 1970s a handful of other serials featured gay characters in minor roles, or as stereotypical gays played for laughs in sitcoms, but otherwise – as we can see from David Wyatt's excellent online guide (see 'Queer TV' box) – television gays were few and far between.

In the 1980s, glamorous US soap *Dynasty* included the regular gay character of Steven Carrington (1981–1986), and although he would never be seen kissing or being especially intimate with a man, the story followed his struggle to get the family – in particular his father, arch patriarch Blake Carrington – to accept his sexuality. In the UK, the BBC's most popular show, the 'gritty' soap *EastEnders*, went further with the character of Colin Russell from 1986–1989, a gay graphic designer who was probably more marginalised for owning a yuppie Filofax than for his sexuality. Colin was seen falling in love with Barry, a working-class gay man; they moved in together, and although their physical relationship as shown on screen was often rather stilted and distant, they were allowed some moments of intimacy including a controversial kiss (1987). The UK's other 'issues' soap of the time, *Brookside*, also featured a young gay character, Gordon Collins (1985–1990), who was bullied about his sexuality in one storyline, and eventually found a lover. Elsewhere in the 1980s, gay characters remained scarce on TV, as marginal bit-players or comic relief – or in the 'other world' of the British aristocracy, as in *Brideshead Revisited* (1981) and *The Jewel in the Crown* (1984).

In the 1990s, lesbians became more visible as leading characters in television series (as opposed to rare appearances as deviants). In Britain, the decade began with the outstanding screen adaptation of Jeanette Winterson's lesbian coming-of-age novel *Oranges Are Not the Only Fruit* (BBC, 1990). In 1993, *Brookside* pioneered the first lesbian kiss in a mainstream soap opera, and went on to show the relationship develop for a few months, on the knowingly controversial Channel Four. The characters, Beth and Margaret, were young, ordinary, attractive women, helping to dispel ignorant stereotypes of what lesbians might look like – although Beth had previously been a victim of sexual abuse, and Margaret later fell in love with a male priest – but that's soaps for you. The previously rather conventional ITV countryside soap *Emmerdale* had a young female character, Zoe, come out in the same year. (*Emmerdale* deserves credit for keeping this character on throughout the 1990s and into the next decade, giving her meaningful relationships with a series of non-stereotyped lesbian partners (first screen kiss: 1995), and not having the character return to heterosexuality.) In 1994, the BBC jumped on the lesbian soap bandwagon in *EastEnders*, where the relationship between a white woman and a black woman, Della and Binnie – both young and attractive, again – was prominent for a while, but didn't last long. Everyday lesbians began to appear in other British drama serials such as *Medics* (ITV, 1994) and *Between the Lines* (BBC, 1993–1995). By 2000, the British public were open-minded enough to *almost* let lesbian ex-nun Anna win the reality gameshow *Big Brother* (C4), and the following year it was a gay man, Brian, who won the prize.

In the USA, a fleeting kiss between women in *LA Law* (1991) and a one-off lesbian kiss for *Roseanne* (1994) were noisily discussed but did not really rock the boat; and the shockwaves of *Ellen*'s outing (1997–1998), mentioned above, might have put American broadcasters off lesbian central characters for a while. In teen hit *Buffy the Vampire Slayer*, Buffy's reliable sidekick, Willow, fell in love with fellow witch Tara in 2000. Their on-screen physical connection is never more than quick kisses on the cheek, but the relationship was sensitively developed. In the internationally popular *ER*, grouchy doctor Weaver began to explore her desire for women in the same year. And James Cameron's sci-fi series *Dark Angel* (2001) gives the lead cop an assertive lesbian sidekick. A small number of other lesbians can be found in supporting or background roles. (See www.glaad.org for latest tracking of lesbian, gay and bisexual characters on US TV.)

The 1990s saw gay men become more commonplace on British TV; for example, in *EastEnders* the young gay couple Simon and Tony (1996–1999) were allowed to kiss without the BBC switchboard exploding with irate calls. The BBC even included a gay art teacher in its long-running drama for children, *Grange Hill* (1993–1998). BBC2's *This Life* (1994–1996) featured gay males Warren and Lenny, as well as bisexual Ferdy, in its twentysome-thing ensemble. The UK's Channel Four financed the production of the San Francisco-based *Tales of the City* (1993), which was followed by *More Tales of the City* (1998) and *Further Tales of the City* (2001). Most spectacularly of all, Channel Four commissioned and heavily promoted *Queer as Folk* (1999–2000), the story of the lives of three gay men (and various friends) in Manchester, extremely well-written by Russell T. Davies. The series was notable for its non-judgemental treatment of interesting gay lives, its gay sex scenes, its emotional depth and its refusal to get bogged down with unhappy 'issues'. In 2001 this was followed by the jolly but less well-crafted *Metrosexuality*, a tale of gay, straight and bisexual lives.

Queer as Folk has boosted the TV visibility of gay men in the USA and Canada too, in its remade form produced by cable channel Showtime (2000–). The show was the topic of numerous newspaper stories from coast to coast, and ran to many more episodes than the UK original. The premiere scored Showtime's best ratings in three years (Miller, 2000). Although cynics had predicted that its transfer across the Atlantic would lead to a more bland production, the US *Queer as Folk* was surprisingly bold and frank.

The 1990s weren't especially kind to gay men on US TV, though. On *Northern Exposure*, occasional characters Ron and Erick operated a bed-and-breakfast, and got 'married' in 1994 – although two TV stations refused to transmit this episode. In the same year, a gay kiss was cut from *Melrose Place* because 'it would cost $1 million in ads' (DeWolf, 1997).

ABC's daytime soap *All My Children* featured a few gay characters, including a high school history teacher, whose presence in the classroom led to 'gay teacher' controversy in the storyline (1995–1998). Carter, one of the Mayor's staff in sitcom *Spin City*, is a gay activist (1996–). *Tales of the City* appeared on PBS in 1994, but *More Tales* did not appear until 1998, on Showtime, after PBS had abandoned it. The Fox network allowed gay characters to appear in its teen shows *Beverley Hills 90210* and *Party of Five* (as well as *Melrose Place*, mentioned above) but in each case the characters became marginalised over time (Hart, 2000).

More recently the sitcom *Will and Grace* (1998–) has dared to include a gay man as a main character – the Will of the title, who shares a flat with Grace, a straight woman. The show was US network TV's fourth-highest rated programme – just below *ER*, *Survivor* and *Friends* – in March 2001 (Wilke, 2001). This indicates a growing acceptance of gay characters, although of course the programme's actual success will be down to the script, cast and production. *Will and Grace* got through two seasons without showing a same-sex kiss, however, allowing *Dawson's Creek* to steal that crown, as mentioned above. The story of the *Creek*'s Jack coming to terms with his sexuality was handled sensitively, and does not seem to have damaged the popularity of the show. Less successful was *Normal, Ohio* (2000–2001), which starred John Goodman as a recently-out gay man returning to his home town to renew his relationship with his adult son. Finally, a small but growing number of TV advertisements have included gay characters – often based around a joke where a woman finds a man to be very attractive but he turns out to be gay, or vice versa. Details of such ads can be found on the website 'The Commercial Closet: The World's Largest Collection of Gay Advertising', at www.commercialcloset.org.

Bisexuals are rarely found on TV. Most notably, Sandra Bernhard's character Nancy in *Roseanne* was seen to date both men and women, and refused to be labelled either straight or gay (1992–1997). A small number of movies, such as *My Own Private Idaho* (1990) and *Basic Instinct* (1992) have featured bisexuality. Transsexuals are even less common in the TV world, although in the UK the long-running ITV soap *Coronation Street* introduced Hayley, a male-to-female transsexual, in 1998. This was a challenging storyline for the traditionally conservative *Street*, and has involved several traumatic plots. For example, Hayley began a successful relationship with a man, Roy, but when she revealed that she had been born a male and was approaching the final stage of her surgical transformation, he was shocked and rejected her for some time – although in due course they were reconciled, and, indeed, got married. Hayley encountered many other problems: *Street* bad guy Mike Baldwin learned of her secret and subjected her to crude taunts and threats to tell everyone. Hayley called Mike's bluff by publicly revealing the information herself, but many insults and jokes at her expense followed. There have been various other incidents where characters have discovered that Hayley is a transsexual and have reacted with shock or abuse. *Coronation Street* has not shown the life of a transsexual to be easy, then, but has frequently shown the cruelty and distressing consequences of people's ignorance and intolerance.

Overall, television broadcasters have been cautious about their use of non-heterosexual characters. For years, lesbians and gays were invisible, and even now, although some reasonable examples are listed above, these instances are exceptional and the vast majority of TV programmes have featured, and continue to feature, a seemingly all-straight set of characters. Bisexuals, and transsexuals, except in a few memorable cases, have been excluded altogether.

GAYS ON FILM

In mainstream movies, there have been very few lesbian or gay *leading* characters. The major examples – such as *The Adventures of Priscilla Queen of the Desert* (1994), *The Birdcage* (1996), *Beautiful Thing* (1996), *Bound* (1996), *Boys On the Side* (1995), *Desert Hearts* (1985), *Flawless* (1999), *Go Fish* (1994), *Jeffrey* (1995), *Kiss of the Spider Woman* (1985), *Priest* (1994), *Torch Song Trilogy* (1988), *Velvet Goldmine* (1998) – tend to be thought of as 'gay-themed films' or 'alternative' anyway, which may detract from their general impact on society. Mainstream release *The Next Best Thing* (2000) had a gay leading man alongside straight Madonna, but the story of the friends having a child together is happiest when they share a home platonically, and all goes wrong when Rupert Everett finds a man – although no doubt this was not intended to be the 'message' of this surprisingly dull film. Some literary stories of English aristocratic homosexuality in the past – *Maurice* (1987), *Another Country* (1984) and *Wilde* (1998) – may have slipped under the radar of more conservative audiences with their attractive 'costume drama' production values. There are, however, a few other exceptional examples, such as *But I'm a Cheerleader* (2000), a teen comedy that makes fun of 'gay rehabilitation' centres. Of course, mainstream filmmakers are increasingly happy to have non-heterosexuals in *supporting* roles – often the familiar 'gay best friend' character, wise and sensitive, who can help to guide the main character towards happiness. See, for example, *True Identity* (1991), *Four Weddings and a Funeral* (1994), *Clueless* (1995), *My Best Friend's Wedding* (1997), *As Good As It Gets* (1997), *The Object of my Affection* (1997), *Primary Colors* (1998) and *Billy Elliot* (2000).

However, perhaps the best-remembered image of a gay man in the movies remains Tom Hanks dying of AIDS in *Philadelphia* (1993). This well-intentioned Oscar-winner is now widely seen as a patronising, bland and overly polite attempt to have a gay character accepted as 'normal' by a 'normal' audience: Hanks is seen as part of a loving family, adores opera, is always polite and pleasant, and never shocks anyone with physical displays of affection for his male partner. The characterisation in *Philadelphia* is the antithesis of that in *Queer as Folk* (see above, p. 84), where gay men were actually allowed to be seen as interesting and funny and different – and not having to imitate middle-class, middle-aged heterosexuality in order to be accepted.

Of course there are a number of 'arthouse' films with gay characters or themes, but it seems reasonable to assert that these will have had a limited impact on the general public consciousness (especially when compared, say, to a central gay character in a popular soap opera on TV). It would seem to be a sad comment on the paucity of good films with lesbian characters that a 'Top Ten' list of the best lesbian movies, published in June 2001 by gay website *Planet Out* (www.planetout.com), has to include grim arthouse fare such as the wilfully gloomy *High Art* (1998). Useful lists of feature films with gay characters can be found at www.queerfilm.com and the 'movies' section of www.planetout.com.

OTHER 'OTHERS': THE QUEER CASE OF THE X-MEN

Some of the most interesting treatments of sexual minorities have been done by allusion (although campaigners would rightly assert that this should not replace better representation of characters who 'actually' do have unconventional sexualities). For example, the blockbuster *X-Men* (2000) showed the 'mutants' as a misunderstood minority, whose human rights were being attacked by politicians and society. One of the obvious parallels is with the anti-racist civil rights movement in America, as peaceful Charles Xavier and his heroic 'X-Men' team represent Martin Luther King and his followers, whereas Magneto and his more violent supporters represent the Malcolm X wing. But just as predominant in the film is the character of Senator Kelly, who is seen campaigning against the mutants using language which very clearly echoes the rhetoric of anti-gay speakers. The film-makers even set up a spoof website, *Mutant Watch* (www.mutantwatch.com), which matches the style and argument of anti-gay websites such as *National Association for Research and Therapy of Homosexuality* (www.narth.com), the *American Family Association* (www.afa.net), the

Family Research Council (www.frc.org), and *Morality in Media* (www.moralityinmedia.org). This comparison also gives us a chance to take a minor detour into the cultural battlefield of homophobic sexual politics.

The *Mutant Watch* site includes an introduction from Senator Kelly entitled 'Protecting Our Children' which begins:

> America is built on the strength of its families. The question is, what are families built on? The answer is people. Ordinary people. Lawyers and doctors, steel workers and schoolteachers. People like you. People like me. As I speak, there is a new and ominous danger facing our families. It is a danger facing every man, woman and child.

Kelly goes on to describe the threat to American families posed by these 'genetic aberrations', and encourages his supporters to 'preserve our heritage'. In another article on the site, Kelly discusses the problem of mutants in the school classroom, and there are links to 'independent scientific studies' which provide medical evidence about the abnormal mutants. There is also an online poll which asks whether unborn children should be tested for 'advanced genetic mutation'.

All of these perspectives and discourses can be seen in the websites of those organisations who feel that it is their duty to stamp out homosexuality to protect 'American families'. For example, a 'position statement' on the website of the Family Research Council states:

> By upholding the permanence of marriage between one man and one woman as a foundation for civil society, the Family Research Council consequently seeks to reverse many of the destructive aspects of the sexual revolution, including no-fault divorce, widespread adultery, and abortion. The council also, however, considers the increased acceptance of homosexuality as a part of that tragic mix. We do not consider homosexuality an alternative lifestyle or even a sexual 'preference;' it is unhealthy and destructive to individual persons, families, and society. Compassion – not bigotry – compels us to support the healing of homosexuals who wish to change their destructive behavior. In addition, we challenge efforts by political activists to normalize homosexuality and we oppose attempts to equate homosexuality with civil rights or compare it to benign characteristics such as skin color or place of origin.
>
> (www.frc.org/iss/hsx, 2001)

To clarify – although the *Mutant Watch* site is a spoof tied to the *X-Men* movie, the Family Research Council is a very real organisation based in Washington, DC, lobbying politicians and the media. It even produces a propaganda site aimed at young people called 'I.E. – Ideas and Energy' (www.frc.org/ie) which describes itself as 'an online webzine written for you, the smart and savvy high school student'. The site contains articles such as 'Gay Rights: Is it Right?' (their answer is: no). Just as Senator Kelly warned that mutants might use their super-powers to gain an advantage in public debate, this article warns that 'According to statistics, homosexuals have a higher average income than your typical Joe Smith, and homosexual activists use it to push the issue in the media, hire lawyers, and campaign for votes' (ibid.).

Finally, Senator Kelly's smooth presentation style – authoritative and reassuring – matches that of all the organisations mentioned above (and indeed there are many more 'family institutes' just like them, across the United States in particular). They all share the desire to appear as respectable policy and research centres. The National Association for Research and Therapy of Homosexuality, for example, has the smart website that befits a national organisation, although its goals, clearly stated on the first page – 'research, therapy and *prevention* of homosexuality' (emphasis added) – give away their extreme intentions. An article on the site explains, 'We don't hate gays; we simply desire to live free of homosexuality' (Davies, 2001), a seemingly unselfconscious echo of the reasoning given by fascists in the past. Similarly, the American Family Association uses various justifications for its anti-gay message. One of these is to assert that gay and bisexual people have a shorter life expectancy than heterosexuals. The solution is given in the article's title: 'Compassionate society should discourage deadly homosexual behaviour'. It explains:

> Paid homosexual activists are invited into our classrooms . . . to offer our kids an early death by teaching them 'How to be Gay' . . . True compassion for our fellow man requires us . . . to discourage such life-threatening choices . . . That's how we'd react to anyone we care about.
>
> (Glenn, 2001)

Their 'compassionate' stance does not stretch as far as allowing gay people to make their own choices, however.

Incidentally, all of these organisations are united behind a 'Boycott Disney' campaign. Although the Disney brand is usually associated with rather conservative and traditional values, these campaigners assert that

Disney is eagerly 'promoting and . . . normalizing the homosexual lifestyle'. Their 'Boycott Disney' campaign leaflet (available at www.afa.net) suggests that the company – and therefore, presumably, all media companies – should never show gay characters, and should focus on traditional Christian families instead. It even implies that employing gay people is a bad idea. The leaflet asserts: 'Disney's attack on America's families has become so blatant, so intentional, so obvious, that American Family Association has called for a boycott of all Disney products until such time as Disney ceases this assault.' The protest was sparked by *Ellen*'s coming-out in particular (the TV network ABC is owned by Disney). The leaflet disdainfully quotes *Ellen*'s executive producer Dava Savel saying 'If this episode helps some child in the Midwest with their sexual identification, we've done our job'. Clearly these organisations would like to 'help' children in a quite different direction.

SUMMARY

Representations of gender today are more complex, and less stereotyped, than in the past. Women and men are generally equals in the worlds of today's TV and movies, although male characters may still be to the fore. Women are seen as self-reliant heroes quite often today, whilst the depiction of masculinity has become less straightforward, and more troubled. Advertising, and the broader world of stars and celebrities, promotes images of well-toned and conventionally attractive women and men, which may mean that *everyone* is under pressure to look good, although women are additionally coerced about make-up, and subjected to even greater paranoia about looking thin. Meanwhile, gay and lesbian characters have started to gain greater acceptance within the TV mainstream, but remain relatively uncommon in movies.

Overall, then, modern media has a more complex view of gender and sexuality than ever before. The images of women and men which it propagates today may be equally valued, but remain different, and diverse. To see how people deal with these ideas and images in their everyday lives, we will now turn to some more theoretical perspectives concerning self-identity.

Chapter 5

GIDDENS, MODERNITY AND SELF-IDENTITY

I̲N THIS CHAPTER, and the next two, we consider some theoretical approaches which provide us with ways of looking at how people form their sense of self and identity. This will be fleshed out in the discussions of actual media, and actual audiences, in the subsequent chapters. Here, we look at the work of Anthony Giddens, on how people understand and shape their self-identity in modern societies, and how the media might feed into this. We'll begin with some background to his approach, so that it all makes sense.

COOL AND CLASSICAL

Anthony Giddens combines an old-school, 'classical' sociological style with a very contemporary awareness of changes in society, and he is happy to mix new theories with more established sociological perspectives. He was born in 1938, but doesn't fit into a category of older, conservative men. He hasn't tried to marginalise the impact of feminism in his understanding of society, and considers change in gender relations to be important. People criticise him for being too eclectic and for not going into things in enough depth, but those people are normally trying to turn their own narrow-minded lack of progression into a virtue, and therefore cannot be trusted. In interviews he seems pleasant and self-effacing, which is nice because he's so prolific that you wouldn't expect him to have had time to develop social skills. (His website is at: www.lse.ac.uk/giddens.)

Giddens manages to create the impression that he is continuing the

---

FOUR THINGS ABOUT ANTHONY GIDDENS

- Giddens enterprisingly co-founded Polity Press in 1984, to exercise more power in academic publishing.
- The University of Cambridge rejected Giddens's applications for promotion to a Chair for ten years, before finally making him a Professor in 1987, after he had published 13 books.
- In 1996, Routledge published a four-volume set entitled *Anthony Giddens: Critical Assessments*, which discussed his work over some 1,800 pages.
- In 1997 Giddens was appointed as Director of the London School of Economics. He is often seen as the architect of Tony Blair's 'Third Way', although Blair doesn't seem to share several of Giddens's beliefs.

---

grand sociological traditions, whilst dealing with the issues of today. The 'founding fathers' of sociology, Durkheim and Weber, cast shadows across his work. The other 'founding father' is, of course, Marx, whom Giddens finds less significant for sociology today. Although Giddens had published analyses of Marx in the 1970s, his textbook, *Sociology* (several editions from 1989), shocked the world of sociology teachers by barely mentioning him – especially in contrast with other sociology textbooks, which had previously been obliged to outline a Marxist perspective on every area of sociology. Marxists find this kind of thing to be proof that Giddens is useless, but their reasons are basically Marxist ones, so their argument gets caught in an embarrassing circular loop.

KEY THEMES

The main Giddens themes are:

1. the fusion of individual actions and grand social forces in one theoretical approach ('structuration').
2. the impact of 'late modernity', where all activity is the subject of social reflection, on social actors, relationships and institutions.
3. the consequent 'democratisation' of everything from big organisations to intimate relationships.
4. some other interests, such as globalisation, the state, and the 'third way' in politics, which are of less interest to us here.

LEFT AND RIGHT

Giddens would not deny that Marx was very important in the development of 'social science', and his instincts seem to be the nice-to-other-people ones which can be found at the theoretical heart of 'the left'. But he is frustrated at the left/right divide in social analysis, and these days is identified as one of the architects of the 'third way', which Tony Blair and Gerhard Schroeder are supposedly interested in – although Giddens's idea of it seems to be more original and complex than Blair's mix of left and right traditions (see Giddens's *The Third Way: The Renewal of Social Democracy* (1998), *The Third Way and its Critics* (2000)).

In sociology there has been a long-standing divide between those theorists who prioritise 'macro level' studies of social life – looking at the 'big picture' of society – and those who emphasise the 'micro level' – what everyday life means to individuals. Giddens always had an interesting relationship with this dichotomy. He seemed to admire Durkheim's preference for broad statements about society and sociology itself (his 1976 treatise on methodology even bore the cheekily grand Durkheim-style title *New Rules of Sociological Method*). But Giddens rejects Durkheim's idea that we should be able to identify laws which will predict how societies will operate, without looking at the meanings understood by individual actors in society. Giddens is here much closer to the other 'grandfather' of sociology, Weber, who argued that individuals' own accounts of social action were paramount. But Giddens recognised that both perspectives had value – and since the 'macro' and 'micro' levels of social life naturally feed into each other, you shouldn't have to choose between them. So he came up with the theory of 'structuration,' which bridges this divide.

THE THEORY OF STRUCTURATION   *next p.*

Giddens's theory of structuration notes that social life is more than random individual acts, but is not merely determined by social forces. To put it another way, it's not *merely* a mass of 'micro'-level activity – but on the other hand, you can't study it by only looking for 'macro'-level explanations. Instead, Giddens suggests, human agency and social structure are in a relationship with each other, and it is the repetition of the acts of individual agents which reproduces the structure. This means that there *is* a social structure – traditions, institutions, moral codes and established ways of doing things; but it also means that these can be changed when people start to ignore them, replace them, or reproduce them differently.

In the book *Conversations with Anthony Giddens* (Giddens and Pierson,

---

STRUCTURATION

Human agency (micro level activity) and social structure (macro level forces) continuously feed into each other. The social structure is reproduced through repetition of acts by individual people (and therefore can change).

1998), we find Giddens untroubled by his critics' efforts to find problems in the detail of how this might actually work. His 'oh, you're making it very complicated, but it's perfectly simple' attitude might frustrate some, but you can't really argue with it, because the whole idea of structuration is perfectly straightforward and, like many Giddens arguments, eminently sensible.

SOCIAL ORDER AND SOCIAL REPRODUCTION

If individuals find it difficult to act in any way that they fancy, what is the nature of those invisible social forces which provide resistance? Giddens finds an answer by drawing an analogy with language: although language only exists in those instances where we speak or write it, people react strongly against others who disregard its rules and conventions. In a similar way, the 'rules' of social order may only be 'in our heads' – they are not usually written down, and often have no formal force to back them up – but nevertheless, people can be shocked when seemingly minor social expectations are not adhered to. Harold Garfinkel's sociological studies in the 1960s showed that when people responded in unexpected ways to everyday questions or situations, other actors could react quite angrily to this breach of the collective understanding of 'normal behaviour' (see Garfinkel, 1984 [first published 1967]).

In the case of gender this form of social reproduction is particularly clear. When a boy goes to school wearing eyeliner and a dash of lipstick, the shockwaves – communicated through the conventions of punishment and teasing – can be powerful. Yet he only supplemented his appearance with materials which are used by millions of women every day. Women who choose not to shave their legs or armpits may be singled out in a similar way, treated as deviants for ignoring a social convention about feminine appearance.

People's everyday actions, then, reinforce and reproduce a set of expectations – and it is this set of *other people's expectations* which make up the 'social forces' and 'social structures' that sociologists talk about. As Giddens puts it, 'Society only has form, and that form only has effects on people, in so far as structure is produced and reproduced in what people do' (Giddens and Pierson, 1998: 77).

But why should we care about maintaining this shared framework of reality? Would it matter if other people were surprised by our actions? Giddens argues that people have 'a "faith" in the coherence of everyday life', which is developed very early in life – when we have to place absolute trust in our carers – and sustained by our ordinary interactions with others (Giddens, 1991: 38). It is because of this faith – a kind of routine trust, extended without a second thought – that some people are so shaken when others challenge the taken-for-granted consensus about how, say, women and men should behave.

We could say, for example, that this explains why some men are disturbed – even angered – to see other men acting in an 'effeminate' manner, because this behaviour challenges their everyday understanding of how things should be in the world. (TV entertainers in drag, on the other hand, pose no threat as they are just 'entertainment' which can easily be read as a *confirmation* of gender stereotypes.) People have an emotional investment in their world as they expect it, and for some, certain aberrations are most unwelcome. Others, of course, don't mind at all. Unfortunately, this account does not explain exactly why appearance or behaviour which crosses traditional *gender* boundaries can be so much more contentious than other unexpected things, such as unusual forms of hair colour or politeness.

The performance of gender appears here – as it does throughout this book – as something which is learned and policed, and which has to be constantly worked on and monitored.

GIDDENS, LATE MODERNITY AND POSTMODERNISM

We are not in a postmodern era, Giddens says. It is a period of *late modernity.* He does not necessarily disagree with the characterisations of recent social life which other theorists have labelled as postmodern – cultural self-consciousness, heightened superficiality, consumerism, scepticism towards theories which aim to explain everything ('meta-narratives' such as science, religion or Marxism) and so on. Giddens doesn't dispute these changes, but he says that we haven't really gone beyond modernity. It's just developed.

So it's inappropriate to call it *post*modernity. It's just modernity with bells on: late modernity. Giddens is undoubtedly right that postmodernity isn't a completely new era. But most major theorists of postmodernity, such as Lyotard, did not actually say that postmodernity replaced, and came after, modernity, anyway.

Nevertheless, the focus on modernity is useful because the most important contrast for Giddens is between pre-modern (traditional) culture and modern (post-traditional) culture. The phenomena that some have dubbed 'postmodern' are, in Giddens's terms, usually just the more extreme instances of a fully developed modernity.

POST-TRADITIONAL SOCIETY

It is important for understanding Giddens to note his interest in the increasingly *post-traditional* nature of society. When tradition dominates, individual actions do not have to be analysed and thought about so much, because choices are already prescribed by the traditions and customs. (Of course, this does not mean that the traditions can never be thought about, or challenged.) In post-traditional times, however, we don't really worry about the precedents set by previous generations, and options are at least as open as the law and public opinion will allow. All questions of how to behave in society then become matters which we have to consider and make decisions about. Society becomes much more *reflexive* and aware of its own precariously constructed state. Giddens is fascinated by the growing amounts of reflexivity in all aspects of society, from formal government at one end of the scale to intimate sexual relationships at the other.

Modernity is post-traditional. A society can't be fully modern if attitudes, actions or institutions are significantly influenced by traditions, because deference to tradition – doing things just because people did them in the past – is the opposite of modern reflexivity. Because of this, Giddens suggests that societies which try to 'modernise' in the most obvious institutional sense – by becoming something like a capitalist democracy – but which do not throw off other traditions, such as gender inequalities, are likely to fail in their attempt to be successful modern societies.

MODERNITY AND THE SELF

In modern societies – by which we mean not 'societies today' but 'societies where modernity is well developed' – self-identity becomes an inescapable issue. Even those who would say that they have never given any thought to questions or anxieties about their own identity will inevitably have been compelled to make significant choices throughout their lives, from everyday questions about clothing, appearance and leisure to high-impact decisions about relationships, beliefs and occupations. Whilst earlier societies with a social order based firmly in *tradition* would provide individuals with (more

Figure 5.1   Thinking about identities with lifestyle magazines

or less) clearly defined roles, in *post-traditional* societies we have to work out our roles for ourselves. As Giddens (1991: 70) puts it:

> What to do? How to act? Who to be? These are focal questions for everyone living in circumstances of late modernity – and ones which, on some level or another, all of us answer, either discursively or through day-to-day social behaviour.

The prominence of these questions of identity in modern society is both a consequence and a cause of changes at the institutional level. Typically, Giddens sees connections between the most 'micro' aspects of society – individuals' internal sense of self and identity – and the big 'macro' picture of the state, multinational capitalist corporations and globalisation. These different levels, which have traditionally been treated quite separately by sociology, have influence upon each other, and cannot really be understood in isolation.

Take, for example, the changes in intimate relationships which we have seen in the last 60 years – the much greater levels of divorce and separation as people move from one relationship to another, the substantially increased openness about sexuality and much more conspicuous sexual diversity. These changes cannot be understood by assuming they were led by social institutions and the state, not least of all because conventional thinking on both left and right has been that both capitalism and the 'moral authorities' of the state would prefer the population to have stable, monogamous family lives.

But these changes cannot be explained by looking only at the individual level, either: we couldn't just say that people spontaneously started to change their minds about how to live. A serious explanation must lie somewhere within the network of macro and micro forces. The changes in marriage, relationships and visible sexuality are associated with the decline of religion and the rise of rationality – social changes brought about by changes in how individuals view life, which in turn stem from social influences and observations. These developments are also a product of changes in the laws relating to marriage and sexuality (macro); but the demand for these changes came from the level of everyday lives (micro). These, in turn, had been affected by the social movements of women's liberation and egalitarianism (macro); which themselves had grown out of dissatisfactions within everyday life (micro). So change stems from a mesh of micro and macro forces.

The mass media is also likely to influence individuals' perceptions of their relationships. Whether in serious drama, or celebrity gossip, the need for 'good stories' would always support an emphasis on change in relationships. Since almost nobody on TV remains happily married for a lifetime – whether we're talking about fictional characters or real-life public figures – we inevitably receive a message that monogamous heterosexual stability is, at best, a rare 'ideal', which few can expect to achieve. We are encouraged to reflect on our relationships in magazines and self-help books (explicitly), and in movies, comedy and drama (implicitly). The news and factual media inform us about the findings of lifestyle research and actual social changes in family life. This knowledge is then 'reappropriated' by ordinary people, often lending support to non-traditional models of living. Information and ideas from the media do not merely *reflect* the social world, then, but contribute to its shape, and are central to modern reflexivity.

FEATURES OF LATE MODERNITY

- The self is not something we are born with, and it is not fixed.
- Instead, the self is reflexively made – thoughtfully constructed by the individual.
- We all choose a *lifestyle* (even if we wouldn't call it one).
- Relationships are increasingly like the 'pure relationship' of equals, where everything has to be negotiated and there are no external reasons for being together.
- We accept that all knowledge is provisional, and may be proved wrong in the future.
- We need *trust* in everyday life and relationships, or we'd be paralysed by thoughts of unhappy possibilities.
- We accept *risks*, and choose possible future actions by anticipating outcomes. The media adds to our awareness of risks.

THE REFLEXIVE PROJECT OF THE SELF

If the self is 'made', rather than inherited or just passively static, what form is it in? What is the thing that we make? Giddens says that in the post-traditional order, self-identity becomes a reflexive project – an endeavour that we continuously work and reflect on. We create, maintain and revise a set of biographical narratives – the story of who we are, and how we came to be where we are now.

Self-identity, then, is not a set of traits or observable characteristics. It is a person's own reflexive understanding of their biography. Self-identity has continuity – that is, it cannot easily be completely changed at will – but that continuity is only a product of the person's reflexive beliefs about their own biography (Giddens, 1991: 53). A stable self-identity is based on an account of a person's life, actions and influences which makes sense to themselves, and which can be explained to other people without much difficulty. It 'explains' the past, and is oriented towards an anticipated future. This narrative can always be gently revised, but an individual who tells conspicuously different versions of their biography to friends may be resented and rejected, and acute *embarrassment* is associated with the revelation that one has provided divergent accounts of past events.

> The existential question of self-identity is bound up with the fragile nature of the biography which the individual 'supplies' about herself. A person's identity is not to be found in behaviour, nor – important though this is – in the reactions of others, but in the capacity *to keep a particular narrative going*. The individual's biography, if she is to maintain regular interaction with others in the day-to-day world, cannot be wholly fictive. It must continually integrate events which occur in the external world, and sort them into the on-going 'story' about the self.
>
> (Giddens, 1991: 54)

A self-identity is not an objective description of what a person is 'like', and we would not expect it to be. Take, for example, a middle-aged man who has recently left his wife and moved in with his new lover, a younger woman. His biography covering these events might say that he was the victim of a failed and ultimately loveless marriage, and that his rational move into this new relationship has brought the happiness which he always sought and, indeed, deserved. His wife's biography, on the other hand, might assert that she did everything she could to make the marriage work, but her pathetic husband was enticed by younger flesh. The younger woman's account might view her lover as misunderstood, or exciting, or something else. None of these views is 'correct', of course – they are merely interpretations of a situation. Nevertheless, each person's own view is true as far as they are concerned, and they retain pride in their self-identities.

The ability to maintain a satisfactory story, then, is paramount: to believe in oneself, and command the respect of others, we need a strong narrative which can explain everything that has happened and in which, ideally, we play a heroic role. This narrative, whilst usually built upon a set of real events, needs to be creatively and continuously maintained. Pride and self-esteem, Giddens says, are based on 'confidence in the integrity and value of the narrative of self-identity' (1991: 66). Shame, meanwhile, stems from anxiety about the adequacy of the narrative on which self-identity is based – a fear that one's story isn't really good enough.

This, again, is all very *modern*. Giddens links the rise of the narrative of the self with the emergence of romantic love. Passion and sex have, of course, been around for a very long time, but the discourse of romantic love is said to have developed from the late eighteenth century. 'Romantic love introduced the idea of a narrative into an individual's life,' Giddens says (1992: 39) – a story about two individuals with little connection to wider social processes. He connects this development with the simultaneous emergence of the novel – a relatively early form of mass media, suggesting ideal (or less than ideal) romantic life narratives. These stories did not construct love as a partnership of equals, of course – instead, women were associated with a world of femininity and motherhood which was supposedly unknowable to men. Nevertheless, the female protagonists were usually independent and spirited. The masculine world, meanwhile, was detached from the domestic sphere, both emotionally and physically, and involved a decisive sense of purpose in the outside world.

Whilst passionate affairs might come and go rather unpredictably, the more long-term and future-oriented narrative of romantic love created a 'shared history' which made sense of two lives and gave their relationship an important and recognised role. The rise of this 'mutual narrative biography' led individuals to construct accounts of their lives, so that, even if the relationship with their partner went awry, a story still had to be maintained. And so now the biography of the self has taken on a life of its own, encouraged by a range of narratives suggested by popular media. Feature films, for example, often include the story of two people who are 'destined' to be together – they have found 'the one', and are happily united as the credits roll. Soap operas, on the other hand, almost always feature characters who move from one relationship to another, and sometimes even back again, because of the demands of the continuous serial form. Lifestyle magazines, as we will see in Chapters 8 and 9, have yet another vocabulary for relationships, which places a heavy emphasis on sexual fulfilment. These sources suggest a (potentially confusing) mix of ways of considering oneself and one's relationships.

THE REFLEXIVE SELF AND SEXUALITY

Freud famously argued that society sought to repress sexuality. Foucault later suggested that sexuality was not repressed but was more of a social obsession – any efforts to 'repress' sex reflected a fascination with it, and would always create even more awareness and talk about it. (More on this in the next chapter.) But Giddens argues that neither of these views is particularly satisfactory. His own argument is that during the nineteenth and twentieth centuries, sexual behaviour became 'hidden away' not because of prurience, but because it was being connected to the newly emergent sphere of intimate relationships – partnerships characterised by love and trust (which, we are told, were not common features of marriages in earlier times). 'Sexual development and sexual satisfaction henceforth became bound to the reflexive project of the self,' Giddens says (1991: 164). This is really a view shared with Foucault, although Giddens's emphasis here is more on the recent development of intimate relationship discourses which are fitted into autobiographical narratives (whereas Foucault's emphasis is more on discourses of the individual sexual body).

With sexuality and sexual identity being regarded, in modern societies, as so central to self-identity, issues in this area take on a profound level of importance. The question of one's sexual orientation, for instance, is of much more fundamental concern to us than taste in music or preference for certain kinds of foods. To have a 'problem' in the sexual department can lead people to declare that they no longer feel like a complete man or woman. This is heightened because sexual feelings are the subject matter of a huge number of songs, films, books, dramas and magazine articles. Other topics of everyday concern, such as food, shopping, pollution, work and illness, do not feature in anything like as many popular media products.

CONSUMERISM AND IDENTITY

Modernity does not, of course, offer up an unendingly diverse set of identities for citizens, newly freed from the chains of tradition, to step into. Many social expectations remain – although these are perhaps the remnants of the traditions which modernity is gradually shrugging off. But in addition, there is *capitalism*. Here, think not of the dirty factories we associate with Marx's critique, but of fashion and glamour, must-have toys, blockbusting bands and movies, fine foods and nice houses. As Giddens puts it, 'Modernity opens up the project of the self, but under conditions strongly influenced by the standardising effects of commodity capitalism' (1991: 196). The stuff we can buy to 'express' ourselves inevitably has an impact upon the project of the self.

Advertising promotes the idea that products will help us to accent our *individuality*, but of course the market only offers us a certain range of goods. The project of the self is redirected, by the corporate world, into a set of shopping opportunities. Giddens sees this as a corruption of, and a threat to, the true quest for self. At the same time, he notes that people will react *creatively* to commodification – they will not be compelled to accept any particular product in one specific way. Nevertheless, he says that the reflexive project of the self 'is in some part necessarily a struggle against commodified influences' (1991: 200), since the identities which are directly 'sold' to us are, by their very nature, similar to the fixed identities of tradition, which the reflexive citizen will question.

LIFESTYLE

Consumerism is one of the clearest ways in which we develop and project a *lifestyle*. Again, this is a feature of the post-traditional era: since social roles are no longer handed to us by society, we have to make choices – although the options are not, of course, unlimited. 'Lifestyle choices' may sound like a luxury of the more affluent classes, but Giddens asserts that everyone in modern society has to select a lifestyle, although different groups will have different possibilities (and wealth would certainly seem to increase the range of options). 'Lifestyle' is not only about fancy jobs and conspicuous consumption, though; the term applies to wider choices, behaviours, and (to greater or lesser degrees) attitudes and beliefs.

Lifestyles could be said to be like ready-made templates for a narrative of self. But the choice of one lifestyle does not predict any particular type of life story. So a lifestyle is more like a *genre*: whilst movie directors can choose to make a romance, or a western, or a horror story, we – as 'directors' of our own life narratives – can choose a metropolitan or a rural lifestyle, a lifestyle focused on success in work, or one centred on clubbing, sport, romance, or sexual conquests. The best-known lifestyle template must be that of the 'yuppie', perhaps because this model emerged in the 1980s as the first radically post-traditional professional identity, based on the individualistic desire to amass personal wealth. This lifestyle stemmed from particular occupations, but also came complete with a handy set of accessories by which would-be yuppies could identify themselves: mobile phone, braces and hair gel (for men), and a conspicuous designer wardrobe. Identifiable yuppie apartments made it easy to decide where to live, and yuppie wine bars gave them somewhere to go in the evening. (Yuppies were effectively satirised by Bret Easton Ellis in *American Psycho* (1991) – and by Mary Harron in the film of the novel (2000) – in which the protagonist finds he can get away with satisfying any desire, including killing people, because no one will challenge his smooth designer-label identity.)

Lifestyle choices, then, can give our personal narratives an identifiable shape, linking us to communities of people who are 'like us' – or people who, at least, have made similar choices. The behaviour associated with our chosen lifestyle will likely have practical value in itself, but is also a visible expression of a certain narrative of self-identity.

The choices which we make in modern society may be affected by the weight of tradition on the one hand, and a sense of relative freedom on the other. Everyday choices about what to eat, what to wear, who to socialise with, are all decisions which position ourselves as one kind of person and not another. And as Giddens says, 'The more post-traditional the settings in which an individual moves, the more lifestyle concerns the very core of self-identity, its making and remaking' (1991: 81).

An identity fitted into a lifestyle is not entirely free-floating. A lifestyle is a rather orderly container for identity, each type coming with certain expectations, so that particular actions would be seen as 'out of character' with it (ibid.: 82). However, an individual might have more than one 'lifestyle', each one reserved for certain audiences. Giddens calls these 'lifestyle sectors' – aspects of lifestyle that go with work, or home, or other relationships.

The importance of the media in propagating many modern lifestyles should be obvious. Whilst some ways of life – rural farming lifestyles, for instance – are not reflected too often on television, and will mostly be passed on by more direct means, ideas about other less traditional ways of life will be disseminated by the media – *alongside* everyday experience, of course. For example:

- A young person interested in dance music and clubbing might 'learn' about this scene first of all from the glossy dance music magazines; then real-life experience might lead this view to be adapted or replaced – but the magazines would still exert an influence over associations of the lifestyle with glamour, or drugs, or whatever.
- A young schoolteacher's idea of what it means to be a teacher will mostly be based on their real-life training, experience and observation – not on something they've seen in some TV drama about teachers.

Nevertheless, a meaningful part of their ideal notion of what a teacher *could* or *should* be like may be based on 'inspirational' films or dramas about teachers such as *Dead Poets Society* (1989) or *Wonder Boys* (2000).

- People who have moved into a social group which they were previously unfamiliar with – such as a working-class woman who suddenly lands a job on Wall Street – may (initially, at least) try to acquire some of the personal styles, and possessions, which the media typically associates with them.

The range of lifestyles – or lifestyle *ideals* – offered by the media may be limited, but at the same time it is usually broader than those we would expect to just 'bump into' in everyday life. So the media in modernity offers possibilities and celebrates diversity, but also offers narrow interpretations of certain roles or lifestyles – depending where you look.

THE BODY, AGENCY AND IDENTITY

Just as the self has become malleable in late modernity, so too has the body. No longer do we feel that the body is a more or less disappointing 'given' – instead, the body is the outer expression of our self, to be improved and worked upon; the body has, in the words of Giddens, become 'reflexively mobilized' – thrown into the expanding sphere of personal attributes which we are required to think about and control.

In *The Presentation of Self in Everyday Life*, Erving Goffman (1959) wrote about 'impression management' as the means by which a person may adjust their facial expressions, posture or clothing to suit a particular situation. In every interaction with another person or group, each of us routinely fosters more or less of an illusion (which may or may not reflect how we 'really' feel) designed to give the 'right impression' to our 'audience'. Goffman's argument should apply to human interactions at any point in history – even cavemen must have adjusted their faces and apparel to encourage feelings of affection, admiration, or fear, in those they met.

So in what way is the 'reflexive mobilisation' of the body a new feature of late modernity? Giddens would suggest that it is to do with the ways in which all aspects of the body are now 'up for grabs' to a previously unheard-of extent. At the grandest of extremes, operations can now make people taller, slimmer and bustier. Even sex can be changed. On a more commonplace level, we assume that anyone these days can adopt a regime which will make them look more slim, or athletic, or muscular. Whilst we have to admit that different regimes of the body have existed for thousands

of years, in different forms, the diversity of the different bodily manipula-
tions available today – and in particular the amount of *thought* we put into
these regimes – may be unique. Certainly the level of media coverage of
these possibilities, in magazines and guidebooks, must be unprecedented.
As we will see in Chapters 9 and 10, almost all lifestyle magazines for both
women and men contain advice on how readers can change their appearance so that they can 'feel good' personally, and be more attractive to
others. There are even popular magazines which have the reconstruction of
the body as their primary aim, such as *Celebrity Bodies* ('You can get one
too!') and *FHM Bionic* ('We can rebuild you'), as well as the many specialist
dieting and fitness titles.

Curiously, Giddens is unhappy with Foucault's account of the body and
how we present ourselves in society. Foucault 'cannot analyse the relation
between body and agency' – the relationship between our outer display and
our inner consciousness – 'since to all intents and purposes he equates the
two' (Giddens, 1991: 57). In other words, since Foucault sees people as all
'surface' – with no true 'inner self' (that's nothing but discourse, Foucault
suggests, all that talk about your inner self) – he is unable to conceive of an
inner consciousness driving the external presentations of self. For Foucault,
Giddens complains, 'the body plus power equals agency. But this idea will
not do, and appears unsophisticated when placed alongside the standpoint
developed prior to Foucault by Merleau-Ponty, and contemporaneously by
Goffman' (ibid.).

It's strange that Giddens suggests Goffman is more sophisticated than
Foucault, because everybody normally thinks of Foucault as being at the
height of sophistication and complexity, whereas Goffman's theatrical
metaphor for everyday life – 'all the world's a stage', basically, with everybody presenting a performance for their various audiences – is simple and
almost obvious (which doesn't mean it's actually wrong, of course). Foucault's argument is relatively difficult to pin down, whereas Goffman presents his case clearly and in detail, with lots of well-observed examples.
Giddens is unimpressed by the challenging vagueness of Foucault and
(refreshingly, perhaps?) plumps for the down-to-earth sociological
reportage of Goffman.

The problem with *The Presentation of Self in Everyday Life*, though,
is that it is very difficult to see what might lie *behind* all of the displays
of self. Apart from the idea of the inner self being basically a cynical actor
who wants to get on comfortably with everyone, in any given situation,
Goffman doesn't give us much to go on. One is reminded, again, of Bret
Easton Ellis's *American Psycho* (1991), where the narrator, Patrick
Bateman, says:

There is an idea of a Patrick Bateman, some kind of abstraction, but there is no real me, only an entity, something illusory, and though I can hide my cold gaze and you can shake my hand and feel flesh gripping yours and maybe you can even sense our lifestyles are probably comparable: *I simply am not there.* [...] I am a noncontingent human being. [...] But even after admitting this – and I have, countless times, in just about every act I've committed – and coming face-to-face with these truths, there is no catharsis. I gain no deeper knowledge about myself, no new understanding can be extracted from my telling.

(1991: 376–377)

Bateman is troubled by the apparent lack of a coherent 'self' at his core – 'Is evil something you are? Or is it something you do?' he wonders (ibid.) – and, like the reader of Goffman, is aware of his own successful performances, but doesn't know where any of them come from. Since Giddens sees people, in a rather 'common sense' way, as thoughtful actors making choices, he is able to skip past this problem.

THE TRANSFORMATION OF INTIMACY

In the post-traditional society, as mentioned above, relationships are entered into for the mutual satisfaction of emotional needs – unlike in the marriages of traditional cultures, which (we are told) were primarily for economic and symbolic convenience. Even if love was an element of such a marriage, the partnership would not be disbanded just because one or both parties felt that it was not bringing them complete fulfilment. By contrast, post-traditional relationships are consciously constructed, analysed, or broken up, according to how the participants are feeling. This is what Giddens calls *the transformation of intimacy*, in which an intimate, democratic partnership of two equal 'soulmates' becomes important for members of modern society. The traditional idea of 'marriage for life' is here replaced with the 'pure relationship', in which communication between equal partners (of whatever sex) ensures the couple are always oriented towards mutual satisfaction. The pure relationship is typical of reflexive modernity, where people's actions are oriented towards the achievement of personal satisfaction. Lest this seem extreme, Giddens admits (1998: 124) that the pure relationship is an 'ideal type', and that in real life today there is still a strong pull of tradition, as well as a consideration for the feelings of others.

Giddens is interested in sexuality and intimacy *within* – importantly – the contexts of modern everyday life. He criticises Foucault, for example, for putting too much emphasis on sexuality, while failing to come up with adequate accounts of gender, romantic love and the family (Giddens, 1992: 24), all of which are linked with sexuality in different ways. He also suggests that Foucault isn't that great on sexuality either. The Frenchman's account doesn't really explain the explosion in sexual awareness within the past century, for example: how did we get from the dry texts written and studied by a small number of male doctors at the start of the twentieth century, to the mass appeal of sizzling sex specials in popular magazines at the start of the twenty-first? Giddens, in typically sensible and sociological mode, points to the arrival of effective contraception as an important turning-point: once sex was separated from reproduction, sexual pleasure and variety could come to the fore. Reliable birth control paved the way for the 'sexual revolution', women's liberation and the emergence of 'plastic sexuality' – sexuality you can play with.

Whilst contraception (in the days before AIDS) had a direct impact on heterosexual sex, it had a knock-on effect on homosexual lives and sexuality generally, as the idea of sexual pleasure in society became more open and less riddled with anxiety. Furthermore, although in traditional societies the important function of reproduction was necessarily focused on heterosexual couples, in more modern times, once reproduction had come under human control, heterosexuality lost its primacy. This, Giddens suggests, is part of the long march of modernity; more and more areas of life come under social control, and so choice and diversity may prosper. (This may be optimistic, and Giddens admits that a point of blithe sexual diversity has not yet been reached – lesbians and gay men still face prejudice, abuse and violence, generally from those people we rightly call 'unreconstructed'.)

The media has continually reflected – and may have partly led – the changing status of different sexual activities, attitudes and sexualities, spreading awareness of different expectations and the existence of diversity. The private world of sex, however hidden or visible it had been at different points in the past, has certainly been thrown into the popular public domain in the past two or three decades, by the mass media, in a way which is quite unprecedented. Formal studies of the changing face of sexuality, alongside the representations of sexuality in films, magazines, news reports, pop videos, soap operas, and so on, all form part of what Giddens calls the *institutional reflexivity* regarding sex – society talking to itself about sexuality. This greater openness about sex has meant that there is a greater awareness of sexual skills, techniques and possibilities; and as examples of 'good sex' and 'bad sex' become more conspicuous, so sexual performance becomes more central to relationships overall, and a factor in whether they thrive or fail. Consequently, magazines, books and TV shows contain more sex advice than ever before. Even magazines for men, which were previously happy to admire women's bodies and assume that the male readers would know how to show the women a good time, are today full of advice for men on how they can impress women in and out of the bedroom (see Chapter 8).

SELF-HELP, POPULAR CULTURE AND THE IDEAL SELF

Self-help books are another source of lifestyle information in the modern world. These populist guides would usually be sneered at by academics, but Giddens has studied them to gain some insight into the more popular ways in which modern living is discussed. (I will be discussing self-help books, too, in Chapter 10.) In one such book, *Self-Therapy* by Janette Rainwater (1989), Giddens finds support for his idea that therapy is basically about helping individuals to sort out a strong self-identity based on a coherent and fully understood narrative of the self: a thoroughly modern and reflexive 'methodology of life-planning' (Giddens, 1991: 180). The language of self-help offers new elements, too, such as 'being true to oneself', which means that the reader has to construct an ideal self which they can then try to be 'true' to. Self-help books are typically about self-actualisation (fulfilling personal potential), and so the self, and the narrative of the self, then has to be directed towards particular *goals* which, of course, have to be selected. So from self-help books we acquire a picture of the self as based on a quest for particular achievements, seeking happiness, and trying to put together a narrative in which obstacles are overcome and fulfilment is ultimately reached.

Self-help books, of course, are only the most explicit purveyors of life advice. Many other forms of popular media offer images of what good relationships look like, what constitutes attractiveness and what makes life worth living. Characters in films usually have clear goals, which we are expected to identify with. Magazines offer specific advice on how to impress and succeed. Game shows, as well as some dramas, equate wealth with happiness (although the dramatic cliché that money brings misery is also popular). If we all have an 'ideal self' which is the aspirational heart of self-identity, and which informs our construction of narratives of self-identity, then the mass media must surely play a part in its development in modern societies. Therefore we will consider actual media examples and their relationship with the construction of self-identity in Chapters 8–10.

STORY STRUCTURES

Another influence of the media might be found not in the *content* of stories, but in the promotion of coherent stories themselves. We come to expect strong, clear narratives, where the motivations of different characters can be identified. For example, Giddens says of soap operas: 'The form is what matters rather than the content; in these stories one gains a sense of reflexive control over life circumstances, a feeling of a coherent narrative which is a reassuring balance to difficulties in sustaining the narrative of the self in actual social situations' (Giddens, 1991: 199).

In his book *Story*, Robert McKee (1999) sets out a template for the structure of a satisfying mainstream movie. Maybe this will show us the archetypal story which people connect with, and which they would want to live their own lives by? The point of the book is not to tell screenwriters what their movies should be *about*, but describes the general way in which a well-told story should unfold. The model can be applied to any story, from a domestic period drama to a sci-fi action thriller. Whilst McKee welcomes all kinds of variations, he suggests that the 'classic' kind of story involves an initially reluctant protagonist who is drawn into a world of challenges, faces various crises, gets to a point where all seems lost, but ultimately arrives at a climax (beginning 20 minutes before the end, please) where the hero and/or the situation is changed forever. We can see that this is the basic structure of many popular movies, old and new, from *The Wizard of Oz* (1939) to *The Parole Officer* (2001). Whether you have Mel Gibson in the historical action epic *The Patriot* (2000) or Mel Gibson in contemporary romantic comedy *What Women Want* (2000), this story structure remains present and correct.

In a book from the same screenwriting shelf, *The Writer's Journey*, Hollywood 'story consultant' Christopher Vogler (1999) draws on ancient and supposedly 'universal' myths and archetypes to suggest a rather more precise sequence of elements which should make a successful film – one which is able to touch hearts around the world. The 'Hero's Journey' described by Vogler, drawing upon the work of mythologist Joseph Campbell, comes in 12 stages. A hero is introduced in their everyday environment (the 'ordinary world'), where they receive a 'call to adventure', which is refused. Encouraged by a mentor, however, they enter the 'special world' of the story, and encounter tests, allies and enemies. The hero approaches the heart of the story, and has to survive a traumatic (ideally, life-threatening) ordeal. They get a reward, but are pursued on 'the road back' to the ordinary world. Finally the hero experiences a transformative 'resurrection', and returns with a prize which will benefit the ordinary world.

Although this may look like a very prescriptive formula, Vogler insists that there is no fixed order for these elements, and that they can be applied to any kind of story. Vogler is not providing a *new* recipe for shaping stories, but rather feels that he is distilling the story elements which have been present in many super-popular stories in the past, from ancient myths and fairy tales to the *Star Wars* saga (1977–) and almost every other block-buster.

But what do these Hollywood story tips have to do with our discussion? Both Robert McKee and Christopher Vogler consider the connections between popular stories and everyday life to be strong. McKee suggests that 'our appetite for story is a reflection of the profound human need to grasp the patterns of living, not merely as an intellectual exercise, but within a very personal, emotional experience' (1999: 12). He quotes Kenneth Burke's assertion that stories are 'equipment for living'. Vogler goes even further:

> I came looking for the design principles of storytelling, but on the road I found something more; a set of principles for living. I came to believe that the Hero's Journey is nothing less than a handbook for life, a complete instruction manual in the art of being human.
>
> (ibid.: ix)

The key story elements described by the two authors do not appear as a result of coincidence or chance. Indeed, George Lucas has acknowledged the influence of Joseph Campbell's studies of mythology upon the *Star Wars* plots, and director James Cameron accounted for the phenomenal international success of his *Titanic* (1997) by noting that it 'intentionally incorporates universals of human experience that are timeless . . . By dealing in archetypes, the film touches people in all cultures and of all ages' (quoted in Vogler, 1999: 243).

Whether truly 'universal' or not, these 'classic' story structures and character types do certainly seem to be appealing and meaningful to many people around the world. They are stories which we can relate to, and which we enjoy. It seems likely, then – to return to the Giddens terminology – that we would borrow from these stories when shaping our narratives of the self. It must be common for narratives of the self to be influenced by the heroic, assertive style of the protagonist in such films. This is difficult to demonstrate empirically, however, since most people would not admit to having fashioned any aspects of their life on movie star role models, if you simply asked them. Magazines, and self-help books, as mentioned above, tend to be more direct in talking about ways to live life – actively encouraging their readers to act like the confident and assertive characters, with clear goals, that we like to watch on screen.

THE ANTI-GIDDENS: STJEPAN MEŠTROVIĆ

Much of the appeal of Giddens's work rests on his belief in people's own capacities – he sees people as rational agents, in control of their lives, who have the ability to evaluate received ideas and creatively bring shape to their own lives. I should perhaps note, or admit, that – although I happened not to have studied Giddens until recently – my own work has also always favoured this approach. For example, in previous books – based on empirical research – I have emphasised the ability of people to resist media messages (Gauntlett, 1995, 1997; Gauntlett and Hill, 1999), the ability of young people to make their own creative media texts (1997), the ability of audiences to make television programmes relevant to their own lives (Gauntlett and Hill, 1999), and the ability of ordinary people to make expressive websites (Gauntlett, 2000). It seems preferable to assume that people are thoughtful and creative beings, in control of their own lives – not least of all because that is how most people surely see themselves. A sociology which disagrees with this view of people, and claims to 'know better', would seem to be almost inhumane.

Here, then, it is instructive to look at Stjepan Meštrović's critical polemic, *Anthony Giddens: The Last Modernist* (1998). The author implies that it is Giddens who is inhumane because his model of social life is far too rational, and excludes emotions and sentiment. The continuing popularity of nationalism, leading to violence and genocide, in many parts of the world, shows that people do not act on a purely rational basis. Nationalism, Meštrović suggests, is just one of many unruly and irrational emotions which people harbour – and which have deadly consequences – and which Giddens's model of the sophisticated, thoughtful, rational actor is unable to explain.

> [Giddens's] glib optimism, popular sociology rhetoric, and shallow treatment of theory resonate with the current climate of feel-good-optimistic ideology in sociology ... Giddens and many other mainstream sociologists have been singing a merry tune of global democratisation even as genocide raged in Bosnia, Russians expressed a nostalgia for Communism, the European Community began unravelling almost as soon as it was formed, and 'ethnic cleansing' became a metaphor for our times.
>
> (Meštrović, 1998: 4–5)

Meštrović suggests that Giddens offers an account of social life which is appealing to comfortable, middle-class Western sociologists, but which is weak when faced with the plight of the poor and the dispossessed. Giddens's recent, more directly 'political' books (1999, 2000) show awareness of, and discomfort about, ethnic conflicts and social problems, but Meštrović would no doubt say that his solutions are simplistic, optimistic and unconvincing.

A judgement about whether Giddens or Meštrović is right or wrong about this may ultimately rest on whether one agrees with Giddens's hope for optimism or Meštrović's inclination towards pessimism. Meštrović makes the surprising mistake of confusing his own interpretation of modernity with Giddens's use of the term. Meštrović understands modernity in the usual sociological way, as the time following the Enlightenment, which means we have been living under modernity for a couple of centuries at least. But Giddens, as we have seen, uses the term rather differently as part of his opposition between tradition and modernity, where tradition still plays a (decreasing) role in contemporary society. So Meštrović thinks that Giddens's account of modernity is flawed because it cannot account for irrational nationalist feelings, but actually Giddens is fine on this point because he wouldn't count those nationalist sentiments as part of modernity anyway – they are remnants of tradition which have not yet been discarded. (We could also note that nationalists no doubt feel themselves to be rational, and will have rational-sounding arguments to support their views.) So Giddens does have grounds for optimism, on his own terms, because we can see that tradition is in decline and that modernity is a more tolerant way of living. The kinds of oppression that concern Meštrović, whether they stem from tradition, and/or irrational thought, should cease to occur as rational modernity gets an even firmer grip.

Meštrović has no sympathy for this rational model, however. 'Giddens's agent is all mind and no heart,' he says (1998: 78). 'Giddens's knowledgeable human agent is ultimately a rationalist, a modernist caricature of what it means to be human' (ibid.: 80). The discussion of how people can creatively engage with their emotional lives through contemporary resources such as self-help books and other media, in *The Transformation of Intimacy* (Giddens, 1992), had seemed to me to be a liberating analysis of modern living. But for Meštrović it is quite the opposite:

> Previously, modernists got as far as Fordism and the assembly line in applying the machine model to social life. Giddens goes a step further: in *The Transformation of Intimacy* and other works, he advocates the self-diagnosis of emotional problems and the

remedy to such problems in much the same manner that one would fix a faulty carburettor.

(Meštrović, 1998: 7)

Whilst the machine analogy seems to be an effective put-down, it isn't really clear what is wrong with the idea that people can try to heal their own affairs of the heart. Meštrović clearly reads Giddens as unemotional and 'heartless', but I find Giddens to be refreshingly willing to consider emotions and feelings within his sociology. The 'pure relationship', for example, could cynically be seen as a selfish and rational approach to partnerships, where a person stays attached to another only when it is rewarding to do so. But on the other hand, it is a model concerned with people following their *feelings*, staying together if they are in love, or seeking an alternative if they are not – an honest, emotional approach.

Meštrović rejects Giddens's belief that people typically know what they are doing, and can account for their actions, asserting instead that people 'most of the time function as if they were on auto-pilot' (ibid.: 34). Both scholars could, no doubt, point to empirical evidence which appear to back up their claims; so it becomes a question of taste. Personally I prefer Giddens's model of the thoughtful, self-aware modern individual, to Meštrović's idea of the unreflexive conformist. Nevertheless, readers who feel seduced by Giddens's upbeat sociology – dismissed as 'a processed "happy meal" of social theory' by Meštrović (ibid.: 212) – should find it useful to at least consider the latter's arguments.

SUMMARY

In this chapter we saw that with the decline of traditions, identities in general – including gender and sexual identities – have become more diverse and malleable. Although sometimes limited by vestiges of tradition, modern lives are less predictable and fixed than they were for previous generations, and identities today are more 'up for grabs' than ever before. Everyone has to choose a way of living – although some people feel more enabled to make more unusual choices than others. The mass media suggests lifestyles, forms of self-presentation, and ways to find happiness (which may or may not be illusory). To interpret the choices we have made, individuals construct a narrative of the self, which gives some order to our complex lives. This narrative will also be influenced by perspectives which we have adopted from the media. Our relationship with our bodies, our sexual partners, and our own emotional needs, will all also be influenced by media representations, but (of course) in complex ways which will be swayed and modified by our social experiences and interactions.

FURTHER READING

Conversations with Anthony Giddens: Making Sense of Modernity (Giddens and Pierson, 1998) is a very readable introduction to Giddens's ideas on self-identity, and modernity, as well as other matters. The most important book on these issues is *Modernity and Self-Identity* (Giddens, 1991), which offers an excellent detailed discussion, whilst *The Transformation of Intimacy* (Giddens, 1992) further develops some of those ideas. Ulrich Beck and Elisabeth Beck-Gernsheim have pursued related interests in their book, *Individualization* (2002).

There are two recent, good and readable introductions to Giddens: *Anthony Giddens and Modern Social Theory* by Kenneth Tucker (1998) and *Anthony Giddens: An Introduction to a Social Theorist* by Lars Bo Kaspersen (2000). See also *Theorising Modernity: Reflexivity, Environment and Identity in Giddens' Social Theory* edited by O'Brien *et al.* (1999) and *The Contemporary Giddens: Social Theory in a Globalizing Age* edited by Bryant and Jary (2001).

MICHEL FOUCAULT
Discourses and Lifestyles

MICHEL FOUCAULT IS an elusive figure. Not in the literal, physical sense – he was buried in Vendeuvre, France, in 1984, after a shortish life of 57 years. Not in the sense that nobody talks about him, either – his influence in sociology, cultural studies, politics and literature has been enormous, and he was clearly one of the most-discussed scholars of the twentieth century. But Foucault's arguments can't really be reduced to a clear-cut list of assertions; the power of Foucault's work stems more from the way he suggests we look at things – which itself is often more implicit than explicit. In this chapter I will attempt to give a relatively straightforward introduction to Foucault's ideas about the self, identity and sexuality, and show how these, and his interest in 'modes of living', can help to develop our understanding of identities and the media in modern society.

The study of Foucault's thought is made additionally difficult because his ideas developed and changed over time. This means that it's best to understand his ideas as different (but related) bodies of thought associated with each of his different major publications. Thus the Foucault who wrote *Madness and Civilisation* (1961 in France) did not have quite the same set of ideas as the Foucault who wrote *The Archaeology of Knowledge* (1969 originally); and the Foucault who wrote *The History of Sexuality* (1976–1984) was thinking something rather differently again. It's important to know this, or else you get confused by people talking about an era of Foucault that's different to the one you'd just been thinking about. Of course, there's nothing wrong with Foucault changing his approach; in a 1982 interview, he remarked that 'When people say, "Well, you thought this a few years ago and now you say something else," my answer is … [laughs] "Well, do you think I have worked [hard] all those years to say the same thing and not to be changed?"' (2000: 131). This attitude to his own work fits well with his theoretical approach – that knowledge should transform the self. When asked in another 1982 interview if he was a philosopher, historian, structuralist, or Marxist, Foucault replied: 'I don't feel that it is necessary to know exactly what I am. The main interest in life and work is to become someone else that you were not in the beginning' (Martin, 1988: 9).

If we can be a little simplistic, though, we can divide the work broadly into an earlier and a later phase. In his earlier studies, Foucault was concerned with the ways in which the discourses of institutions, and their formally recognised 'experts', worked to constrain certain groups – limiting their opportunities by promoting certain views about them. (For 'discourses', read 'ways of speaking and thinking' about something.) The clearest example of this is in his first book *Madness and Civilisation*, where Foucault shows how the discourses of psychiatrists, from the seventeenth century to the start of the nineteenth, served to define and confine those people seen as mad. Other works such as *The Birth of the Clinic* (1963) also look, albeit somewhat more obliquely, at how historical changes in the 'expert' understanding of the human body had effects on the treatment of people by the state and its agents.

In his later works, on the other hand, Foucault shifted emphasis away from the ways that external forces and discourses might constrain people, towards a focus on how discourses might bring people to *police themselves*. At the turning point between these approaches was *Discipline and Punish* (1975), which might have originally been about how prisoners and criminals were defined by experts and institutions, but also came to describe how the disciplines and surveillance of prisoners affected their own behaviour. Subsequently, *The History of Sexuality* was concerned with ways in which social constructions of sexuality were internalised by people, leading them to see sexuality as the (possibly shameful) 'truth' about themselves, at the core of identity. Sexuality, then, did not have to be actively regulated by the state, as such, because people would be very careful to monitor their own behaviour themselves.

Foucault's emphasis changed, then, from a world constructed from *without* – external discourses imposed on people – to a world constructed from *within* – the individual's own dynamic adaptation to their surroundings. Note that the wider social environment remains significant; but Foucault had, perhaps, become more interested in people's subjective responses to it, both as internalised constraint, and more creative resistance.

FOUCAULT'S PARIS

Paris offers a range of treats for the discerning follower of Foucault. At www.theory.org.uk/foucault, there is an illustrated *Foucault's Paris* walking tour, which takes tourists to several key Foucault locations. Starting on the south side, at the Bibliothèque du Saulchoir – where the philosopher worked on volumes II and III of the *History of Sexuality* during the last five years of his life – the walk takes in various cafes which he 'probably' visited; the École Normale Supérieure where Foucault both studied and taught; and the Collège de France, where Foucault was elected to a special Chair in the 'History of Systems of Thought' in 1969. It would be fitting to end the tour at Foucault's grave, but that's 200 km away in Normandy.

In general the Foucault tourism opportunities have been poorly exploited by the French; *Foucault's Paris* suggests they should get top bald Foucault lookalike actor Patrick Stewart to record highlights of Foucault's works to CD for sale in a nice *Boutique de Foucault* somewhere near the Eiffel Tower.

FOUCAULT ON POWER

To understand why Foucault's model of power caught the attention of many scholars and activists, it helps considerably to remind ourselves of what had come before. Prior to Foucault, power was largely seen as a 'thing' which was 'held' by certain dominant groups. For Marxists, and people on the Left generally, power was seen as something held by the dominant class, the bosses, the owners of the means of production. The workers, in this system, were powerless, because in order to earn money to live they had to surrender to their exploitation by the dominant class. For feminists, it was men in patriarchal society who had the power; women were the powerless.

Foucault's understanding of power is quite different. For Foucault, power is not an asset which a person can *have*; rather, power is something *exercised* within interactions. Power *flows through* relationships, or networks of relationships. You couldn't really say that someone was powerful, per se, then; but you could say that they frequently found themselves in a powerful position, or had many opportunities to exercise power.

Foucault's clearest description of power occurs in Chapter 2 of Part 4 of *The History of Sexuality, Volume One: The Will to Knowledge* (1998 [1976]). Here he says:

> Power is everywhere; not because it embraces everything, but
> because it comes from everywhere ... Power is not an institu-
> tion, and not a structure; neither is it a certain strength we are
> endowed with; it is the name that one attributes to a complex
> strategical situation in a particular society'.
>
> (1998: 93)

This doesn't mean that everybody has equal access to power, though. Foucault falls back on talk of 'force relations' as the general social background
of inequality against which all the power interactions are played out. Power,
he says, 'is the moving substrate of force relations which, by virtue of their
inequality, constantly engender states of power, but the latter are always
local and unstable' (ibid.: 93). This part of the argument seems a little
poorly defined – is Foucault trying to sneak back the old idea of power,
here, by re-introducing it as 'force relations'? He explains it better elsewhere
(Foucault, 2000: 283) when he says that we may find 'states of domination'
where power relations have become so entrenched that they can seem
entirely one-sided and unchangeable. Nevertheless, Foucault says, such situations can be resisted and changed. The central point remains: power simply
cannot be *held* by one group; power is everywhere and plays a role in all
relationships and interactions (though this may be to a large or small extent
in each case). Power does not exist outside of social relationships; it's
exactly *within* these relationships that power comes into play. So it *is* a very
different model of power.

But when I was first introduced to this idea, as a student, it was hard to
see its value. If power is everywhere, doesn't that mean we can hardly talk
about it – or, perhaps, that there's nothing to talk about? And with power
slipping and sliding all over the place, it was difficult to see either what this
really meant, or what the implications would be.

This view of power also, unsurprisingly, upset those who were attached
to the previous model. To see power as a *force* held by a dominant group –
as in the traditional view – is valuable, from a political point of view,
because it highlights the inequality between the dominant people and
everybody else, and it emphasises exploitation. Sometimes it was hard to see
what it really *meant*, though, and it was always based on a one-dimensional
definition of power. For example, it would seem clear-cut to say that your
boss at a workplace has more power than you – they can tell you what to
do, and they can even sack you. (The boss can exercise power due to *institutional* arrangements of power, that can be called upon and used.) So
that's power, and this simple case alone seems to suggest that the traditional
left-wing view – that power is held by bosses and owners of companies –

FOUCAULT'S FANS AND FOES

In a book entitled *Saint Foucault*, David Halperin makes no secret of his admiration for the late thinker. In 1990, Halperin says, he conducted 'an admittedly unsystematic survey of various people I happened to know who had been active in [AIDS activist organisation] ACT UP/New York during its explosive early phase in the late 1980s'. He asked them to name the one book or resource that had most inspired them, and 'received, without the slightest hesitation or a single exception, the following answer: Michel Foucault, *The History of Sexuality, Volume I*' (1994: 16).

Halperin notes that Foucault's popularity with activists would surprise those who felt that his argument that 'power is everywhere' took away the opportunity to criticise injustices or oppose inequality. In the 1980s, Halperin muses, who would have guessed that Foucault 'was about to be canonized as the founding spirit of a newly militant form of popular resistance' (ibid.)?

Marxist critic Frank Lentricchia, for example, had said that: 'Foucault's theory of power, because it gives power to anyone, everywhere, at all times, provides a means of resistance, but no real goal for resistance', and therefore courted despair (Lentricchia, 1982: 51–52). In 1981, Jürgen Habermas had dismissed Foucault, along with other supposed 'antimodernists' such as Jacques Derrida, as a 'Young Conservative' (Halperin, 1994: 22). Edward Said was also frustrated by what he saw as Foucault's circular and self-defeating approach to power (Said, 1983: 245–246).

Halperin has little time for these views. If Foucault was making a covert case for 'political quietism', this was certainly lost on the ACT UP activists who had taken Foucault as an inspiration for all kinds of resistant demonstrations and actions (1994: 22–23). Halperin also notes that: 'The quietist reading of Foucault is also at stark odds with Foucault's own well-documented practice of political engagement. At the very time that he was crafting formulations about power, in fact, the fifty-year-old philosopher was regularly engaging in street battles with the police', and was very actively involved with campaigns and demonstrations throughout his working life (ibid.).

was a strong one. However – to continue the example – maybe your boss would go home and be beaten by their partner, who would dominate their home and make your boss feel miserable and useless – and suddenly, your boss is no longer 'a powerful person' per se; we find that the idea of them as powerful only made sense in one particular context.

Similarly, whilst women could point to ways in which patriarchal society supported the continuation of men's power, on the level of individual relationships it would always be easy to find instances where women seemed to have more power than men. In particular, the idea of all men having power, whilst women were united in their global powerlessness, never really worked – especially when a middle-class feminist academic would have much more in common with her male colleagues than she had with a woman living in poverty in the Third World.

So the idea that power is not actually a glorious substance held by dominant groups makes sense. But this is a disappointment if we liked to be able to oppose domination and support minorities; the old model allowed us to jeer at nasty powerful groups, whereas Foucault's model seems to have taken that opportunity away. At the same time, though, we know it makes sense. Whilst it may have been thrilling to condemn all men for their global conspiracy of power, for example, this was always difficult to reconcile with the pathetic examples of men that feminists would encounter in their everyday lives. Meanwhile, Foucault is not saying that there are no inequalities in society, or no marginalised groups. In fact, Foucault himself was quite an activist in support of minorities. Foucault's message, then, is not automatically reactionary just because it proposes a new way of looking at how power works. It doesn't *really* say that you can't jeer at nasty powerful groups, either, but it encourages a more practical and sophisticated approach to examining how that power is exercised. It also doesn't imply that feminism or Marxism are useless, it just forces them to become more interesting, complex and realistic.

POWER AND RESISTANCE

Foucault asserted that wherever power is exercised, resistance is also produced. 'Where there is power, there is resistance' (Foucault, 1998: 95). This is an essential part of his approach to power. Points of resistance are 'everywhere in the power network' (ibid.), and resistance does not (simply) occur at one major point, but all over the place. It might take the form of quiet tensions and suppressed concern, or spontaneous anger and protest. Just as power flows through networks of power relations – 'a dense web that passes through apparatuses and institutions, without being exactly localised in them' (1998: 96) – so the 'swarm of points of resistance' appear all over the place too. (This doesn't mean that resistance would always be dissipated and disorganised – revolutions are possible, Foucault suggests, if enough of these points of resistance can be strategically mobilised.)

This may sound like abstract theory, but it's easy to observe in the real world. We know from experience that wherever power needs to be referred to, to make something happen, then grumbles of discontent accompany it. If a boss has to make menacing reference to the terms of someone's employment, to make them work harder or in a particular way, this creates resentment. If one member of a couple has to allude to all the money they are bringing into the household, in order to get their partner to do something, then resistant feelings will be aroused. If an 'expert' places a contentious label on a situation, this will produce oppositional feelings amongst the people involved, or other concerned parties.

These examples help to show why Foucault says that power is *productive*. Whilst the traditional view of power would see it as a negative force, and a dampener on interesting things happening, in Foucault's eyes the exercise of power *might* have positive or negative consequences, but most importantly is productive, bringing things into being – whether as a result of the original action, or the effects of resistance to it, or both. This does not mean that Foucault is saying that acts of power are always 'good', as such – just that they cause things to happen, and are rarely one-dimensional.

This brings us to Foucault's argument in *The History of Sexuality, Volume I*, that it was precisely the discourses about sexuality, in Victorian times and the early twentieth century, which sought to *suppress* certain kinds of behaviour, which simultaneously gave an *identity* to them, and so (ironically) launched them into the public eye:

> There is no question that the appearance in nineteenth-century psychiatry, jurisprudence, and literature of a whole series of discourses on the species and subspecies of homosexuality, inversion, pederasty, and 'psychic hermaphrodism' made possible a strong advance of social controls into this area of 'perversity'; but it also made possible the formation of a 'reverse' discourse: homosexuality began to speak in its own behalf, to demand that its legitimacy or 'naturality' be acknowledged, often in the same vocabulary, using the same categories by which it was medically disqualified.
>
> (Foucault, 1998: 101)

The exercise of power on the one hand – the labelling of 'deviant' sexualities by authority figures – actually *produced* the resistance which would drive gay liberation movements in the twentieth century. The discourses about sex should not be viewed just as a form of domination, then, Foucault suggests, because in fact by making such a fuss about sex they were contributing to the vibrancy of the subject – stoking the fires of sexual discourse, as it were. (One of the broader arguments in *The History of Sexuality, Volume I*, is that far from being a time when no one could bear to think about sex, the Victorian era was absolutely *obsessed* with sexuality, which is why it was talked about as a problem so much.)

SEX AND IDENTITY

In *The History of Sexuality*, Foucault dismissed the common view that sex had been a freely-expressed, unproblematic part of life throughout history until it had been suppressed and hidden from public view within the last couple of hundred years. Tracing the history of discourses about sex, Foucault argues that sex was brought *into* the spotlight by Christianity in the seventeenth century, when it was decreed that all desires – not just forbidden ones, but all of them – should be transformed into discourse, in the form of the Christian confession. Desires suddenly acquired great importance. This idea of sex as the inner 'truth' about the self spread through Western culture, becoming further reinforced by carefully-worded studies in the eighteenth century, when sex became a 'police' matter, and also rested at the core of the newly-emergent political and economic concern about 'population' (Foucault, 1998: 20–25). Sex became a social and political issue – as it still is today, when teenage pregnancy, AIDS, sex education and pornography, for example, are thrust into the news by an interested party. From the start of the twentieth century, of course, the idea of sex as being at the core of identity was further reinforced by Freudian and psychoanalytic discourses, in which sexual urges and conflicts are the driving force of child development, and at the root of most problems. These ways of thinking about the self are not limited to the readers of Freud's books, or the clients of psychotherapists, but are widely dispersed through the kind of popular general knowledge you gain by reading magazine articles, watching sit-coms or seeing Woody Allen films.

Does it make sense to say that sex is at the heart of identity today? The answer is surely yes, and more so than ever before. As we have seen already, and will consider in more detail in later chapters, the discourses of magazines and self-help books, as well as many screen dramas, make knowing one's sexual identity of crucial importance to inner happiness. The media clearly suggests that, in order to be fulfilled and happy, you should:

- understand your own sexuality,
- have sex often,
- seek help for sexual problems,
- have a satisfactory sexual partner – or get a new one.

Talk shows, dramas, magazines, newspaper problem pages and other media all relay these points. We cannot assume that these messages have a direct impact on people, of course; and it is not necessarily the case that the mass media are *adding* these messages into society – perhaps the media are only circulating ideas which already seem like common sense to many people. But whatever their origins and power, these notions seem stronger than ever. Between 1961 and 1999, the divorce rate in England and Wales grew from 25,400 to 144,600 per year (having peaked at 165,000 in 1993 – more than a six-fold increase between the early 1960s and the early 1990s). Whilst divorce rates are not a perfect indicator – they only tell us about the kind of heterosexual people who are (or were) interested in getting married – this statistic clearly makes the point that people are no longer staying in relationships which no longer satisfy them. (So statistics for *divorce* – where people have made the dramatic step of disbanding a relationship which they previously swore to stay in forever, at a formal ceremony – are particularly telling here.) Whilst a general explanation for these divorces would be over-simplistic, we can say with some confidence that the modern proliferation of discourses of self-fulfilment, in terms of both sex and relationships, are likely to play a part in the termination of these marriages.

The high percentage of divorced people who *re*-marry indicates that these people have not gone off the ideals of romantic love per se – they just wanted a better partner, someone who would understand them better, and satisfy their true needs. (In 1999, 41 per cent of UK marriage ceremonies were for couples where one or both of them had been previously married.) Also, of course, marriage itself is in decline, partly because being 'locked' into marriage does not correspond, for a growing number of people, with the modern discourses of self-fulfilment. An official UK *Population Trends* report notes: 'There have been steady trends over the last quarter century, both in the increasing proportion [of couples] cohabiting, and the decline in the relative numbers married – and these trends seem set to continue' (National Statistics, 2001: 15). Major government surveys have found that two-thirds of the UK adult population agree that 'it is all right for a couple to live together without intending to get married' (ibid.: 7), and those opposed to this idea are clearly shown to be largely clustered within the older generations – those born before 1935 – who are, of course, on the decline.

All in all, we see from these statistics that couples are increasingly unlikely to get married – due in part to an uncertainty that this will bring self-fulfilment – and that those who *are* married, are today much more likely to divorce in order to continue the quest for self-fulfilment elsewhere. Whilst this does not show that sex itself has become more important than a few decades ago, the popular media discourses of self-fulfilment – which refer to relationships in general but include a heavy emphasis on sex in particular – are likely to be feeding these trends.

BACK TO LIFESTYLE: FOUCAULT'S ETHICS

In the previous chapter we discussed Anthony Giddens's interest in *lifestyle* – the idea that in modernity, everyone has to make choices about the shape and character of their lives and identities. A few years before Giddens was publishing in this area, Foucault had come to focus on similar questions, albeit with different emphases, whilst preparing *The History of Sexuality* volumes two and three, in the early 1980s.

In this work, Foucault talks about 'ethics', and it is important to understand that for Foucault this term does not (simply) mean a general moral code; instead, it refers to 'the self's relationship to itself'. To put it another way, ethics here means a person's concern for and care about themselves; the standards they have for how they would like to be treated, and how they will treat themselves. Ethics describes 'the kind of relationship you ought to have with yourself' (Foucault, 2000: 263) – the rules one sets for one's own behaviour. These rules, although personal and subjective, are vitally important; as Ian Hacking (1986: 236) notes, 'It is seldom force that keeps us on the straight and narrow; it is conscience'. A person's own ethics will usually *relate* to, but are unlikely to be exactly the same as, well-known sets of morality codes. For example, society says that it is wrong to be unfaithful to your partner, and says that 'being unfaithful' is having sex with another person. But an individual's own ethics might allow them to have sex with someone other than their partner, as long as that partner will not find out, and so cannot (in theory) be hurt by this action. Someone else might deal with this ethical problem in a different way, by shifting their definition of sex – as did Bill Clinton when, as President of the United States, he insisted he had not had 'sexual relations' with the young intern Monica Lewinsky, because they had (as it later transpired) engaged in oral but not penetrative sex.

TECHNOLOGIES OF THE SELF

Another central term in Foucault's later works is 'technologies of the self'. If ethics refers to a person's concern for the self – a set of internal ideas or loose rules – then the 'technologies of the self' are what is actually done about it: the ways that an individual's ethics are manifested in their mindset and actions. Another definition is that 'technologies of the self' refers to the ways in which people put forward, and police, their 'selves' in society; and the ways in which available discourses may enable or discourage various practices of the self.

Summing up what Foucault means by 'technologies of the self' is not straightforward, though. For a few years my website, www.theory.org.uk, feeling unsure of the best way to summarise the concept in one sentence, has invited users to supply their own attempts. Some of the better entries include:

- 'Technologies of the self are a series of techniques that allow individuals to work on themselves by regulating their bodies, their thoughts and their conduct' (Jennifer Webb, Queensland Art Gallery).
- 'Technologies of the self are methods employed by people resulting in how they will be perceived as "selves" by others and themselves' (Ernst Buchberger, University of Vienna).
- 'Technologies of the self are the specific practices by which subjects constitute themselves within and through systems of power, and which often seem to be either "natural" or imposed from above' (Jason Mittell, University of Wisconsin-Madison).
- 'Technologies of the self are the mechanisms employed by individuals and society, for better or worse, which perpetuate the public consumption of and regulation of individuality' (Jessica Matthews, Sarah Lawrence College).
- 'Technologies of the self are the continuously evolving mechanics of our very "nature" that dictate what we think, say and do, based on our daily experiences' (Charlie Webb, UK).

These are all useful summaries of the same idea. At slightly more length, Simon Kweeday of Liverpool Hope University offered this explanation:

> We try to portray our personality in the best possible light, when in fact our personality is not fixed, is always in flux and may not even exist at all, in any realistic sense. Society and its power constraints, rules and regulations, as well as many other contrasting

and complementary factors all gel into forming technologies of the self. Our portrayal of these facets from within projected towards society and from outside projected within ourselves determines who we are to ourselves and to other people.

In short, I think we might as well understand technologies of the self as the (internal and external) practice of our (internal) ethics. The ethics are our set of standards to do with being a particular sort of person; the technologies of the self are how we think and act to achieve this. Such acts, though, are not necessarily done 'for show', to give an impression to an audience; they may be practiced for the individual's own sake.

In *The History of Sexuality* volumes two and three, *The Use of Pleasure* and *The Care of the Self*, Foucault explores Ancient Greek and early Christian approaches to ethics, pleasure and technologies of the self. In an interview from 1983, he states most explicitly the meaning of this project and its relationship to the present. He explains, 'What strikes me is that in Greek ethics people were concerned with their moral conduct, their ethics, their relation to themselves and to others, much more than with religious problems' (2000: 255). They were very unconcerned about the nature of the gods, or the afterlife, Foucault asserts, as these were not ethical questions. The Greeks were concerned to 'constitute a kind of ethics which was an *aesthetics of existence*' (ibid., my emphasis) – which, again, has little relation to religion. Furthermore, Greek ethics were cultivated by the individual and were not governed by any formal or institutional regulations. 'For instance,' says Foucault, 'the laws against sexual misbehaviour were very few and not very compelling' (ibid.). His studies showed how Christianity brought a different set of technologies of the self, where sexuality was reconceptualised as being closer to the inner self, the soul, and an object of regulation. Desires had to be monitored and understood, and confessed to in a whole new discourse of the 'truth' about oneself which required a person to understand their faults and temptations, in order to be able to confess and therefore cleanse the soul (Foucault, 1980; 2000: 242–243).

To put it very simply, the Greeks wanted to cultivate a decent and beautiful life, in the present, and their ideas of what would make a good life were not bound by universal or normalising prescriptions about sex (such as fidelity to one partner, or a requirement of monogamous heterosexual marriage). The Christians, by contrast, had to worry about maintaining a pure soul, and had to avoid a clear list of sins in order not to be tarnished. The sins, of course, featured sexual desires – not only acts, but mere temptations as well – prominently.

Foucault felt that all this is relevant to people in modern Western societies because, with the decline of Christian religion, we find ourselves facing similar questions regarding how to create a satisfactory ethics for living a good life. These are issues which we come up against when we watch *Oprah*, read magazines, view dramas, or try to relate to news stories about the private lives of public figures. In a 1983 interview, Foucault mused:

> I wonder if our problem nowadays is not, in a way, similar to [that of the Greeks], since most of us no longer believe that ethics is founded in religion, nor do we want a legal system to intervene in our moral, personal, private life. Recent liberation movements suffer from the fact that they cannot find any principle on which to base the elaboration of a new ethics. They need an ethics, but they cannot find any other ethics than an ethics founded on so-called scientific knowledge of what the self is, what desire is, what the unconscious is, and so on. I am struck by this similarity of problems.
>
> (2000: 255–256)

Asked whether he thought, then, that the Greeks offered 'an attractive and plausible alternative', however, Foucault was adamant that one cannot find solutions to contemporary problems by copying the solutions of other times or cultures. We can't borrow the ancient Greek lifestyle for use today; we need to address today's problems directly. So it emerges that Foucault was interested in ancient attitudes to life and ways of being – technologies of the self – partly for their own sake (of course), but partly because these histories show people coming to terms with those same questions of identity and lifestyle which keep coming up in this book, namely: 'How should I live? Who shall I be? Who should I relate to? Can I find a comfortable self-identity?'

In fact Foucault, who liked to re-describe his previous work in the light of his current concerns, managed in one 1982 seminar to re-present all of his work as different approaches to self-awareness:

> My objective for more than twenty-five years has been to sketch out a history of the different ways in our culture that humans develop knowledge about themselves: economics, biology, psychiatry, medicine, and penology. The main point is not to accept this knowledge at face value but to analyse these so-called sciences as very specific 'truth games' related to specific techniques that human beings use to understand themselves.
>
> (2000: 224)

Here, each of the 'so-called sciences' of human behaviour is seen ultimately as a technology of the self – a way of looking at what it means to be a person. The reason for looking at *several* historical and cultural perspectives on the self is not simply a desire for a bit of variety – it is a means of demonstrating that no particular way of conceptualising the person is fixed or necessarily correct. Today's view of sexuality as an attribute, for example, may seem like common sense to most people here and now, but to the ancient Greeks would not have made sense. Today we have the idea that you are heterosexual, or homosexual, or perhaps bisexual – and, regardless of whether or not you are comfortable with different sexualities, we expect people to stay within one category. If, for example, you saw your gay friend passionately kissing a person of the opposite sex, there would probably be some confusion – 'Are they still gay? Have they gone straight? Are they now trying "bi"?' But the Greeks, who (according to Foucault) did not see sexuality as something you 'were' but rather something you 'did' – an activity rather than an identity – would not have had, or even understood, this concern. Foucault would not presume that this was because people in the past were *wrong*; he did not believe that our current forms of knowledge and understanding were necessarily better than any others. Such a 'different' way of viewing sexuality was not unique to ancient Greece. For example, in his historical study *Gay New York*, George Chauncey (1994) shows that in the early decades of the twentieth century, working-class New York culture did not recognise the categories of 'homosexual' and 'heterosexual' (or 'bisexual', which by meaning 'both' supports the binary division). Although some effeminate men identified as 'fairies' – a subculture well integrated into working-class communities – many other typically masculine men would have sexual relations with other men without this affecting their identity as a 'normal man'. The 'fairies' and 'normal men' were therefore divided by their gender style, rather than sexual activity.

What Foucault wanted to show was that – not only in relation to sexuality, but many other aspects of social life and living – today's practices are but one option among many, and our ways of 'understanding' ourselves do not necessarily represent the truth, as such. Rather, they are *strategies* – not necessarily bad ones – for making sense of modern life.

ADVERTISING AND TECHNOLOGIES OF THE SELF

In an article entitled 'Consumerism and "compulsory individuality"', Anne Cronin (2000) argues that the discourses of advertising emphasise *choice* and the power of the individual to transform themselves — through the purchase of certain products. These choices are seen as expressions of our individual identities. Consumerism is a *technology of the self*, then: through purchasing particular products, the adverts tell us, we can become like the liberated, aspiration beings seen in the ads. Nike's 'Just Do It' campaign, for example, suggests a do-it-yourself ethos of bodily regimes and willpower through which one can become a streamlined, fit, independent, self-directed being. Advertising and women's magazines position women, in particular, as both the subject and the object of consumerism, Cronin says

> Consumerism promises women self-transformation and appears to validate women's choices. Yet, even as subjects, women have faced an impossible imperative 'to be ourselves' through 'doing ourselves' mediated by 'doing' make-up (making yourself up), fashion (fashioning yourself), dieting and exercise (re-forming yourself).
>
> (2000: 279)

These regimes — these technologies of the self, as Foucault would call them, promoted through the media — remind us of the 'ethical duties to the self' that Foucault discusses in historical times. Advertising and the media often suggest that women have an ethical duty to monitor their appearance, make sacrifices to achieve a better body, and 'treat' themselves to a range of cosmetic treatments and adornments. Cronin warns that these regimes can never make women truly individual; indeed, as more and more messages tell us to 'just be yourself' or 'express yourself', this 'compulsory individuality' takes women further and further away from truly being 'an individual'.

THE ART OF LIFE

Whilst Foucault was indeed interested in a range of different ways of viewing the self, and he was genuinely keen to study them as a way of revealing the divergent possibilities, it is also clear that he preferred some models to others. Whilst he resented being categorised as an anti-psychiatrist, for instance, it is safe to say that Foucault thought that the pro-cedures of early psychiatry were pretty rubbish. The ancient Greek view of life as a work of art, on the other hand, is clearly appealing to him:

> Greek ethics is centred on a problem of personal choice, of the aesthetics of existence. The idea of [one's body, and one's life] as a material for an aesthetic piece of art is something that fasci-nates me. The idea also that ethics can be a very strong structure of existence, without any relation to [external laws or] a discipli-nary structure. All that is very interesting.
>
> (Foucault, 2000: 260)

Foucault is very interested in the idea that there is not necessarily any con-nection between our personal ways of living – social and sexual ethics – and the broader functioning of politics and society. Ethics can be 'a very strong structure of existence' without the need for external laws or disciplinary structures. Since the self is not 'given' but has to be actively created, then life itself could be developed and treated as a work of art (ibid.: 261–262).

But what does 'life as a work of art' really mean? In Foucault's terms, it is nothing to do with physical appearance – *looking* beautiful; rather, it is about a beautiful way of living. This does not mean surrounding oneself with beautiful things, either; it's about behaviour. Foucault seemed to admire the Greek ethics which led to a control of the self, in particular in regard to sexuality, where *self-restraint* became an art. Sex acts were not morally limited in the ways that we would recognise today, but their timing and quantity was important. (The opposite of this 'beautiful' restraint would be gross over-indulgence). Since a variety of sexual practices were 'allowed' – such as sex between men and boys – it was *moderation* and control of desire that gave a certain beauty to life. As Foucault explains in *The Use of Pleasure* (1992: 250–251), the impetus to be

> this self-disciplined subject was not presented in the form of a universal law, which each and every individual would have to obey, but rather as a principle of stylization of conduct for those who wished to give their existence the most graceful and accom-plished form possible.

These were suggestions on how to live a fine life, then, but not rules binding all members of society. As a set of principles that you could opt into, they were not like (what we now call) traditional morality, but had more in common with a high-status diet.

Not all aspects of Greek life are admired by Foucault. Although he has been criticised for not seeming very interested in the lives of Greek women, he did recognise that they were badly treated in that society (Foucault, 2000: 256–257); and he is not even convinced that sexuality between men was unproblematic (ibid.). But as we have noted before, Foucault is not suggesting that modern societies should copy the Greek model. His interest is in revealing that certain forms of freedom and choice are possibilities, and that nothing is 'given' from the start.

GAY LIFESTYLE

In the early 1980s, Foucault also became more publicly 'out' as a gay man (although to a large extent he managed to avoid having his sexuality turned into an 'explanatory' label – as in 'the gay scholar Michel Foucault'). In interviews conducted during this time, we find Foucault talking about how a gay relationship can be negotiated and created, in the absence of an established lifestyle model for such a partnership. Here, Foucault is concerned with finding a 'mode of life' in which such a relationship could work, and this is very close to Giddens's interest in 'lifestyle' (see previous chapter) developed a few years later. (Like Giddens, Foucault is interested in the idea of people having to forge their own models of sociability – he doesn't actually want to *prescribe* particular models for anybody.) For example, in a 1981 interview for *Gai Pied* (Foucault, 2000: 137–138), he ponders:

> Is it possible to create a homosexual mode of life? This notion of mode of life seems important to me … A way of life can be shared among individuals of different age, status, and social activity. It can yield intense relations not resembling those that are institutionalised. It seems to me that a way of life can yield a culture and an ethics. To be 'gay', I think, is not to identify with the psychological traits and the visible masks of the homosexual but to try to define and develop a way of life.

Here, we see that being gay is of interest to Foucault because it does not come packed with ready-made lifestyle patterns as (to an extent) heterosexuality does; instead it presents the freedom, and the challenge, to develop a meaningful lifestyle. Considering how such a lifestyle might be set out in a public forum, Foucault interestingly picks *magazines* as valuable communicators (2000: 139):

> Something well considered and voluntary like a magazine ought to make possible a homosexual culture, that is to say, [make available] the instruments for polymorphic, varied, and individually modulated relationships.

Magazines seem to be mentioned here because they can playfully make suggestions about lifestyles without being overly prescriptive. Foucault did not want anything as rigid as 'a program of proposals', because it could become a set of laws which would be quite contrary to the openness and creativity needed: 'There ought to be an inventiveness special to a situation like ours and to these feelings.' Warming to his topic, and giving an unusually clear-cut summary of what we might call 'the Foucault project', he asserts (139–140):

> We have to dig deeply to show how things have been historically contingent, for such and such reason intelligible, but not necessary. We must make the intelligible appear against a background of emptiness and deny its necessity. We must think that what exists is far from filling all possible spaces. To make a truly unavoidable challenge of the question: What can be played?

Foucault is here emphasising the motivation behind his historical studies, which sometimes is left so implicit (but not explicit) that readers ask of their Foucault paperbacks, 'What's your point? Why are you telling me all this history?' But here it is made clear: the histories of madness, or punishment, or sexuality, are designed to show *why* things were organised a certain way, on the one hand; but on the other hand to show that things didn't *have* to be that way at all.

A text like a magazine – which can be picked up and flicked through in any order, and which is treated in a relaxed, non-reverential way – might indeed offer the best way of exploring 'what can be played', as Foucault puts it, and magazines are discussed in more detail in the Chapters 8 and 9. Meanwhile the idea of giving a *performance* leads us into the next chapter, on queer theory, which directly builds upon Foucault's work.

SUMMARY

Femininity / pressure put on women to look good)

Foucault shows that particular ways of talking about things (discourses) shape the way that we perceive the world and our own selves. Today, popular media are obviously primary channels for the dissemination of prevailing discourses. The ability to influence a certain discourse is a form of power that can be exercised (although power is not a property held by a particular group, but is something that flows through social processes and interactions). The exercise of power always produces resistance, and so in this sense power is *productive* because it causes things to happen (which will not necessarily be the consequences intended by the original agent). The discourses about sexuality and identity are strong ones, enthusiastically spread by the media and consumed by audiences. Sexuality is seen as the key to happiness and knowing your 'true self'. In modern life, Foucault suggests, we have to establish an ethics and a mode of living – not dissimilar to Giddens's ideas about lifestyle – and he hints that the possibilities are virtually endless, but are not always visible to us.

FURTHER READING

Using Foucault's Methods by Gavin Kendall and Gary Wickham (1999) is a surprisingly good introduction to Foucault and how his ideas can be applied to different areas. It's important to read Foucault in his own words, of course. The interviews reproduced in *Ethics: Essential Works of Foucault 1954–1984 Volume 1* (Foucault, 2000) offer the best introduction to his ideas in this sphere, and then *The History of Sexuality, Volume I: The Will To Knowledge* (Foucault, 1998) is very important and reasonably short. See also Bristow (1997), Sarup (1996), Gutting (1994), Halperin (1994), and Foucault (1980, 1990, 1992).

Chapter 7

QUEER THEORY AND FLUID IDENTITIES

Q UEER THEORY, DESPITE one interpretation of its name, is not a theory of homosexuality (although it does have some things to say about that). It is an approach to sexuality and, more generally, identity, which builds on some of the ideas developed by Foucault (see previous chapter). The first and, in my view, the most valuable version of queer theory was put forward by Judith Butler in her book *Gender Trouble: Feminism and the Subversion of Identity* (1990). Butler, born in 1956, is Professor of Comparative Literature and Rhetoric at the University of California, Berkeley. It should be pointed out that Butler herself didn't label her *Gender Trouble* argument as 'queer theory'. Indeed, in a 1993 interview (Osborne and Segal, 1994), she recalled:

> I remember sitting next to someone at a dinner party, and he said that he was working on queer theory. And I said: What's queer theory? He looked at me like I was crazy, because he evidently thought that I was a part of this thing called queer theory. But all I knew was that Teresa de Lauretis had published an issue of the journal *Differences* called 'Queer Theory'. I thought it was something she had put together. It certainly never occurred to me that I was a part of queer theory.

This really is odd, though, because almost everybody regards Butler as the creator of modern queer theory. She owes a debt to Foucault and other earlier figures, but the thing we call 'queer theory' today definitely starts with *Gender Trouble* by Judith Butler. (Also important, within the version of queer theory which is concerned with literature rather than social identities, is the work of Eve Kosofsky Sedgwick, which challenges assumptions about sexuality in literature.)

It is also worth mentioning that Butler is unlikely to win any awards for clarity of writing style. (On the contrary, indeed, she once won an annual international award for having produced the most incomprehensible academic text.) Her prose is unnecessarily dense and long-winded, and almost never fails to use jargon even where much more accessible vocabulary is available. Some people defend this, saying that academics should be allowed to develop complex terminology to express their sophisticated ideas – after all, nobody expects to read journals about rocket science and understand all of it straight away. However, although Butler's writing is like an explosion in a dictionary factory, if one takes time to dig through the rubble one finds that her ideas are actually quite straightforward. So let's get started.

THE EASY BULLET POINT SUMMARY

We'll need to look at each of these points in more detail to fully understand their meaning and implications, but here's the simple summary of what queer theory is about:

* Nothing within your identity is fixed.
* Your identity is little more than a pile of (social and cultural) things which you have previously expressed, or which have been said about you.
* There is not really an 'inner self'. We come to believe we have one through the repetition of discourses about it.
* Gender, like other aspects of identity, is a performance (though not necessarily a consciously chosen one). Again, this is reinforced through repetition.
* Therefore, people can change.
* The binary divide between masculinity and femininity is a social construction built on the binary divide between men and women – which is also a social construction.
* We should challenge the traditional views of masculinity and femininity, and sexuality, by causing 'gender trouble'.

QUEER STUDIES

There is a strand of literary and film studies which is related to queer theory, and which entertains itself by 'queering' texts, which generally means coming up with alternative sexualities for the characters in a text. This is perfectly good fun, but – as with all studies which spend time inventing alternative readings of texts which the author probably didn't intend and which most audiences probably won't think of – might be a bit of a waste of time.

In this book we are concerned with queer theory as a tool for thinking about identity which is relevant to everybody.

QUESTIONING SEX AS WELL AS GENDER

Butler begins *Gender Trouble* with her concerns about the way that feminism had treated 'women' as a single and coherent group. On the one hand, it is pretty obvious that in order to make its arguments about the domination and mistreatment of women, feminism had to talk about women as one group, who were unfairly treated by the other group – men. The problems with this had been noted before – black feminist bell hooks, for example, had forcefully argued that white middle-class feminists had very insensitively ignored the fact that poor black women tended to have more in common with poor black men than they did with white academic feminists (hooks, 1982, 2000). The idea that women were united as a group, regardless of race, class or other differences, was therefore starting to look like the dream of women who didn't have any other oppressions to worry about. Of course, women might well have unique experiences in common – experiences of childbirth, of menstruation, or of being discriminated against for being female, for example; but it was the feminist implication that being a woman was *the defining factor* in identity that had come under fire. This argument does not just apply to sex and gender, but to other axes of identity such as race, class or sexuality, none of which can be broken from its context and singled out as a person's primary identity. Butler says that 'the singular notion of identity [is] a misnomer' (1990: 4). Furthermore:

> By conforming to a requirement of representational politics that feminism articulate a stable subject [i.e. 'women'], feminism thus opens itself to charges of gross misrepresentation.
>
> (ibid.: 5)

Butler asks whether feminism, in seeking to construct 'the category of women as a coherent and stable subject', might actually be performing 'an unwitting regulation and reification of gender relations' (ibid.). To put it another way: one of the initial ideas behind feminism was that we wanted a society where everyone was just treated as an equal person, without their sex making any difference. But by creating a binary 'women versus men' opposition, feminists were confirming the notion of women as a unique species – a notion which, in other contexts, would be seen as sexist. ('Binary' is used here to indicate that something is either one thing or the other – you are either female or male, and there are no other options.) The emphasis on 'women' as a group has partly worked 'to limit and constrain in advance the very cultural possibilities that feminism is supposed to open up' (ibid.: 147).

Butler notes that feminism and sociology more generally had come to accept a model, which she calls the 'heterosexual matrix', in which 'sex' is seen as a binary biological given – you are born female or male – and then 'gender' is the cultural component which is socialised into the person on that basis. Although Butler herself didn't present it as a diagram, we can draw it like this:

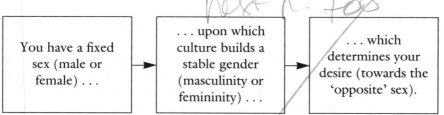

| You have a fixed sex (male or female) . . . | . . . upon which culture builds a stable gender (masculinity or femininity) . . . | . . . which determines your desire (towards the 'opposite' sex). |

Butler's overall argument is that we should not accept that these follow from each other – we should shatter the imagined connections. The above model would have to be replaced with something like this:

| You have a body. | You may perform an identity. | You may have desires. |

Note that in this model, not only have the words become very undeterministic – they assume very little – but also the arrows have gone, so your body does not determine your gender or identity, and this will not help us to predict your desires.

Butler argues that if 'sex' – the binary division of people into male or female – has a history, if people were not always divided in this way, if scientific discourses have formed our view of the duality of 'sex', then it is not a universally fixed term (1990: 7). Histories of science and sexuality have shown that this view of sex did not develop without discussion and contestation; and in particular the well-known fact that some people are born who cannot easily be categorised as either male or female – hermaphrodites – shows that there is at least a *third* category in this supposed binary world of sex. (Such cases may be a minority, but that is not relevant to the straightforward question of how many categories there are.)

Butler therefore goes on to argue that the binary nature of sex is seen as a given, but this itself is a construction – a way of viewing bodies. It is our view of gender (which everyone agrees to be culturally constructed) which leads to this view of sex. So, if we see sex as a questionable category which has no necessary link to any particular gender or personality or identity, and which in turn cannot dictate desire, then we come to a new conclusion:

> If a stable notion of gender no longer proves to be the foundational premise of feminist politics, perhaps a new sort of feminist politics is now desirable to contest the very reifications of gender and identity, one that will take the variable construction of identity as both a methodological and normative prerequisite, if not a political goal.
>
> (Butler, 1990: 5)

In other words, feminism cannot assume that people will have certain kinds of identity just because they are 'female' or 'male', and indeed it should perhaps campaign *for* this proliferation of identities. Furthermore, Butler specifically warns that feminists should avoid making generalisations about sex: 'Feminist critique ought to explore the totalizing claims of a masculine signifying economy, but also remain self-critical with respect to the totalizing gestures of feminism' (ibid.: 13). She suggests that feminists are right to criticise generalisations about 'men' and 'women' made by those they identify as patriarchs and sexists – and so should avoid making such generalisations themselves. None of us should make universal assumptions. Butler soon follows this with a similar warning: 'The insistence [by some feminists] upon the coherence and unity of the category of women has effectively refused the multiplicity of cultural, social, and political intersections in which the concrete array of "women" are constructed' (ibid.: 14). The assertion that women make up one united, oppressed group, then, has not enabled a realistic understanding of women (or others) in society. In her 1993 interview, Butler reasserts her connection with feminism, and says that she is concerned that queer theory has come to mean something quite anti-feminist. Nevertheless, whilst we can understand that she might not want to be seen to be *attacking* feminism as such, it is difficult to see how 'feminism' could be meaningful to Butler, since she has undermined its one universally defining feature – an emphasis on women.

GENDER AS A PERFORMANCE

The ways that we think and talk about gender and sex, Butler notes, tend to 'presuppose and preempt the possibilities of imaginable and realizable gender configurations within culture' (1990: 9). We are constrained by existing discourses. Most humanist views of the person see gender as an *attribute*, which – once installed by culture, at least – becomes fixed, a permanent part of that person's self. But Butler prefers 'those historical and anthropological positions that understand gender as a *relation* among socially constituted subjects in specifiable contexts' (ibid.: 10). In other words, rather than being a fixed attribute in a person, gender should be seen as a fluid variable which can shift and change in different contexts and at different times.

Gender, then, is a *performance* – and nothing more. 'There is no gender identity behind the expressions of gender; . . . identity is performatively constituted by the very "expressions" that are said to be its results' (ibid.: 25). Butler is here saying that we do not have a gender identity which informs our behaviour; on the contrary, that behaviour is all that our gender is. Gender, then, is what you *do* at particular times, rather than a universal *who you are*. (Ten years later, Madonna sung of love in the same terms: 'Tell me love isn't true, it's just something that we do' (*Don't Tell Me*, 2000) – wishing it to be more of a cultural construction rather than an inescapable 'given'.) We already recognise gender as something of an achievement. If a woman puts on a new dress and make-up, she might declare, 'I feel like a *woman* tonight'; similarly, a man who has put on overalls and picked up a power drill might see himself in the mirror and say, 'What a *man*!'. The fact that these expressions are not wholly meaningless shows that mostly people are at least partly aware that gender is some kind of performance (ibid.: 22).

It follows from this that no kind of identity is more 'true' or 'real' than any other. Thus, for example, where gay relationships seem similar in style and structure to heterosexual partnerships, this only reveals to Butler the 'utterly constructed status' of both types. 'Thus, gay is to straight *not* as copy is to original, but, rather, as copy is to copy. The parodic repetition of "the original" . . . reveals the original to be nothing other than a parody of the *idea* of the natural and the original' (ibid.: 31). Similarly, of course, there can be no 'real' or 'authentic' male or female performance. There are identity patterns that we have become familiar with, through their frequent repetition, but, Butler suggests, there is nothing fixed or predetermined about them.

Of course, the mass media conspicuously circulates certain kinds of male and female performance as preferable, thereby making the gender categories more 'real'. At the same time, though, the changes in gender representations in the past three or four decades (see Chapters 3–4) show that the recommended expressions of gender are eminently flexible. Within particular moments, then, the media might make gendered behaviours seem more 'natural', but when considered over time, the broad changes reveal the very constructedness of gender performances.

SUBVERSION

If gender is a performance, then, it can be turned on its head – or turned into *anything*. We do not have to wait for a feminist revolution, or for society to become more liberal or different before gender roles can be transformed, Butler suggests (ibid.: 30):

> If sexuality is culturally constructed within existing power relations, then the postulation of a normative sexuality that is 'before,' 'outside,' or 'beyond' power is a cultural impossibility and a politically impracticable dream, one that postpones the concrete and contemporary task of rethinking subversive possibilities for sexuality and identity within the terms of power itself.

Gender and sexuality can be reinvented in the here and now, in other words. Some commentators have focused on Butler's suggestion that existing gender forms could undermined through *parody* – as can be done by the drag performer who parodies the stereotypical routine of the other gender. But Butler is also aware that drag artists can easily be incorporated by traditional and even conservative humour, where sex roles are recognised with laughter, but not challenged. In fact Butler's ideas for undermining traditional understandings of gender go well beyond obvious parodies in any case; she welcomes any alternative performances of identity. As she explains in typically verbose style at the end of her introductory chapter:

> This text continues, then, as an effort to think through the possibility of subverting and displacing those naturalized and reified notions of gender that support masculine hegemony and heterosexist power, to make *gender trouble*, not through the strategies that figure a utopian beyond, but through the mobilization, sub-

versive confusion, and proliferation of precisely those constitu-
tive categories that seek to keep gender in its place by posturing
as the foundational illusions of identity.

(ibid.: 33–34, my emphasis)

So Butler is proposing that if society were to witness unpredictable, seemingly 'random' performances of identity, which challenge our expectations
about gender – that's the proliferation of 'subversive confusion' that she's
talking about – then our taken-for-granted gender categories would be
shaken and, if subjected to enough challenges, might eventually fall apart
altogether. This manifesto for radical change, almost buried in the heart of
her unexpectedly popular book, is the call for 'gender trouble' of its title.

Butler reminds us that we do not face a choice of *whether* to give a
performance, because identity is a performance already – it's *always* a
performance. The self is always being made and re-made in daily interactions, so the decision to steer it in a different direction might not be such a
big deal. Or, in Butler's prose:

> To enter into the repetitive practices of this terrain of significa-
> tion is not a choice, for the 'I' that might enter is always already
> inside: there is no possibility of agency or reality outside of the
> discursive practices that give those terms the intelligibility that
> they have. The task is not whether to repeat, but how to repeat
> or, indeed, to repeat and, through a radical proliferation of
> gender, *to displace* the very gender norms that enable the repeti-
> tion itself.
>
> (ibid.: 148, original emphasis)

This is, in effect, Judith Butler's mission statement. By giving a different
form to our daily performances of identity, we might work to change
gender norms and the binary understanding of masculinity and femininity.
Everyday life, then, is a political project, and one which everyone can work
on and potentially transform.

DID BUTLER *REALLY* SAY THAT?

After *Gender Trouble* was published, some people interpreted it as saying
that sex and gender were just social constructs that we could 'wish
away'. Indeed, my preferred reading of the book, given above, is quite
close to that optimistic view. As we have seen, Butler *does* suggest, at
the very least, that current understandings of gender can be challenged and

subverted through alternative performances of identity. However, this argument also got Butler into trouble with people who thought that this was a very idealistic view of how sexual politics in modern societies could be transformed. The entrenched forces of patriarchy, it was suggested, would not vanish just because a few queer theory fans made fun of them. And this point seems, in part, to have been accepted by Butler. Interviewed in 1993, she said:

> One of the interpretations that has been made of *Gender Trouble* is that there is no sex, there is only gender, and gender is performative. People then go on to think that if gender is performative it must be radically free. And it has seemed to many that the materiality of the body is vacated or ignored or negated here – disavowed, even. [. . .] So what became important to me in writing *Bodies that Matter* [1993] was to go back to the category of sex, and to the problem of materiality, and to ask how it is that sex itself might be construed as a norm. [. . .] I wanted to work out how a norm actually materialises a body, how we might understand the materiality of the body to be not only invested with a norm, but in some sense animated by a norm, or contoured by a norm. So I have shifted. I think that I overrode the category of sex too quickly in *Gender Trouble*. I try to reconsider it in *Bodies That Matter*, and to emphasise the place of constraint in the very production of sex.
>
> (Osborne and Segal, 1994)

So Butler started thinking that, although there are possibilities for subversion, we still need to attend to why it is that being male or female, defined by biology, feels like a specific reality to many people. This doesn't contradict her previous work, although it was clearly more depressingly focused on 'realism' rather than liberation.

Furthermore, we do not have to worry too much about this: every thinker puts forward tools which we can choose to use, or modify, or reject. I feel that the tools in *Gender Trouble* are more useful, relevant, and exciting than some of the more cautious ideas in Butler's later works, and would argue that it's not particularly important to worry about what Butler has thought about her own previous ideas since. We can also note that in some recent more pieces, such as Butler (1999), she has written again about the excitement generated by the idea that sexuality could be seen in terms of 'bodies and pleasures' (as Foucault had put it), with no necessary connection to existing categories of gender or sexuality. In any case, Butler has not *disowned* the *Gender Trouble* thesis; she has simply added some sensible notes of caution, acknowledging the complexity of social life.

USING BUTLER

An obvious criticism of Butler is that she doesn't really spell out how people should resist genders, or cause 'gender trouble', beyond the broad assertions quoted above. Monique Deveaux (1994) has complained that it's not clear how Butler's idea of everyday resistance would work in practical terms, for example, and in a review of *Gender Trouble*, E. Ann Kaplan (1992) noted that she would have liked 'more concreteness, particularly in relation to Butler's proposed politics of repetitive parodic gender performance'. On the other hand, it's not hard to *imagine* what these forms of resistance would involve, even though Butler doesn't provide illustrations. Feminists and gender theorists were quick to spot, rightly, that in the early 1990s, the pop icon Madonna seemed to be the living embodiment of Butler's manifesto. The *Sex* book (1992), the videos for *Express Yourself* (1989), *Justify My Love* (1990) and *Erotica* (1992), and the whole *Erotica* album, did it all – the blurring and confusion of genders, fluidity of sexuality, transgression of masculine and feminine stereotypes, were all what Butler appeared to be calling for (see Frank and Smith, 1993; Lloyd, 1993; Schwichtenberg, 1993; Brooks, 1997; Faith, 1997). Madonna's communications were on a global media canvas, of course – on a different level to the everyday interactions we mentioned above. (In her everyday life, most interviews and articles suggest, Madonna was usually more conventional.) Nevertheless, Butler's proposed gender challenges would gain much strength if a lead was taken by popular media figures – and the idea of a 'proliferation' of identities makes much more sense if we can assume that the mass media would play a key role in spreading these images. To destabilise the taken-for-granted assumptions about the supposedly binary divide between female and male, masculinity and femininity, gay and straight, what could be more powerful than a two-pronged attack, on the levels of both everyday life and popular media? The potential connections between queer theory and popular media will be discussed a little more in Chapter 11.

THE ANTI-BUTLER: MARTHA NUSSBAUM

To help us think about Butler it may be useful to consider a much-discussed review article by Martha Nussbaum, published in the American current affairs magazine *The New Republic* in February 1999. The article is a sustained attack on Butler's work, which contrasts the goals of activist feminists, who have sought to make life better for women in the real world, with Butler's stance, which Nussbaum seems to think involves fighting against nothing, merely playing with parodies of gender in the margins of society. She asserts:

> The new feminism [led by Butler] . . . instructs its members that there is little room for large-scale social change, and maybe no room at all. We are all, more or less, prisoners of the structure of power that have defined our identity as women; we can never change those structures in a large-scale way, and we can never escape from them. All that we can hope to do is to find spaces within the structures of power in which to parody them, to poke fun at them, to transgress them in speech.
>
> (Nussbaum, 1999)

This seems to be a serious misunderstanding of Butler, however. The call for 'gender trouble', as we have seen, is one which seeks to shatter the whole idea of gender throughout society – 'large-scale social change', in other words. Gender parody, and subversive performances, are not just a way of playing in the margins of social oppression to cheer oneself up; they are the tools by which, Butler suggests, we might overthrow the oppressive constraints of sex and gender roles altogether. Nussbaum, though, repeatedly reads Butler's ideas of subversion as quiet play rather than radical protest. She suggests that Butler is saying that 'We are doomed to repetition of the power structures into which we are born, but we can at least make fun of them' (Nussbaum, 1999), but this hardly tallies with Butler's assertion at the end of *Gender Trouble* that:

> If identities were no longer fixed as the premises of a political syllogism, and politics no longer understood as a set of ready-made subjects, a new configuration of politics would surely emerge from the ruins of the old. Cultural configurations of sex and gender might then proliferate or, rather, their present proliferation might then become articulable within the discourses that establish intelligible cultural life, confounding the very binarism of sex, and exposing its fundamental unnaturalness.
>
> (Butler, 1990: 149)

In her typically wordy way, Butler is clearly saying the *opposite* of what Nussbaum claims she says – we are *not* 'doomed to repetition of the power structures into which we are born', and these must be actively *challenged* and *transformed*.

Nussbaum is enthusiastic about feminist social changes brought by laws and other political action on the 'macro' level; maybe this is why she is unable to see Butler's ideas as a real challenge working on a different level, from the grass roots 'micro' level of everyday life. Nussbaum wants the state to force people to change, whereas Butler (in my interpretation) wants the popular culture of everyday people to be transformed from *within*. There isn't really any reason why, if she understood it more sympathetically, Nussbaum should object to Butler's contribution.

This is similar to the difference of opinion between Giddens and Meštrović, discussed in Chapter 5. Butler, like Giddens, would like to assume that people have the power to transform their own lives and make the world a better place. Nussbaum, like Meštrović, takes the more authoritarian view that the world isn't going to get any better unless a critical elite forces the population in a particular direction.

Nussbaum does have one democratic card to play though – her critique of Butler's writing style. In addition to the standard criticisms of its lack of charm ('ponderous and obscure . . . exasperating'), Nussbaum argues that if Butler really wanted to encourage people to challenge the prevailing norms then she wouldn't write in such a frustrating and inaccessible style. She has a point there. She is also right to point out that Butler's failure to clarify how she is using complex terms makes her books difficult to interpret, even for the most scholarly of readers:

> A further problem lies in Butler's casual mode of allusion. The ideas of these thinkers are never described in enough detail to include the uninitiated (if you are not familiar with the Althusserian concept of "interpellation," you are lost for chapters) or to explain to the initiated how, precisely, the difficult ideas are being understood. Of course, much academic writing is allusive in some way: it presupposes prior knowledge of certain doctrines and positions. But in both the continental and the Anglo-American philosophical traditions, academic writers for a specialist audience standardly acknowledge that the figures they mention are complicated, and the object of many different interpretations. They therefore typically assume the responsibility of advancing a definite interpretation among the contested ones, and of showing by argument why they have interpreted the figure as they have, and why their own interpretation is better than others.
>
> (Nussbaum, 1999)

Nussbaum concludes that Butler is addressing an uncritical audience of 'young feminist theorists' who are so much in awe of Butler's dense prose that they cannot see that there's not much there:

> The ideas in these books are thin. When Butler's notions are stated clearly and succinctly, one sees that, without a lot more distinctions and arguments, they don't go far, and they are not especially new. Thus obscurity fills the void left by an absence of a real complexity of thought and argument.
>
> (ibid.)

I would not agree that Butler has failed to give us new and interesting things to think about. The arguments I outlined above are genuinely innovative, challenging and useful. (We have also seen that Nussbaum didn't really seem to understand what Butler was calling for anyway, which weakens her critical position.) Nevertheless, Nussbaum may be right to suggest that Butler's good ideas are thinly spread through some pretty horrendous and pretentious texts. And in the decade since *Gender Trouble* was published, Butler has just got worse, not better. Reading *The Psychic Life of Power* (1997), for example, is tough for even the best-educated reader. It is a struggle to determine what she is talking about, and when you have, you wonder why it matters. She often seems to be discussing minutiae in great depth when there are much bigger questions to be tackled. But then a lot of academic work is like that. Overall I think that Nussbaum's attack on Butler is wrong and fails to appreciate the radical challenge to social life, to be fought on the everyday fields of interaction and communication (and, potentially, the media), which Butler puts forward. Her comments on the elitism and arrogance of Butler's style, however, are probably more justified. Nevertheless, Butler has provided tools which others can take up and popularise, and has therefore made a valuable contribution.

ANOTHER ATTACK ON QUEER THEORY

In an article published in the journal *Sexualities*, Tim Edwards provided what he called 'a strong critique of queer theory and politics' (1998: 471). Considering this article may, again, help clarify what queer theory stands for, and illuminate possible misunderstandings of it. For clarity, I have broken Edwards's argument into a set of numbered points:

1 Identities are usually stable

Edwards notes that the definition of queer theory is not clear-cut, but rightly observes that 'queer theory is primarily defined as an attempt to undermine an overall discourse of sexual categorisation and, more particularly, the limitations of the heterosexual-homosexual divide as an identity' (ibid.: 472). The author is unhappy with this 'utopian' orientation, however. 'The reality for many people much of the time is that their sexualities remain remarkably constant and stable over time even when lived experience may contradict this' (ibid.). This may be true – although Edwards doesn't actually provide any evidence for his assertion – but nevertheless, sociologists and cultural critics are left with a choice which they have faced for centuries: do we look at the world optimistically, assuming that people and conventions can change, or pessimistically, assuming that the world will stay as we already think it is? Edwards takes the supposedly 'realistic', pessimistic view, as is his right, but this seems to be a matter of personal choice rather than the necessarily 'correct' view that he seems to think it is.

2 Queer theory cheats, by focusing on fancy theories and cultural texts rather than real life

Edwards notes that some versions of queer theory make use of poststructuralist and psychoanalytic theories which are not founded on conventional kinds of empirical study. This is true, but it doesn't make the theories wrong. Indeed, the arguments may not rely on these elements anyway – for example, although Butler draws on psychoanalytic theories a lot, I outlined her approach above without feeling the need to mention them, as I do not consider them to be necessary for the basic argument (there's no point making a theory more pretentious and speculative than it needs to be). Queer theory makes sense with or without psychoanalytic elements.

Edwards also complains that many queer theorists are from a literary background and that their gender-bending arguments are supported by examples from literary texts, rather than real life. This is a fair point: illustrating an argument by reference to a few novels does not equate with decent research in the real world. So Edwards is right to suggest that this is a weakness within queer theory's claim to broad social relevance at this time, but again it does not actually show that queer theory is *wrong* about anything in particular. Furthermore, if the pioneers of queer theory happen to come from a background in literary studies, it's not really a surprise if they focus, in part, on literature. If queer theory has no sociological relevance, it will wither on the sociological vine anyway.

3 Queer theorists gaze optimistically at popular culture

Edwards notes that some of the followers of queer theory have found comfort in their analysis of certain texts carefully selected from the worlds of popular culture and art:

> What is perhaps most striking concerning such works is the comparative lack of attention paid to the oppression of sexual and even racial minorities in favour of a form of cultural optimism focused primarily upon issues of representation from Rock Hudson's movies to Della Grace's photography.
>
> (ibid.: 477)

Clearly Edwards is on safe ground arguing that an academic study of some 'transgressive' art photos is not going to change the world. But it's a cheap shot. The implications of the queer studies of cultural representations – films, pop stars, art, advertising – are that a proliferation of alternative views of gender and sexuality in popular culture will eventually lead to some changes. They are emphasising the importance of *culture* alongside more heavy-handed ways of changing society through legislation and regulation.

I would agree with Edwards that very detailed academic studies of challenging texts do not, in themselves, get us very far, and are possibly even a waste of time, but such studies are not at the heart of queer theory in any case. You wouldn't dismiss Marxism *as a body of thought*, for example, just because some English Literature professors had published a few rather pointless Marxist analyses of some novels.

4 Seeing gender as a discourse ignores its real-world significance

Edwards says that Butler's argument that gender exists at the level of discourse ignores its significance as 'an institutionalised social practice'. This sounds like a legitimate concern, but it doesn't really stand up, because Butler is *well aware* that gender and sexuality are firmly established as seemingly 'real' and robust social phenomena. It is the discourses of gender and sexuality which make them real. And Butler's argument is precisely aimed at *collapsing* the institutionalised power which Edward is concerned about.

5 The celebration of diversity may lead to individualism and fragmentation

Edwards seems to think that marginalised groups should 'stick together' rather than focusing on differences. This makes sense. However, it's also what white feminists used to say to black women to keep them quiet – race had to be ignored as an issue so as not to split the women's movement.

Queer theory certainly does question the idea of clear-cut identities, and the idea that 'women' or 'gay people' necessarily have something in common. This is liberating and powerful in some ways, but also, as Edwards warns, seems to take away the case for getting equality for women (as a group) or gay people (as a group), even if society is discriminating against them *as a group*. On the other hand, queer theorists might assert that they would like to see an end to all discriminations *and* all groupings.

6 By celebrating difference, queer politics reinforces the idea of gays and lesbians as marginal and 'alternative'

This is an odd criticism, based on some misunderstandings that we have to pick apart. Edwards argues that several difficulties emerge if activists emphasise *difference* as a political strategy, and play up the significance of alternative lifestyles:

> The first and more theoretical [problem] centres on the ambiguous sense of gay and lesbians as intrinsically different, which seems to play straight into the essentialist trap of seeing the gay man or lesbian as a specific type of person.
>
> (ibid.: 479)

This point is easily dispensed with, as queer theory emphatically *rejects* the idea of gay people as 'intrinsically different'. The point of the celebration of diversity and difference is that *everybody* is a little different from everybody else (and that we are happy about that). So this is quite contrary to the kind of 'heterosexuals versus homosexuals' ideology that Edwards is trying to link with it. He goes on:

> A secondary and more empirical factor is that while for some gay men and lesbians their sexuality is about a way of life and a central part of their identity, for others it amounts to little more than preferring tea or coffee. Neither is intrinsically right or wrong, yet there is a clear emphasis in queer politics upon the former approach.
>
> (ibid.: 479–480)

Having previously worried that queer theory might lead to apolitical fragmentation, then, Edwards is here concerned that the approach might be *too* political in relation to individual identities. This criticism is thin, at best, and since queer theorists support a proliferation of different identities – which do not all have to be 'radical' ones – it holds little sway. It is reminiscent of when the excellent gay drama series *Queer as Folk* was first shown on British television in 1999: a gay man complained on the viewer feedback programme *Right to Reply* that the characters were not 'normal' enough. 'I don't know anyone like that,' he protested, as though the three (very different) central characters in the drama should be compelled to represent an average, blanded-out spirit of uncontroversial gayness.

7 Queer theory celebrates pleasure, sex, the visual, the young and trendy

In his final set of points, Edwards argues that queer theory should place less emphasis on *pleasure* and the *visual*. He acknowledges that there is a place for pleasure to be emphasised as an uplifting alternative to the stigmas of AIDS, homophobia and purely 'political' identities, but worries that this places too much emphasis on sex. This is a pointless, miserable complaint – what can be wrong with aspirations to pleasure? – and even Edwards keeps this bit quite short. His concern about the visual is similar: we see quite a lot of images of sexy gay people these days, he notes unhappily, but this seems to be a general complaint about the uniformity of media images of attractiveness in general. Surely it is good if gay people are portrayed as being as sexually attractive as straight people, I would say; in the media of contemporary societies, it's the best you can expect.

These jibes tie into a more general problem for Edwards:

> Contemporary gay and lesbian politics are, in their entirety, centred upon the needs and activities of a minority of a minority: namely, those who are usually young, often affluent and frequently living in major cities where they adopt a gay (or queer) identity as a way of life. This quite clearly either excludes and/or under-represents the interests of those who are older, poorer, live outside of major cities, and who do not run their lives around their sexual orientations.
>
> (ibid.: 480–481)

It is clear that this would be a problem, but again I think that Edwards has either accidentally confused himself, or is misleading his readers. The criticism quoted above might work as an attack on some of the glossy gay lifestyle magazines, but it has nothing at all to do with *queer theory*. Queer theory celebrates diversity and variety. No theory could be happier with asexual, elderly blind people. All in all, I hope I have shown that Edwards's critique of queer theory – based on an inventive variety of misrepresentations and misunderstandings – carries little weight; and hopefully this has illuminated what is good, rather than bad, about the approach.

SUMMARY

Jersey 4

Queer theory is a radical remix of social construction theory, and a call to action: since identities are not fixed – neither to the body nor to the 'self' – we can perform 'gender' in whatever way we like. Although certain masculine and feminine formations may have been learned, these patterns can be broken. By spreading a variety of non-traditional images and ideas about how people can appear and act, the mass media can serve a valuable role in shattering the unhelpful moulds of 'male' and 'female' roles which continue to apply constraints upon people's ability to be expressive and emotionally literate beings.

FURTHER READING

Butler's *Gender Trouble* (1990) is a good next step, although not an easy read. Other short introductions to her work appear in Segal (1997) and Bristow (1997). *Sex Acts: Practices of Femininity and Masculinity* by Jennifer Harding (1998) provides a useful discussion, and links Butler's ideas to other related theories and areas. Diane Richardson's *Rethinking Sexuality* (2000) discusses queer theory and mounts a defence of radical feminism. See also *Performativity and Belonging* edited by Vikki Bell (1999), and *Revisioning Gender* edited by Ferree, Lorber and Hess (1999). Finally, *PoMoSexuals* edited by Carol Queen and Lawrence Schimel (1997) – the title refers to postmodern sexualities – offers some lively, journalistic writings that bring queer theory to life.

Chapter 8

MEN'S MAGAZINES AND MODERN MALE IDENTITIES

LIFESTYLE MAGAZINES FOR men are a relatively new phenomenon. In this chapter we will consider the ideas of manhood conveyed by the magazines, and see whether they are simply mainstream vehicles for old-fashioned attitudes and 'soft porn' pleasures, or whether they are offering new models of male identity to modern men. In her book *OverLoaded: Popular Culture and the Future of Feminism* (2000), Imelda Whelehan argues that magazines like *Loaded*, *FHM* and *Maxim* are an attempt to override the message of feminism, promoting a laddish world where women are sex objects, and changes in gender roles can be dismissed with an ironic joke. Whelehan recognises that these magazines may not have straightforward effects – she notes that 'to assume that these readers internalise the lad credo in its entirety is to underestimate the uses to which popular culture is put by individual consumers' (2000: 6). Nevertheless, she says, 'it is impossible to ignore the growth of this image and its depiction of masculinity ... its prevalence offers a timely warning to any woman who felt that gender relations were now freely negotiable' (ibid.). It's a persuasive and worrying argument, especially when illustrated with some unpleasant sexist quotes from *Loaded*. However, whilst I for one would not want to defend the dumb excesses of some of the men's titles, this remains a rather superficial analysis, based on a caricature of what modern men's magazines are about. Their 'depiction of masculinity' can be regressive and cringeworthy on some pages, but overall is clearly not as one-dimensional as Whelehan suggests. Furthermore, Whelehan's assumptions of how the magazines will have an impact on men's identities is too casually damning and

Figure 8.1   Men's magazines: seeking masculinities for the modern world

pessimistic. Although it is easy to empathise with Whelehan's concerns – not wanting to see men pushed into a laddish stereotype, or see sexism rein-forced – but we really need a better understanding of the types of masculini-ties projected by the various magazines before we can even begin to try to assess their potential impact.

In Chapter 6, we saw that Foucault argued that identities were formed from the materials available to people in popular discourses. Tony Schirato and Susan Yell, in their discussion of men's lifestyle magazines in Australia, assert that magazines are a central point for discourses of male identity:

> It is interesting to consider how this change in the profile of men's magazines impacts on discourses of masculine subjectivity. Magazines certainly constitute a significant site within the culture for the discursive production of subjectivity – to para-phrase Janice Winship (1987: 162; writing on women's maga-zines), they operate within a nexus of 'identity – consumption – desire'. Consequently, changes in the market and profile of mag-azines indicate shifts in the 'available discourses' ... for con-structing identities.
>
> (1999: 84)

Of course, not all men read these magazines, and every person who *does* look at them will make a selective, active reading. Nevertheless, the magazines are indeed a 'significant site' for discourses of masculinity, which are reflected, reproduced and perhaps manipulated on their pages. We should therefore begin with a quite detailed look at where the magazines came from, and what they're about.

ABOUT THE INTERVIEWS WITH READERS

In this chapter and the next, I will be referring to some qualitative interviews which I conducted by email with various magazine readers in February and March 2001. Twenty women and twenty men, predominantly from the USA and UK, were interviewed. These respondents were found by sending out requests to various (non-academic) email mailing lists, asking for readers of women's or men's lifestyle magazines to contact me. Comments from these interviews are used here to illustrate and flesh out my arguments, and to show certain reactions to the magazines. The interview data does not reflect a scientific sample of magazine readers – at best, we have responses from a reasonably random bunch of self-selected people who are readers of lifestyle magazines, who are email users, and who (as in all studies) are people who were willing to convey their responses to a researcher. The interviewees were encouraged to give their honest views and opinions, and discouraged from trying to make deliberately 'analytical' points just to look intellectual. (See also 'A note on methodology' in Chapter 1).

THE EMERGENCE OF MEN'S LIFESTYLE MAGAZINES

The men's magazine market is relatively new. It's not that men never bought magazines in the past, of course – they were the primary purchasers of *What Car*, *Hobby Electronics*, *Angling Times* and numerous other titles dedicated to a particular hobby or interest. There were also the 'top shelf' pornography magazines such as *Playboy*, *Penthouse*, and *Men Only*. But there was not really a general 'men's interests' magazine to parallel the numerous 'women's' titles. Publishers were aware of the gap in the market but felt that men would not want to read general 'lifestyle' material – glossy magazines were seen as rather feminine products, and 'real men' didn't need a magazine to tell them how to live. For instance, Joke Hermes found that the whole idea of a problem page was generally 'loathsome' and laugh-

able to men, when she interviewed women and men about women's magazines in the early 1990s (1995: 52).

Commentators such as Tim Edwards (1997) and Sean Nixon (1997)
trace the emergence of men's lifestyle magazines in the UK back to the
launch of *Arena* in 1986. *Arena* was an upmarket fashion and style magazine for the urban man, which built upon the success of style magazines
such as *The Face*, *i-D* and *Blitz*. These three titles had all been launched in
1980, and covered fashion, design and music for an audience of trendy
young men and women. As publishers Wagadon noted that *The Face* was
selling to more men than women, it encouraged its creator, Nick Logan, to
launch *Arena* for slightly older style-conscious men (Nixon, 1997). *GQ*
(*Gentlemen's Quarterly*), also centred on expensively stylish living and
fashion, followed in 1988. These magazines were profitable but did not
really smash open the market for most men. The staff of *Arena* were pleased
with their early circulation figure of 65,000 (ibid.: 141) but the magazine
was not reaching a significant slice of the population – and, indeed, had
never intended to. *Arena* and *GQ*, as well as *Esquire* (launched in 1991),
were seen as 'fashion for posh blokes – advertising executives,' as one of my
email interviewees put it, although all three had upmarket lifestyle and literary aspirations as well.

The men's market as we know it today *really* took off with the launch of
Loaded in 1994. *Loaded* is widely recognised as the cornerstone of the
modern British 'lad' culture, and for years now UK journalists have regularly used '*Loaded* reader' as a shorthand for a kind of twenty-something,
beer-drinking, football-loving, sex-obsessed male stereotype. However, sales
of the less macho *FHM* (*For Him Magazine*) overtook those of *Loaded* in
1996, and it now sells almost twice as many copies each month. (*FHM* had
a former life as a relatively unsuccessful fashion publication, before being
relaunched as a lifestyle magazine in 1994.) Further titles, *Maxim* and
Men's Health, were launched in 1995, and both sold well. Since then, publishers have sought to make the men's market even bigger and broader,
with varying degrees of success. Overall, though, the expansion of this area
has been incredible – market research by Mintel reported that by 2000, the
UK men's magazine market had grown to ten times its 1993 size. And
unusually, these British inventions have crossed the Atlantic: *Maxim* and
then *FHM* have broken open a significant market for young men's lifestyle
magazines in the USA.

WHAT'S IN THEM

All of the men's lifestyle magazines cover aspects of men's lives today, which previous literature for men (the hobby and special-interest magazines) did not discuss. They all include reviews of films, music, video games and books (except *Men's Health*). But the magazines otherwise differ quite a lot: *Loaded* celebrates watching football with a few beers, for example, but the *Men's Health* reader would forego the drink, and play the game himself. *FHM* encourages quality sex, whilst *Front* stands for quantity. Here we'll look at each magazine in a little more detail, with an emphasis on titles with the highest UK circulation figures. (Circulation figures are per monthly issue, for the period 1 July to 31 December 2001, and come from official auditors ABC (Audit Bureau of Circulations); see www.abc.org.uk and www.accessabc.com.)

1 *FHM*

UK circulation: 571,000; US circulation: 844,000
Websites: www.fhm.com, www.fhmus.com

FHM is an extremely successful magazine by any standards. In the UK, it's the biggest lifestyle magazine, selling more copies than any other men's or women's title. A US version was launched in February 2000, with the circulation topping one million in July 2001 (Emap, 2001). By 2002 *FHM* had become an international success in some 15 countries including Australia, Singapore, Malaysia, Turkey and France. There are some signs that readers may become tired of the formula – the UK circulation fell from 700,000 in the first half of 2001, to 571,000 in the second – but it remains hugely successful.

Why has *FHM* done so well? The editor who oversaw its rise to power, Mike Soutar, argued in 1999 that '*FHM* understood how men communicate, and principally that's through humour ... In a group of men there's no-one more respected than the funniest guy.' He also said that the key to its success was capturing the essence of being a twenty-something man, 'when part of you wants to settle down and get a mortgage, but part of you thinks your mates are more important and you want to shag anything that moves' (Varley, 1999). He also added, tellingly, that 'whatever [men are] like on the outside, on the inside we're just a seething mass of insecurities and we are simply unable to do things in the house very well.'

Announcing the launch of the US version, editor Ed Needham promised that 'if men can do it, read it, buy it, think about it, or spend their money on it – they will find it in *FHM*. We created our publication based on three guiding principles. Everything in the magazine must be one or more of the following: funny, sexy, useful' (WriteNews, 2000). The mantra of 'funny, sexy, useful' had been established by Soutar at the UK edition in the mid-1990s (Garratt, 1997). In another article, Dana Fields, US *FHM*'s executive publisher and 'a self-described ardent feminist', said that the magazine would 'address personal issues that men would never talk about among themselves, like relationships and face cream' (Crabtree, 2000). She says, 'The magazine is like a male *Cosmo*. It freely acknowledges that men are insecure and have a lot of questions about their bodies.'

These nods towards men's insecurities are important: *FHM* is built around a complex and sometimes contradictory mix of cockiness and knowing uselessness, with the odd bit of genuine misery and euphoria thrown in. The implied reader of *FHM* is not the super-confident know-all of masculine stereotypes; on the contrary, his magazine is always giving him advice, in a multitude of ways. Problem pages are no longer a turn-off; indeed, *FHM* includes more than one, in the 'Hospital' section for health, sex and relationship problems, and the 'Expert Dads' section where experts-as-father-figures offer solutions to everyday challenges as well as more intimate advice. There is also sex advice from lesbians – on the rational basis that they know best how to please a woman – in the regular 'Letters from Lesbos', and typically in another article such as those highlighted on the cover as 'Blow her mind! Treat her to the deadliest sex moves ever!' (August 2001), 'Transform your puny love life with a week at the *FHM* Sex Camp' (July 2001), 'Help! My woman is broken! Her sexual malfunctions – and how to mend them' (May 2001) and 'Ladies' Night! How to deliver the ultimate "lovemaking" performance' (January 2001). Love and rela-tionships are treated in a somewhat goal-orientated way – which isn't that different to the approach of women's mags like *Cosmo* – in features such as 'Woo her pants off! Be romantic – without puking' (March 1997), ' "You complete me, darling" – How women spot a tosser' (July 1998), 'How to get dumped with dignity' (February 2000), the helpful 'How to master polite conversation' (August 2001) and 'They can be yours! Seduce any girl with FHM's Miracle Pulling Guide' (January 2002). Whilst cynics might expect these 'advice' pieces to be mere excuses for sexist jokes, this is not the case: a typical article on how to appeal to women (January 2002) sug-gests that men should listen to what women actually say, be clean, display an ability to be responsible and caring, be able to cook, avoid getting drunk and avoid 'hunting in man-packs'.

Health advice is also given each month, although the dour tone of tradi-tional medical warnings is (predictably) replaced with cheerful joshing about disappointing bodies and ways to look less horrific. Health-related cover stories have included 'On tonight's menu: You! Meet the loathsome parasites that call your body home' (July 2001), 'Lose your lard and get fit for the beach!' (June 2001) and 'Heal ladies' problems! Your girlfriend's health explained' (February 1999). Various helpful quizzes have given men the chance to find out if they are in a 'doomed relationship', 'crap in bed', 'mental', 'boring', and other modern malaises. Those upset by the apparently humorous treatment of serious conditions should note that the magazine does suggest sensible treatments and solutions.

The advice doesn't stop there: men are not expected to be particularly competent at everyday chores, either, and *FHM* has offered pages of easy-but-impressive cooking, basic DIY, housework, cleaning and even gardening (August 2001). Elsewhere, a monthly 'bloke test' interviews two male celebrities and compares their responses to questions about pointless macho achievements ('Can you open a beer bottle with your teeth?'), which may or may not be a wry satire on contemporary masculinity.

Of course, there are also pictures of scantily-clad women – actresses and models – accompanied by superficial 'titillating' interviews; and the general tone, as in all of these magazines, is heterosexual – notwithstanding *FHM*'s rather stereotyped but gay-friendly special feature in February 1999 ('They dress better. Have great hair. They get more sex. Women love them. Let's face it – homosexuals have more fun. So why not join them?'). But there are also many pages of attractive, well-turned-out men in each issue's substantial fashion section.

FHM's international editions vary somewhat. The Singapore edition is slightly more conservative, for example, and more easily shocked-and-amused by the idea of people having sex. The US version is slightly more wary of homosexuality, but retains most features of the British original, including the worries about sexual incompetence. ('Chances are FHM's Sex-o-Meter proved you're not a stud after all,' the August 2001 issue notes frankly. 'Take a tip or two from these ladies and re-educate yourself in the sack'). The French version has slightly more risqué photography than other editions – including more frightening photos of penis ailments in the 'FHM Hospital' section ('Relaxez-vous et dites tout au docteur!') – and the section which UK and US editions call 'Grooming', in their masculine way, is called 'Beauty' by the less anxious French. The 'Amour!' section hints that this version takes a more sensitive approach to affairs of the heart, but this turns out to be photos of *filles les plus sexy* and readers' 'Sex Questions'. Overall, in these different editions the mix of material remains more or less the same. Meanwhile, back in the UK, an occasional spin-off health and fitness title, *FHM Bionic*, went monthly in July 2001 but then was axed altogether at the end of the year.

FHM SUMMARY

What people think it is: Women in bikinis.

What it really is: Advice on sex, relationships and everyday life, plus interviews, reviews, and women in bikinis, all delivered in good humour, and mixed up in a way which doesn't quite address one coherent personality, but which seems to makes sense.

FHM's ideal man: Good in bed, happy in relationships, witty, considerate, skilled in all things.

---

2 Loaded

UK circulation: 309,000

The archetypal 'lad's mag', *Loaded* was originally conceived as a celebration of 'the best fucking time of your life', emphasising excess, football, cars, drinking and music – the rock'n'roll lifestyle (Southwell, 1998; Jackson *et al.*, 2001). Contrary to popular perception, the magazine was not obsessed with naked women; its attitude to women was often surprisingly indifferent, preferring to focus on macho achievements, gangsters and sport (particularly in the early issues of 1994–1996; of the first 30 issues, only eight had a woman on the cover). *Loaded* unapologetically sought to reclaim 'traditional male pleasures', following a feeling in the early 1990s that feminists didn't want men to enjoy themselves. In this sense, *Loaded* was correctly seen as part of a 'backlash' against feminism, even though feminists had never actually been much opposed to things like football or drinking, and *Loaded*'s creators insisted that they had no interest in such a counter-attack; deputy editor (and later editor) Tim Southwell said in an interview, '*Loaded* isn't clever enough to be a rebellion against feminism or anything else, there's no thesis behind [the magazine] . . . I don't care one way or the other, it's of no interest to me or to anyone else at *Loaded*' (Carter, 1996: 15). Nevertheless, the magazine led a cultural change which made it increasingly acceptable and 'mainstream' to display or look at pictures of women wearing very little, influenced by the *Loaded* view that this was harmless; and being a 'lad' became an entertainment rather than a curse within mainstream culture. Southwell's explanation of its success, in 1996, was as follows:

> Life's just too short to think about changes in masculinity . . . *Loaded* is successful because for the first time readers have got an amazing empathy with the writers of the magazine. The writers

> of *Loaded* are just the same as anybody else that reads it ...
> Readers love the fact that *Loaded* just went fuck that, fuck every-
> thing, we're just going to do exactly what we want ... We
> tapped into something that's true to most young men in Britain.
>
> (ibid.: 14)

During 2001, things began to change slightly. Where the original editor, James Brown, had warned that 'grooming is for horses' (*Loaded* editorial, July 1995), the magazine now has pages headed 'Grooming'. New editor Keith Kendrick was reported to have upset the staff by proposing that they include *FHM*-style tips and advice, and material about relationships (Hodgson, 2001c). When appointed in January 2001, he declared that 'Men and women are not the opposite sex. That was then, this is now. We're friends with each other' (Hodgson, 2001b). He also said that 'Men have a more sophisticated attitude to life and relationships. *Loaded* should be a magazine that celebrates young men without being insulting to women' (Hodgson, 2001a).

Changes in the magazine were slight but noticeable. Throughout 2001, the regular 'Platinum rogues' section continued to chart the rise and fall of macho heroes, and Howard Marks, '*Loaded*'s smuggling legend', discussed drugs and criminality each month. In August 2001, the 'Rogue' section suggested it was business as usual, boasting 'Everything you probably don't need to know about women, sport, telly, drugs, sex, mobile phones, sheds, swearwords, fire, music, criminals, ice cream, biscuits, [and] films,' but the magazine's long-standing website was axed. By December 2001, an 'all new and improved' *Loaded* was trying to revive its flagging fortunes by going overboard on sex and relationships advice – sometimes in the *FHM* helpful style, but more often veiled in the 'raunchy' tone of articles like 'Sex tips from barmaids' and 'What models want in bed'. The February 2002 issue offered 'How mental is your girlfriend? Rapid response quiz' alongside features on war, naturism and strippers. The cover in April 2002 even suggested, 'Weep! Gossip! Go shopping! Flex your feminine side and succeed with women', although the actual article – written by a woman – was merely an 'entertainment' piece based on a pack of sexist assumptions about the 'differences' between men and women, and how these could be cynically exploited to 'get sex'. *Loaded*'s makeover therefore leaves it like a slightly more childish, less intelligent version of FHM.

The publishers of *Loaded*, IPC, launched *Later* in 1999: a magazine for the older former reader of *Loaded*, aged 25–40. The magazine was not a big success, and closed in 2001.

LOADED SUMMARY

What people think it is: Football, beer, naked women.

What it really is: Predictably masculine themes including sport, drinking, gangsters, silliness, some 'joke' sexism, a few scantily-clad women. Plus fashion. The singularity of its conception of manhood makes *Loaded*, arguably, more boring than it is offensive.

***Loaded*'s ideal man:** A single guy who can go out and 'have a laugh' at any time. Qualifications in extreme sports or drug smuggling an advantage.

---

3 *Maxim*

UK circulation: 277,000; US circulation: 2,554,000
Websites: www.maxim-magazine.co.uk, www.maximonline.com

Maxim in the UK looked for several years like a less well-designed hybrid of *FHM* and *Loaded*, although its circulation now rivals the latter. When launched in the USA in 1997, however, the magazine took off massively and became the best-selling men's lifestyle title, with a circulation three times that of established US favourites like *GQ* and *Esquire*, and double that of the famous music paper *Rolling Stone*. There are also editions published in a growing number of countries including France, Greece, The Netherlands, Italy, South Africa, Spain and Poland.

To consider the original, UK edition first: *Maxim*, it has to be said, does not have a clear 'unique selling point'. The August 2001 cover lists 'sex, gadgets, fashion, crime, beer, skittles' along the top; nothing distinctive there. *Maxim* combines the macho crime, derring-do and sports of *Loaded* with the sex and health advice, fashion and lifestyle stuff from *FHM*, plus the photo-interviews with famous attractive young women found in both. This perhaps adds up to a confusing picture of masculinity: the same reader who discovers armed robbery and extreme mountaineering in one part of the magazine also learns anatomy basics in the regular 'Nightschool' and reads an awestruck interview with a top model elsewhere. The 'How To' section offers monthly advice on the broadest range of topics, on everything from escaping a Mafia hit and winning at tennis, to wine-making and anger management (August 2001).

The US edition has a clearer identity, partly by virtue of being the first and most successful magazine of its type, and partly by playing to the clear-cut masculinity of the American 'jock' market. Commenting on the new phenomenon in 1999, *Time* magazine said:

> *Maxim* . . . is ironic about its dumbness in the manner of a show like *South Park*, which is to say that the irony is often barely discernible, white noise for a generation that likes to laugh unapologetically at poo and look at pictures of breasts without feeling that [famous feminist] Patricia Ireland is peeking over anyone's shoulders.
>
> (Handy, 1999)

Mike Soutar, who followed the success of *FHM* in Britain by having another smash hit as editor of the US *Maxim*, left that job to return to the UK in May 2000, and in an article for the *Guardian* newspaper noted that:

> The most striking thing about the US men's publishing business in 2000 is how much it resembles the UK men's publishing business back in 1995. Remember how British *GQ* and British *Esquire* – the established, snooty, advertiser-worshipping titles – were usurped so quickly by the funny, reader-driven men's upstarts led by *Loaded* and *FHM*? Well, it's happening all over again in the US. Only this time *Maxim* leads the brash upstarts. And this time, the established, snooty, advertiser-worshipping titles are – American *GQ* and American *Esquire*! Shouldn't they be sacking people over at [publishers] Condé Nast and Hearst for screwing up so badly? Twice in a row?
>
> (Soutar, 2000)

The US version of *Maxim* has a similar mix of content to the UK edition described above – and of course, since it started with no *FHM* or *Loaded* in sight, it looked more distinctive. Although it offers relationship advice, articles in today's US *Maxim* tend to assume that women are a different species – to a greater extent than the UK magazines do – and that a woman will try to trap the unwilling man into a relationship. There is also a strong element of homophobic anxiety in the pitiable way that the magazine cannot accept physical contact between men. For example, a photo of rock band Blink-182 hugging each other is given the caption, 'We're just giving him the Heimlich! We swear!', and a guide to male conduct warns that two men may never share an umbrella, stand at adjacent urinals, or compliment each other on looks (July 2001). Although supposedly humorous, these unattractive macho insecurities are unlikely to play well with the intelligent and attractive young women that *Maxim* man wants to take to bed.

MAXIM SUMMARY

What people think it is: Some kind of combination of *FHM* and *Loaded*.
What it really is: Some kind of combination of *FHM* and *Loaded*. Added macho factor and homophobia in the successful US edition.
***Maxim*'s ideal man:** Good at everything. Has sex with lots of attractive women. Somewhat lacking in clear identity.

4 *Men's Health*

UK circulation: 216,000; US circulation: 1,631,000
Websites: www.menshealth.co.uk, www.menshealth.com

The only magazine in this selection to regularly feature semi-naked men, instead of women, on the cover, *Men's Health* has a broader remit than its title suggests, and it is perhaps the publication which most closely parallels women's lifestyle magazines. The magazine has much on the body and appearance, unsurprisingly, including fitness routines, healthy eating and ways to lose weight. There is also a strong strand of psychology, including a lot of advice on positive thinking, improving self-esteem and using mental techniques for success. *Men's Health* also includes articles on how to keep romance and passion alive in a relationship – formerly the exclusive province of women's magazines – and sex advice, from erection problems to advanced techniques. In the US, the magazine has spawned a junior version, *MH-18* – boasting 'Tons of useful stuff for teenage guys' – a complete (and unusually healthy-living) lifestyle guide for young men.

MEN'S HEALTH SUMMARY

What people think it is: Health and fitness information for men.
What it really is: A clever 'masculine' packaging of everything that women's magazines are expected to be about – looks, sex, relationships, diets, psychology, lifestyle.
***Men's Health*'s ideal man:** Supremely fit and good in bed, knowledge-able, considerate. *Men's Health*'s ideal man is *everybody*'s ideal man – although this is potentially intimidating.

5 *Front*

UK circulation: 154,000

Launched in 1998, *Front* is the lad's mag most obsessed with sex and 'babes'. It's a lifestyle magazine with most of the 'lifestyle' stuff ripped out. Relationships and health are given little space. Think *Loaded*, but delete half the male role models, and add more female lingerie models. To a certain extent, *Front* is aware that its projected readership is unlikely to get close to actual women. 'A bloke is rarely happier than when he's with a few mates, drinking, laughing and taking the piss out of each other,' the editor assures them (February 2002).

FRONT SUMMARY

What people think it is: Sex and women.
What it really is: Sex and women, clubbing and drugs, interviews with some men, more women and sex.
***Front*'s ideal man:** Surrounded by lusty, attractive, naked women.

---

6 *GQ*

UK circulation: 126,000; US circulation: 759,000
Websites: www.gq-magazine.co.uk, www.gq.com

Describing itself as 'the most stylish men's magazine in the world', upmarket *GQ* is theoretically at the opposite end of the sleaze scale to *Front*. *GQ* prides itself on having well-known writers and the sharpest suits. But to avoid failure in the circulation wars, the magazine nowadays combines old-fashioned upper-class masculinity (expensive fashion, posh restaurants, smart grooming) with a substantial dash of laddish populism (women in bikinis, supermodels, nudity). The August 2001 issue featured ridiculously slavish prose to accompany a Claudia Schiffer photo feature ('she has to be the most coveted and eligible woman in the world,' the editor writes, idiotically, declaring her 'a quintessential *GQ* woman'), plus an overbearing article on how women should behave, and a greater number of exposed breasts than in the same month's *Loaded*.

GQ SUMMARY

What people think it is: Posh clothes and upmarket articles for 'gentlemen'.

What it really is: Expensive fashion and style features, some decent articles, plus embarrassing middle-aged lust and lots of scantily-clad women.

GQ's **ideal man:** Smartly dressed, well-read, and married to Claudia Schiffer, apparently.

The rest

There are, of course, several other less successful men's magazines. These include *Esquire* (USA and UK) and *Arena* (UK only), both of which are literate, reasonably classy style magazines, including music and celebrity interviews, fashion, and the reliably popular sex-related articles. Both take 'grooming' seriously: *Arena* advises that 'A man with grubby nails is a man who spends too much time under the bonnet and not enough in front of the mirror', whilst *Esquire*'s Grooming Panel tests out facial skincare products and 'age rescue therapy' creams (both August 2001). Both magazines have the confidence to be less insistently macho; for example, the same issue of *Arena* includes a substantial profile and interview with gay fashion designer Patrick Cox, a thoughtful discussion with political journalist John Pilger and a (serious) tribute to cashmere knitwear. Like its brothers, of course, the magazine also features a handful of awestruck photo-based pieces on beautiful women.

More unique is the American *Men's Journal*, which caters for the more 'rugged', outdoorsy man who seeks travel and adventure, and doesn't want photo-features of celebrities in swimwear. Exercise and fitness is good for its own sake (rather than being a way to impress the 'ladies'), and grooming products are presented as protection against the elements. Because the emphasis is so clearly on conquest of the great outdoors, traditional masculinity is not challenged much by this magazine, although the idea that men would read a glossy lifestyle magazine which includes a 'Mind and Body' section at all remains mildly eyebrow-raising. With a well-heeled readership about two-thirds the size of the American *GQ*'s, *Men's Journal* is not doing badly in its field.

Finally, there are also technology-and-lifestyle magazines, such as *Stuff for Men* (USA and UK) and *T3* (UK), where the more traditional idea of a magazine for men about gadgets and electronics is welded to the newer idea of men's general-interest lifestyle coverage, plus the near-ubiquitous photographs of women in bikinis.

SO WHAT'S IT ALL ABOUT?

The new men's magazines have been given predictably rough treatment by some cultural critics. Pro-feminist and left-wing writers often seem to see the provocative picture of a scantily-clad woman on the cover and assume that the meaning of the entire magazine can be 'read off' from that image alone – it's a sexist repositioning of soft porn, and that's all there is to be said. Even those who glance inside are quick to judge. For example, Andrew Sullivan (2000), writing in the liberal US current affairs magazine *New Republic*, dismisses contemporary men's magazines as plain 'dumb'. He has evidence from one issue of the US market leader, *Maxim*:

> The June issue features a primer on penis size ('How It's *Really* Hangin''), [and] a moronic guide to becoming a millionaire ('Rule #4: Ditch your loser friends').

Sullivan's smug rejection of these features ignores the humour and self-consciousness that riddle these magazines. Articles such as the one on becoming a millionaire are meant to be read as humourous, jokily aspirational but fundamentally silly; to sneer at the quality of their advice is to miss the point. Meanwhile, it would be wrong to see the penis article as a restatement of phallic dominance; on the contrary, surely a very un-macho cloud of *insecurity* hangs over the male audience for articles on penis size. It is difficult to imagine a masculine archetype like Clint Eastwood settling down to study *Maxim*'s guide to how he measures up in the trouser department.

The most perceptive and sensitive analysis of the 'new' men's magazines and their readers has been produced by the research team of Peter Jackson, Nick Stevenson and Kate Brooks, in work published 1999–2001 (Jackson *et al.*, 1999; Stevenson *et al.*, 2000; and most notably the book *Making Sense of Men's Magazines*, Jackson *et al.*, 2001; see also Kenny and Stevenson, 2000). These researchers thankfully do not assume a moral superiority to the magazines or their readers, and do not try to 'prove' that the magazines are mere trash, enjoyed by a large audience of mindless fools. Instead, they take the huge growth of men's magazines to be a cultural phenomenon worthy of serious consideration, which should be able to tell us something about men and masculinity today. In the following sections I will discuss some of the points made by Jackson, Stevenson and Brooks, whilst also making my own argument that the magazines really show men to be *inse-*

cure and *confused* in the modern world, and seeking help and *reassurance*, even if this is (slightly) suppressed by a veneer of irony and heterosexual lust.

ISN'T IT IRONIC?

Jackson *et al.* rightly note that the men's magazines usually address the reader as a 'mate', of the same status as the magazine journalists themselves. The tone is generally 'friendly, ironic and laddish' (2001: 77). The irony is used as a kind of defensive shield: the writers *anticipate* that many men may reject serious articles on relationships, or advice about sex, health or cooking, and so douse their pieces with humour, silliness and irony to 'sweeten the pill'. (I do not mean 'silliness' to be a criticism: the way in which *FHM* combines serious advice with funny and 'inappropriate' humour is often quite clever.) This use of irony is no secret. As publishers EMAP launched *FHM* in South Africa – just one part of the global expansion of the title – their internal marketing blurb proudly explained:

> Before *FHM*, conventional wisdom had it that women read magazines from an introspective point of view, seeking help and advice for, and about, themselves. Men on the other hand, read magazines about things like sport, travel, science, business and cars. *FHM* realises that men will read magazines about themselves if you give them the information in the right context: irreverent, humorous and *never* taking itself too seriously. The articles in *FHM*, although highly informative, are written tongue-in-cheek. The fashion is accessible, the advice humorous and empathetic.
>
> (www.natmags.com, 1999)

Jackson *et al.* note that the magazines 'are careful to avoid talking down to their readers' (2001: 76), and their focus group interviews confirm that men like to feel that they are flicking through the magazines and not taking them too seriously, which they believe is in contrast to women who read magazine advice 'religiously' (ibid.: 126). In fact, research on female magazine readers indicates that they too like to treat their magazines lightly and with little commitment (Hermes, 1995), but the fact remains that male readers seem to be extremely wary of being told what to do – they like to feel they know best already – which is why humour and irony have to be deployed. Jackson *et al.* note that the exception is *Men's Health* (and to a lesser extent we can add *FHM Bionic*), where the magazine takes the role of a trusted health advisor, and (perhaps inevitably) has to use a more 'expert' tone. At the same time, *Men's Health* has become increasingly successful as it has started to mimic, in some parts but not others, the anti-serious tone of *FHM* – for example, a mental health quiz in the December 2001 issue was promoted with the cheerful cover line 'Will You Lose Your Marbles?'.

The fact that humour and irony is required in the magazines does not, of course, show that today's men do not 'really' want to read articles and advice about relationships, sex, health or other 'personal' matters. After all, the magazines could easily forget about these areas altogether, and focus on cars and guns and white-water rafting. So we have to conclude that many men *want* articles like this, but do not want others – or even perhaps themselves – to think that they *need* them. The humour of the lifestyle articles means that they can be read 'for a laugh' although, I would argue, men are at the same time quietly curious to pick up information about relationships and sex, and what is considered good or bad practice in these areas. It's difficult to prove this assertion, by definition, because men are not eager to admit to this curiosity – and indeed, in the focus groups conducted by Jackson *et al.*, many of the men said dismissive things about the magazines, but at the same time appeared to be familiar with their contents.

Irony provides a 'protective layer', then, between lifestyle information and the readers, so that men don't have to feel patronised or inadequate. But irony has other functions too. Jackson *et al.* assert that one of these is 'to subvert political critique' (ibid.: 78) – in other words, feminists or others who criticise the content of the magazines can be said to be 'missing the joke', making their complaints redundant. This is true, but I would say that irony is used in order to provide a 'get-out clause' against critics. Although the sexism of some of the less popular magazines (such as *Front*) can sometimes appear genuine, in *FHM* and its imitators I would say that it is the *irony* which is genuine. The *FHM* writer, and their projected reader, *do actually know* that women are as good as men, or better; the put-downs of women – such as jokey comments about their supposed incompetence with technology – are knowingly ridiculous, based on the assumptions that it's silly to be sexist (and therefore is funny, in a silly way), and that men are usually just as rubbish as women. In an analysis of an Australian 'lad's' magazine, *Ralph* – similar to *Loaded* or *Front* – Schirato and Yell concur with this kind of diagnosis, writing that '*Ralph*'s performances of "stereotypical" masculinity are self-conscious "over-performances" of a set of discourses and subjectivities which it recognises are already in a sense obsolete' (1999: 81).

The idea that the underlying assumptions of these magazines are more anti-sexist than sexist may not always be true, of course, and is optimistic; and it is always possible for readers to read the sexist jokiness literally. But I would say that this 'sexist jokiness' of *FHM* is based on thoroughly non-sexist assumptions – the *intended* laugh, more often than not, is about the silliness of being sexist, rather than actual sexism because, in the world of *FHM*, men are aware, however quietly or embarrassedly, that it's only fair to treat women and men as equals in the modern world, and that sexism is idiotic.

Having said that, it has to be admitted that many *FHM* readers may be sexist, in one way or another, and their reading of *FHM* may not challenge their sexism, and might indeed support it. That's sadly true. At the same time, though, *FHM* consistently teaches men to treat their girlfriends nicely, to try to be considerate and to give satisfaction, both sexually and in more general terms. It also teaches men various domestic skills – even if the justification is that it will 'impress your lady'. You could even say that *FHM*'s general project is to create a man who is competent in the home and kitchen, skilled in the bedroom, not overly dependent on his partner, healthy, interested in travel, able to buy his own fashionable clothes, a good laugh and a pleasure to live with. Based on this list, we have the kind of man that feminists would surely prefer to have around. The pictures of beautiful members of the opposite sex wearing little clothing, and the emphasis on sex rather than relationships, don't fit within this thesis, of course, although we can at least point out that several women's magazines contain the same kind of material today too.

WHY IRONY?

Jackson *et al.* do recognise that men's magazines are complex and contradictory (and indeed this view is emphasised most in their book (2001) compared to their earlier, slightly more antagonistic articles). Nevertheless, they generally tend to play down the nuances and conflicting elements, preferring to treat the magazines as more-or-less relentlessly laddish and 'masculine'. This leads them to get some things, in my view, exactly right, and other things wrong. For example, they provide a definition of irony, by Richard Rorty, which suggests that a person using irony does so to indicate an awareness that they are using terms which are uncertain, not necessarily 'true', and open to challenge. Jackson *et al.* ruminate that this would mean that men's magazines are not really being ironic at all, but are using a discourse of 'common sense' – although they find this account unsatisfactory too (2001: 104):

It is precisely the lack of awareness of the constructed nature of masculine identity that seems so pervasive. Yet to argue that the magazines reflect the return of a form of masculine common sense is to treat the texts as less problematic than we believe them to be. Our argument is rather that irony is used as an ideological defence against external attack (only the most humourless do not get the joke) and an internal defence against more ambivalent feelings that render masculine experience less omnipotent and less certain than it is represented here.

Here, I would agree that irony is indeed used for both of the reasons given. The problem is that Jackson *et al.* seem to assume that the irony is *successful* as an 'internal defence' – in other words, that the use of irony really does 'protect' masculinity, and keeps those 'ambivalent feelings' hidden from view. This is also reflected in the authors' assertion, at the start of the quotation above, that there is a 'pervasive' 'lack of awareness of the constructed nature of masculine identity' in the men's magazines. I would argue that this is quite wrong – on the contrary, today's magazines for men are *all about* the social construction of masculinity. That is, if you like, their subject-matter. In the past, men didn't need lifestyle magazines because it was obvious what a man was, and what a man should do, anyway. It is only in the modern climate, in which we are all aware of the many choices available to us, and are also aware of the feminist critique of traditional masculinity, and the fact that gender roles can and do change, that men have started to need magazines about how to be a man today. Jackson *et al.* suggest that the magazines foster a 'constructed certitude' built around the laddish values of responsibility-free sex, drinking and messing about (ibid.: 86) – where this 'constructed certitude' means a sense that 'this is the reliable essence of being a young man today'. But I would say that just as they do this on some pages, the magazines undermine it on others, raising questions about the different ways in which men can present an acceptable face today. (See Chapter 5, on the work of Anthony Giddens, for more on how people in 'late modernity' are increasingly required to choose a lifestyle and construct a 'narrative of the self'). Funnily enough, Jackson *et al.* seem to recognise this elsewhere in their book – noting, for example, that 'the magazines have encouraged men to "open up" previously repressed aspects of their masculinity (including attitudes to health, fashion and relationships)' (ibid.: 22), and that 'the magazines signify the *potential* for new forms of masculinity to emerge even as the magazines are simultaneously reinscribing older and more repressive forms of masculinity' (ibid.: 23, original emphasis).

There is little sign that people buy magazines just to reinforce ideas and assumptions that they are already familiar with. One of the key themes of lifestyle magazines, I would say, is that nothing in life is totally given and fixed. This is a message we welcome. Surveys show that a majority of people in society feel unsatisfied and would welcome change in their lives; having a well-paid job doesn't make respondents any more satisfied, and although many people today spend money in a bid to make themselves happier, this doesn't work (Millar, 2000; Summerskill, 2001). We read magazines partly for the pleasure of the glossy surfaces and attractive photographs, and partly to answer the question, 'What can I do next?'

Of course, talking about men's magazines is made more complicated by the fact that the content of different titles varies considerably. Jackson *et al.*'s view that the magazines are trying to re-assert a stable kind of more-or-less old-school masculinity makes much more sense when applied to *Loaded* than when applied to *FHM*. But since *FHM* sells nearly twice as many copies as *Loaded*, and *Loaded* is trying to revive its fortunes by becoming more like *FHM* (in 2001), it doesn't look like a winning argument. It's also curious to note that Jackson *et al.* quote former *Loaded* editor Tim Southwell describing the magazine as 'a weird mixture of lusting after women, failing to get off with women, thinking about heroes, thinking about childhood experiences' (Stevenson *et al.*, 2000: 374). This doesn't sound like a super-confident masculinity; frustrated desires and nostalgia are quite the opposite of a thrusting agenda. Of course, *Loaded* often *was* quite pig-headedly macho, but this seam of disappointments and memories was always there too.

Finally, on the debatable importance of irony, it is worth quoting one of the men I interviewed by email about their consumption of men's magazines; I asked specifically about whether irony was a dominant theme:

> I've seen articles in the *Guardian* or whatever where they talk about the ironic tone of men's magazines. But everybody knows that, so it's not clever to point that out in the *Guardian* because all of the readers of *FHM* and *Loaded* know that anyway . . . Many if not all of the articles [in the magazines] are written in that jokey tone, where nothing seems to be taken seriously. It's not heartless though because it's like having a laugh with your friends in the pub, so it's quite warm. The interesting thing about men's magazines is not the fact that they have this ironic style, but all the nervous concerns going on underneath. Men don't read the magazines because they are fans of irony! They read them for other reasons.
>
> (26-year-old male from Edinburgh, Scotland)

The 'nervous concerns' would be the questions which *FHM* and *Maxim*, and to a lesser extent *Loaded*, address all the time (within their jokey discourse, of course) – questions which can all be summarised as, 'Am I doing this right?': Is my relationship OK? Is my sexual technique good? These things I do – am I odd or am I normal? Are things always like this? And – how *do* you put up shelves?

FEAR OF INTIMACY?

Another theme in the arguments of Jackson, Stevenson and Brooks is the idea that men's magazines reflect a 'fear' of intimacy or commitment. They say that the magazines which emerged in the 1990s were focused – amongst other things – on 'obsessive forms of independence (read: fear of commitment and connection)' (2001: 78); and are a 'celebration of autonomy and a fear of dependence' (ibid.: 81). Later we are again told that they are 'a desperate defence of masculine independence' (ibid.: 82).

This all makes being independent sound like a psychotic tendency, and some kind of macho neurosis. But women's magazines filled hundreds of pages, over *years*, telling women how to be independent, and it's a message they still carry. And that's fine: the message that you shouldn't depend on a partner for your happiness is widely seen as being a very good one. Being a 'dependent' person is not ideal, and if we think that's true for women, it's true for men too. Calling it a 'fear of dependence' is Jackson *et al.*'s sneaky way of making it sound like a product of dumb macho psychology, but the received wisdom from women's magazines and self-help books is that being wary of becoming dependent is eminently sensible. We can also note that feminism used to criticise men for being too dependent on their female partners, sapping women's energies by selfishly expecting women to tend to their emotional, sexual and domestic needs. That was a valid criticism. But now if we criticise men for being maddeningly independent – as if men are selfishly *refusing* to rely on women for emotional support – it starts to get a bit silly.

To be fair, though, although Jackson *et al.* don't exactly explain *why* they view the promotion of independence as a bad thing in men's magazines, we can infer that they are concerned that the magazines encourage men to be *too* self-contained – the kind of man who couldn't express himself fully within a relationship, perhaps, and who was unable to give love and share his life with someone. We can agree that that would not be good; but do the magazines really encourage men to be excessively insular and unexpressive? Not really. The 'new' feature of many of the top men's magazines, as we've noted, is that they are full of relationship tips, from *FHM* explaining the difference between physical lust and emotional attachment to a reader concerned that his nice girlfriend isn't his ideal physical type (August 2001), US *Maxim* advising on tactful ways to impress a woman (July 2001), and *Men's Health* discussing how to keep a partner interested (August 2001), to all of these magazines offering sex advice and asking famous females what makes them happy in a relationship. There can be no escape from these magazines' emphasis on being a decent, considerate and attentive boyfriend.

The enormously successful US version of *Maxim* does sometimes seem to embrace the idea that women are eager to 'trap' men into a long-term relationship or marriage, and this, of course, is an irritating slice of sexism. The view that a person should not be tied too hastily into an imperfect relationship, however, especially when young, is a perfectly reasonable one. Without wanting to defend the dim sexism of some articles in the US *Maxim*, the advice itself isn't terrible. And we can note that after feminists went to such lengths to argue that marriage was a patriarchal system which trapped women into an unhappy life of exploitation and lack of freedom, it seems (again) a bit odd for us to start complaining that men's magazines are not in favour of marriage or similar tight commitments.

In general, there does not seem to be evidence for a 'fear of intimacy' in men's magazines; there is a *fear of anything that might stop you enjoying yourself*, which includes boring mates, the police, illnesses and partners that do things that prevent you from having a good time. Positive relationships are not to be feared, though, and the all-powerful *FHM*, as we've said, is full of advice about how to keep your girlfriend happy.

REINSCRIBING SEXISM

As already mentioned in the sections on 'irony' above (pp. 167–172), men's magazines are often accused of trying to re-assert sexism and male dominance, and are said to be part of a 'backlash' against feminism. The view that they are sexist is often based on the observation that the magazines usually contain several pictures of women wearing clothes which are small, or not there at all, and in seductive poses (but without 'showing everything' in the style of pornography). One reply to this is that some magazines for women do the same thing back to men these days – in the UK, the young woman's magazine *More* delights in showing pictures of semi-naked hunks, and sells twice as many copies as the men's *Front* – so this can't be a case of sexism as such, since both men and women are shown in these ways. But a counter-argument to this might be that women are sometimes shown in 'fuck me' poses, whilst men are usually not. But we only need to use slightly different words to correctly point out that both men and women are shown in 'I'd like to have sex with you' poses.

Alluring pictures of semi-naked women could specifically be said to be sexist because this feeds into the objectification of women, which is a long-standing form of oppression. Since there is not a comparable historical tradition of the offensive 'objectification of men', pictures of semi-naked men do not have the same impact. This used to be a really good argument, but as time goes by we start to think that since magazines for women *and* those for men celebrate super-attractive people, both women and men, it probably doesn't matter in sexism terms. At the same time we might be annoyed that the same ideas of beauty are being regurgitated over and over again.

As for the idea that 'male dominance' can be resurrected by the magazines, we can quote an interviewee who made this pertinent point:

> Even if a guy, say, read *Front* and took it literally and 'learned sexism' from it, I don't see why feminists would find that threatening or worrying because what is this guy? He's nothing, he's a loser. You don't get on in the world today by being sexist. People will just think he's a stupid twat.
>
> (30-year-old male from York, England)

Another respondent made a similar point:

> Male readers drooling over these women [in the magazines] . . . It's not really an assertion of power is it. Women who can make men go weak at the knees, and make them do stupid things, that's power. Which is fine.
>
> (28-year-old male from Brighton, England)

We can infer from their ages that these respondents are men who have heard the feminist arguments of the late 1980s and early 1990s, when looking at scantily-clad women was clearly quite wrong for any right-thinking man, but have started to change their views as time has moved on and gender relations have changed again (including the development of the new language in popular culture where women can treat men as disposable eye-candy too). As another man commented:

> I used to agree, and I mean I really did agree, with women who said that naked women in magazines was a bad thing. But nowadays I can hardly even remember what the argument was. Women can look at handsome men in films and magazines, and

men can look at attractive women . . . it seems fair. What were
we complaining about again? Is it because we were afraid of sex?

(29-year-old male from New York, USA)

To move on to the remaining question, can all this be seen as a backlash
against feminism? Sometimes it might be: the cruder sexism found in *Front*
and the US *Maxim*, and sometimes *Loaded*, can seem to be fuelled by anti-
feminist feeling, and the sexism in itself is clearly unhelpful. I would argue
that *FHM* and its imitators are not part of a backlash, though: *FHM* is for
men who accept the changes that feminism has brought, and are working
out how to fit into that world. Even the US *Maxim*, in its slow and sometimes backwards way, is trying to work this out. The nuances of modern
identity-seeking are played out very subtly in these most popular magazines.

MEN AND WOMEN AS CLEAR AND OPPOSITE IDENTITIES

Finally, Jackson *et al.* argue that in men's magazines, 'men and women are
[represented as] polar opposites in terms of their sexual identities and
desires' (2001: 84), and suggest that the magazines' model of 'new lad'
masculinity 'acts as a means of enforcing boundaries between men and
women' (ibid.: 86). They go on to say:

> The accompanying fear seems to be that, unless men and
> women are rigidly rendered apart, this would introduce a small
> grain of uncertainty within the representation of masculine iden-
> tity, thereby threatening to undermine it all together . . . 'New
> laddism', as we have seen, leaves no room for doubt, question-
> ing, ambiguity or uncertainty.
>
> (ibid.: 86)

Again, this looks like quite a good argument on paper, but doesn't match
up with the actual content of the magazines – especially as these points are
made in relation to *FHM* in particular. As I have already argued and illustrated, the magazines do *not* assume that their readers have a fixed and
ready-to-wear masculine identity – if they did, they would not fill so many
pages with advice on how to achieve some basic competences in life. *FHM*
in particular is quietly brimming with the 'doubt, questioning, ambiguity
[and] uncertainty' which Jackson *et al.* say is absent. In the late 1990s,
when Jackson *et al.* were looking at the magazines, even the *covers* of *FHM*
were riddled with anxiety: 'Fat? Boring? Crap in bed? Does this sound

familiar to anyone?' (February 1998), 'Look at the state of you!' (February 1998), 'Am I gay?' (February 1999), 'Is your love life just a hollow sham?' (April 1999), 'Are you going mental?' (April 1999), and 'Does your penis horrify women?' (July 1999) are typical examples.

As for the idea that women and men are shown to be 'polar opposites' sexually – Jackson *et al.* note an implication in a few articles that whilst men are perenially eager for sex, women 'would always prefer a candle-lit bath' (ibid.: 84) – this doesn't apply to most articles in most of the magazines, which generally assume that women will be eager and willing partners in sexual activities – especially if men deploy the pleasureable techniques suggested. Meanwhile, it's true that the magazines do often joke about general supposed 'differences' between women and men, although this can be at the expense of either sex. I would also repeat my suggestion that the magazines don't *really* think that the differences are fundamental, and that the 'sexist jokiness' is based on an understanding that men and women are not very different *really* – an idea underlined by the fact that men's and women's magazines are becoming increasingly similar in very obvious ways. Nevertheless, this discourse of difference can be a troubling aspect of the publications. One of my email interviewees, a gay man who enjoyed *FHM*, said this:

> I think the fact that *FHM* – and *Loaded* maybe even more so – suggest men and women are fundamentally different is the thing that annoys me most about them. They generalise too much about the categories 'men' and 'women', and perpetuate the idea that there's a 'sex war' going on. (Having said that, the fact that I feel I can 'adapt' [the magazines] to my (different) lifestyle suggests there's some room for movement in the values they express . . .)
>
> (22-year-old gay male from Leeds, England)

In general it seems most appropriate to see men's magazines as reflecting a frequently imperfect attempt to find positions for the ideas of 'women' and 'men' in a world where it's pretty obvious that the sexes are much more the same than they are different. The magazines sometimes discuss men and women as if they were different species, but this is a way of making sense of reality, rather than reality itself, and readers (hopefully) understand this.

WHAT OTHER RESPONDENTS SAID

A few more comments from my email interviewees are worth mentioning. One young man offered this interesting commentary on the unfulfilled promise at the heart of men's magazine consumption:

> I was thinking about this and there's a lot of disappointment involved in buying men's magazines. You get excited about buying a new copy of a magazine like *FHM*, it's so nice and glossy, and they have a style of photography that makes every-thing look so sparkly and desirable (especially, of course, the women). But then it's a bit disappointing because there's not really much in it, and it's disappointing to find that the women, when interviewed, don't sound that interesting really. And it's disappointing because you see these gorgeous women who wouldn't look twice at you, but then you remember that they probably look quite like people you know, really, and it's the very careful styling and makeup and photography that makes them so irresistible, but then that's quite disappointing too. Most of all, it's disappointing that you fell for it, and will con-tinue to fall for it.
>
> (24-year-old male from Nottingham, England)

The troubling thing for this respondent seems to be his complicity in his own exploitation: the publishers know that he can be tricked into buying each issue with the promise of something 'sparkly and desirable'; the particularly galling thing is that he falls for it month after month, and that in spite of this there is still pleasure in the anticipation, and in the moment of purchase. This was echoed elsewhere too, such as in a London man's observation that he was drawn to the features on beautiful women which 'are tittilating, although contrived'. Another regular reader was troubled by the conflicting signals projected by the magazines:

> Every issue has some article on how to get women in bed. Men who require an article to be able to do this seem to be far from the marketed image of the self-confident, sophisticated male who reads these magazines.
>
> (22-year-old male from Nashville, USA)

There were interesting responses to my question, 'Do these magazines help you to think of yourself as a particular kind of person?'. This man was a regular reader of *FHM*, *Loaded*, *Arena* and *GQ*, and liked the way in which they gave him a sense of fitting in with popular culture:

> [They help me think of myself] as an achiever or wannabe. Part of mainstream culture, doing the things mainstream culture requires . . . They offer examples of 'success', and how to achieve this success.
>
> (23-year-old male from London, England)

Others were more reluctant to identify with the target audience, even where they probably *were* the target audience:

> I don't like to think of myself as the typical reader of these magazines [*FHM*], even though I secretly enjoy it. It makes me smile. I overlook the sexism. The whole magazine is undeniably attractive, I like the fact that it's like a glossy woman's magazine with a bit of everything, except it's for men.
>
> (26-year-old male from Bradford, England)

> I enjoy reading the problems and the advice [in *FHM*]. At school we always read the problem pages in the girls' copies of *Just Seventeen*, for a laugh, we would say, though actually we were curious about the sex advice too. It's good to have problem pages in a men's magazine – we obviously need it really!
>
> (27-year-old male from Cardiff, Wales)

These quotes confirm that men are aware of the changing social construction of masculinity and are willing to welcome the self-help aspect of women's magazines which were previously alien to men's reading culture. Respondents were often keen to show that they didn't take the magazines too seriously, but this gay subscriber to *Men's Health* embraced the publication wholeheartedly and with no sign of irony:

> This magazine definitely reaffirms my masculinity. I see what is going on in the straight man's world, and try to incorporate it into my life to be perceived as more desirable in the gay man's culture. [. . .] I try to become more like the men in the magazine – fitter, muscular, stylish, attractive. I am gay, and this is a straight man's magazine, but much of my style is directly influenced by this magazine. I have been a subscriber for almost five

years, and have used *Men's Health* for information on all sorts of topics revolving around what it means to be a man in the world today.

(24-year-old male from Chicago, USA)

He found particular *value* in *Men's Health*'s enthusiasm for physical improvement:

It gives men a self-conscious sense of style and appearance. It makes them more body conscious. This is not a negative trait, it brings men into the consumer culture of fashion [which] women have always been a part of. I think this is a positive thing, for both men and women. I don't think it will make the world a better place by making us all look beautiful – that is silly, but I do think that it provides men with images that would make them think twice about their appearance, and maybe begin to understand appearance like women do. Maybe it will bridge some kind of gap between the sexes. I don't know.

(as above)

The comments from female readers were also revealing. This woman felt that the magazines reflected a world where men were not coping well:

[Looking at the men's magazines] brings out the mothering in me, because it makes me feel that men are lost. Not that I particularly want to mother a man or a group of men, but it makes me sad and curious.

(34-year-old female from Melbourne, Australia)

This view seems to support my argument that the image of men which emerges from the magazines is not powerful and strong – rather the opposite, that men are seeking help. A younger woman read the magazines in more positive mode, because she found them preferable to the publications aimed at women:

It's annoying that these mags are aimed mostly at men, and I wish that some articles found in men's mags could also be like that in women's mags too! It defines the men as lads in the pub, real male bonding going on, and women as girlfriends and sexual partners, but I have a laugh too in the pub, laughing at men's crude jokes, playing pool (which I'm great at) and drinking pints. (But then sometimes they do have articles with successful and sassy women like [TV presenter] Denise van Outen for example).

(21-year-old female from Bristol, UK)

SUMMARY

In this discussion I have argued against the view that men's lifestyle magazines represent a reassertion of old-fashioned masculine values, or a 'backlash' against feminism. Whilst certain pieces in the magazines might support such an argument, this is not their primary purpose or selling point. Instead, I have suggested, their existence and popularity shows men rather insecurely trying to find their place in the modern world, seeking help regarding how to behave in relationships, and advice on how to earn the attention, love and respect of women and the friendship of other men. To put this into the terms of the theories we discussed earlier in this book, in post-traditional cultures, where identities are not 'given' but need to be constructed and negotiated (see Chapter 5), and where an individual has to establish their personal ethics and mode of living (Chapter 6), the magazines offer some reassurance to men who are wondering, 'Is this right?' and 'Am I doing this OK?', enabling a more confident management of the narrative of the self. At the same time, the magazines may raise some anxieties – about fitness of the body, say, or whether the reader is sufficiently 'one of the boys'. The discourses of masculinity which the magazines help to circulate can therefore, unsurprisingly, be both enabling and constraining. When considered in relation to queer theory's call for 'gender trouble' (Chapter 7), the magazines' conceptions of gender seem remarkably narrow. Nevertheless, the playfulness of the magazines and their (usually) cheerful, liberal attitude to most things – apart from the occasional nasty sting of homophobia – suggests that some fluidity of identities is invited. Furthermore, the humour and irony found throughout these publications doesn't hide a strong macho agenda, but conceals the nervousness of boys who might prefer life to be simpler, but are doing their best to face up to modern realities anyway.

Chapter 9

WOMEN'S MAGAZINES AND FEMALE IDENTITIES TODAY

essay 4/5

IN CHAPTER 3, we traced the history of women's magazines through the second half of the twentieth century, from the traditional publications – with their emphasis on the home, beauty, finding a husband and keeping him – through to the success of the 'independent and sexy' *Cosmopolitan* in the 1980s and 1990s. But what messages do today's magazines convey? And what do readers make of them?

Figure 9.1   Women's magazines: assertive female identities for all

THE DEBATE ABOUT THE MAGAZINES' IMPACT

To establish the background to the debate about women's magazines, it is worth looking at the way that the discussion of their impact on young women has turned around in the past 20 years. The early work of Angela McRobbie, in the late 1970s, is today seen as a case study in how *not* to approach such research. McRobbie had examined various editions of *Jackie*, a magazine for teenage girls, and her criticisms of their stereotypically feminine and romance-obsessed content worked on the assumption that the ideology of the magazines would be absorbed in a direct way by its readers. Nowadays McRobbie happily admits that this assumption was not tenable. For example, she reports:

> Frazer (1987) demonstrated (as did Beezer *et al.* 1986) that my own earlier work about *Jackie* magazine wrongly assumed that ideology actually worked in a mechanical, even automatic kind of way.
>
> (McRobbie, 1999: 50)

The study by Elizabeth Frazer (1987) involved group discussions with teenage girls about selected stories from *Jackie*. Frazer found that rather than absorbing the stories as if they were valuable lifestyle advice, these readers laughed at the tales, and criticised them as unrealistic fictions. This study (and others like it) are sometimes mistakenly taken to 'show' that people are not affected by the texts they read. In fact, that conclusion does not quite follow: just because the readers were able to criticise the text, and were aware that it was a constructed fiction, does not prove that they would never be influenced by its content. However, Frazer's study did successfully show that the effect of magazines could not be assumed or predicted.

A study by Joke Hermes, *Reading Women's Magazines* (1995), complicated matters further by suggesting that readers often didn't attach much meaning to their reading of magazines in any case. Hermes had conducted qualitative research in a bid to find the meaning of women's magazines in their lives; but this had turned out to be difficult because magazine consumption was often described as little more than a pleasurable way to fill moments of relaxation. Magazines were easy to pick up and easy to put down. Although readers did connect with *parts* of the magazines they read, Hermes warns that cultural studies often makes the mistake of assuming that 'texts are always significant' (1995: 148), when in fact the typical reader of any particular magazine article, say, may not be very bothered about it. Many studies of media reception, she suggests, are subject to the 'fallacy of meaningfulness' (ibid.) – the idea that when someone consumes a media text then 'meaning' is always produced. Although Hermes caught occasional 'glimpses' of the interests and fantasies that were related to reading women's magazines, she offers a valuable reminder to researchers that the 'relationships' they are investigating – between media products and consumers – are not always passionate ones.

Dawn Currie conducted another major study in 1993–1994, which involved an analysis of teenage magazines in Canada and interviews with a sample of their readers. This was eventually published as *Girl Talk: Adolescent Magazines and their Readers* (Currie, 1999). The author found her interviewees (48 girls aged between 13 and 17) to be more enthusiastically engaged with the magazines than Hermes's older respondents had been. These teenagers were particularly attracted to the magazines' advice sections, for example, finding them to be both 'useful' and pleasurable. Currie herself is less happy about the magazine content, however, finding that quizzes and advice pages emphasised the value of pleasing others (in particular boys) – although they also highlighted the importance of 'being yourself'. She notes that these pieces typically encouraged their female readers to be selective about who they chose to go out with, but she criticises them for propagating the idea that one should be looking for the 'right guy'. Currie's discussion is interesting, complex and reflexive, but never really doubts its own assumption that the content of the magazines will be 'patriarchal', and although the author asserts, repeatedly and at some length, that researchers should not impose their own meanings on those of their subjects, she nevertheless seems to stamp her own broadly negative feeling about the magazines throughout the study.

During the 1990s, Angela McRobbie (re-)emerged as arguably the most thoughtful and sophisticated commentator on magazines for young women. She has paid close attention to the ways in which the magazines have changed since the 1970s, and has repeatedly asked difficult questions about what kind of magazine feminists would want, if they are unhappy with today's magazines. We will return to McRobbie's arguments in more detail later in this chapter. First, we should examine the content of modern women's magazines.

THE MAGAZINES TODAY

In the men's lifestyle magazine market, we saw that there is a relatively small number of very successful titles. In the longer-established women's market, on the other hand, there is a broader range of popular magazines.

Because there are so many magazines enjoying similar levels of success, the following account of the contents of individual titles is quite brief. To keep things simple, all examples are from the August 2001 issue unless otherwise stated. As in the previous chapter, the circulation figures, from ABC, are for July–December 2001.

Also because there are so many general magazines for women, I have left out those intended for older, more 'settled' women who want to read about parenthood and home-making (although I included *Red* and *Redbook* as samples intended for the younger end of the 'settled' market). The titles covered here are therefore the best-selling lifestyle magazines aimed at a young or youngish woman who has not become absorbed by family and home-making interests:

- *Cosmopolitan* (USA) – Circulation 2,759,000 – Sex, relationships, fashion and beauty, health, celebrities, careers, more sex. Cover stories include: 'Cosmo's summer sex survey: See how you compare', 'Man overload! How to reel in bunches of boys', 'Sexify your look' and '151,497 of you begged to see *this* guy butt naked' (website: www.cosmopolitan.com).

- *Cosmopolitan* (UK) – Circulation 463,000 – Sex, relationships, fashion and beauty, more sex, careers. Cover stories include: 'Ohmigod – they're so rude! Your hottest holiday sex confessions. Meet the lusty lifeguard, the romeo rep, the poolside pulse racer – and other hunks in trunks' and ' "I've had 70 one-night stands this year" – Cosmo goes undercover at Sex Addicts Anonymous' (website: www.cosmopolitan.co.uk).

- *Redbook* (USA) – Circulation 2,321,000 – Sex, and 'Balancing family – work – love – time for you', as it says below the title. A section ties together 'Sex & marriage' (which *Cosmo* would never do); also fashion and beauty, health, celebrities, parenthood. Cover stories include: 'Explosive sex!', 'Will your child suffer if you work?' and 'Stressed about money? 100+ ways you can save'. Disappointingly housewifey on the whole (website: www.redbookmag.com).

- *Glamour* (USA) – Circulation 2,201,000 – Sex, relationships, fashion and beauty, health, 'empowerment', entertainment and celebrities. 'Dos and don'ts' for everything. Cover stories include: 'Be his best ever in bed', 'Summer hair & skin dos and don'ts', and 'Hey, weight obsessers! Shut yourself up – here's how' (website: www.us.glamour.com).

- *Glamour* (UK) – Circulation 437,000 – Sex, relationships, fashion and beauty, entertainment and celebrities. Cover stories include: '686 love, sex, hair, style and celebrity dos', 'Sun, sand & boob jobs – The shocking new trend in package holidays' and 'Men's top sex dos and don'ts' (website: www.glamourmagazine.co.uk).

- *Marie Claire* (UK) – Circulation 382,000 – Fashion and beauty, interviews and real-life stories, relationships, sex, health, plus one or two serious major 'issue' articles per month. Cover stories include: 'Catwalk to closet: 869 fashion and beauty trends' and 'Can men ever really understand women?' (website: www.marieclaire.co.uk).

- *New Woman* (UK) – Circulation 305,000 – Sex, fashion and beauty, relationships, celebrities, men, health, career tips. Cover stories include: '309 fast fashion and beauty fixes', 'Summer = sex! Work out your 28–day cycle and make him a slave to your rhythms', and 'Cheer up love! The scientific way to master your mood swings' (website: www.newwoman.co.uk).

- *Company* (UK) – Circulation 261,000 – Sex, fashion and beauty, relationships, celebrities, health. Cover stories include: 'Will this be your summer of lust?', '191 sexy, slinky, seductive looks', and 'Men confess: The ugly truth about their holiday sexploits' (website: www.company.co.uk).

- *Elle* (UK) – Circulation 211,000 – Fashion, interviews with female stars, beauty, celebrities. Cover stories include: 'Catwalk report: Top 10 trends for autumn', ' "I'd marry him tomorrow" – Girls on their gay best friends', and 'Botox-to-go: The boom in lunch-hour face-lifts'. Like a more accessible *Vogue*, with more celebrities and a bit more emotion (website: www.elle.co.uk).

- *Vogue* (UK) – Circulation 195,000 – Fashion, beauty, interviews, design. Cover stories include: 'Those 14 looks you'll want this season', 'Denim couture', and 'Style buys: Cool sneakers and hot corsets'. Not really a lifestyle magazine like the others, except that you can't miss its obsession with being fashionable and stylish (website: www.vogue.co.uk).

- *B* (UK) – Circulation 193,000 – Sex, relationships, fashion and beauty, celebrities, more sex and relationships. Cover stories include: '1000 women confess! Who's doing what in bed, at work & after dark', 'Sexy holiday hair – 25 quick ways to get it', and '6 love ultimatums and how to use them' (website: www.bmagazine.co.uk).

- *She* (UK) – Circulation 176,000 – Relationships, sex, fashion and beauty, interviews, food, health. Cover stories include: '7 steps to great sex', 'Relax your way to success – Your daily confidence plan', and 'Celebrity special: Nips, tucks and boob jobs' (website: www.she.co.uk).

- *Red* (UK) – Circulation 174,000 – Relationships, interviews, fashion and beauty, interiors, travel. Cover stories include: '150 summer's best buys [clothing and make-up]', 'Zoe Ball on her man, baby, friends & why she's still a party girl at heart', and 'Easy ways to make over your garden'. For women aged 25–50 with a relatively youthful outlook (website: www.reddirect.co.uk).

These two big-selling American magazines, built around the identity of a particular female celebrity, have a broad appeal and are rather in a category of their own:

- *Rosie* (USA) – Circulation 3,613,000 – Rosie O'Donnell's magazine. Real-life stories, interviews, fashion and beauty, political issues, celebrities, health, cooking, crafts and decorating, advice. Cover stories include: 'Sarah Ferguson & Rosie talk about losing their moms, gaining weight & finding a way past the pain', 'Summer crafts for kids' and 'Simple ideas for a home office that works'. This title is really too *Good Housekeeping* to be in this list, but in March 2002, O'Donnell decided to come out as a lesbian mother on ABC TV's *Primetime*, so things may change (website: www.rosiemagazine.com).
- *O – The Oprah Magazine* (USA) – Circulation 2,531,000 – Oprah Winfrey's magazine. Self-help, interviews, fashion and beauty, inspirational real-life stories, relationships, food, advice. Cover stories include: 'You've got a friend: The laughs, the lapses – the essence of the connection', 'The buddy system: Losing weight together' and 'What makes for real happiness?: Oprah talks to the Dalai Lama' (website: www.oprah.com).

And for teenage readers . . .

- *More* (UK) – Circulation 290,000 – Sex, more sex, fashion and beauty, naked men, celebrities. Cover stories include: 'Sex confessions – "I was a female escort" – "I've starred in porn films" – "I had a threesome" – and more', '30 foxy frocks', and 'A-list celebs, Z-list threads – When bad clothes happen to good people'.
- *J-17* (UK) – Circulation 180,000 – Clothes, boys, celebrities, fun, snogging, sex advice, pop music, even a bit on careers. Cover stories include: 'J-17 Confidential: 15 pages of lads, advice & celeb secrets', 'Real life: My boyf is older than my dad', and 'Summer crushin' – Will a slogan T-shirt get you snogs?'.
- *YM (Your Magazine)* (USA) – Circulation 2,206,000 – Pop stars,

boys, beauty and style, celebrities, advice. Cover stories include: 'Actual stories you've never heard from 'NSync', 'Girls who've sworn off sex', and '100+ best jeans: Our obsessive guide' (website: www.ym.com).

- *CosmoGirl* (USA) – Circulation 839,000 – Boys, celebrities and pop stars, beauty and fashion, health, fun, advice. Cover stories include: 'Get sexy shiny hair!', 'The CosmoGirl Dating Bible – Make this the summer you snag the hottest boyfriend ever!', and pop music items. A UK edition of CosmoGirl was launched in October 2001 (website: www.cosmogirl.com).

DON'T JUDGE A BOOK BY ITS COVER?

The covers of magazines are extremely important to their public image and sales. Liz Jones, editor of the UK *Marie Claire* from 1999–2001, says: 'Nowadays, when the average time spent choosing a magazine and lifting it off the shelf is about three seconds, the covers make or break a magazine. You need lots of cover lines [– the phrases like 'Great sex today!' promoting articles in the magazine], and they all have to be compelling' (Jones, 2001a).

KEY THEMES

Women's magazines are, of course, all about the social construction of womanhood today (just as men's lifestyle magazines, as we have seen, are all about the social construction of men). Some of their content is pretty self-evident – the 'fashion and beauty' material, which takes up many pages in all of the above magazines, contains very few surprises in terms of gender representation. Critics would say that these sections represent a not-very-subtle and relentless insistence that women of all ages must do their best, and go to considerable expense, to look as 'glamorous' as possible – and it is difficult to disagree (although we all know from everyday life that many people choose to disregard this message, to greater or lesser degrees). In the following sections we will consider some of the more non-traditional features of modern women's magazines.

Men as sex objects

Women were objectified for decades in men's media, advertising and pornography. But nowadays several women's magazines objectify men using the same kind of language and imagery as the men's magazines – and at times, even in ways which men's magazines might be embarrassed about. For example:

- The US *Cosmopolitan* has a 'Hunk of the Month' feature, and in 'Survival of the Sexiest' (June 2001) the magazine invited readers to vote for which man they wanted to see strip. In the same month the UK edition gave away a 'Naked male centrefolds' supplement. *Company* is similar, for example presenting sporty 'Boys of Summer' in a 'Fit Men' section (August 2001).
- The sex tips in *Company*, *Cosmo* and other titles assume that men will do whatever the woman asks – unlike sex tips in men's magazines, where it is assumed that male readers will need to win the consent of a partner.
- *Elle*'s July 2001 cover offers: 'Hola boys: Eye candy for grown-up girls'; the following month the mag explains 'why a gay best friend is this season's must-have accessory'.
- *More* has a major regular section entitled 'Men Unzipped'. This typically includes 'Blokes' Bits – What's inside men's minds . . . and trousers'; 'The *More* Centrefold'; and several pictures of fit men in underwear or shorts. Sample quote – on actor Heath Ledger: 'Most girls would play the rugged Aussie's didgeridoo anytime'.
- *New Woman* regularly lusts after men in its 'Bloke' section; *B* has a 'Lust' page for male film and media stars; *Company* has a 'Pin Up' page for similar men. Even *YM*, for younger readers, has a 'YM Boys' section – 'The cutest ones we could find this month'.

This approach to men, of course, is done with a smile, and *knowingly* treats men in the way that men have traditionally treated women. Some 'men's rights' groups have objected to this kind of objectification, but inevitably end up looking self-pitying and pompous. The magazines' assumption is that men can't really complain, because men (as a group) have been doing this kind of thing for decades.

Men are not, of course, always treated as just bodies or sex machines. Even the most sex-obsessed magazine, *More*, has a regular feature where ordinary men are asked for their answers to readers' personal problems, and their answers are usually thoughtful and sensitive; and even the 'Men Unzipped' section includes parts exploring the feelings of sample men about delicate or emotional issues. The approach of *More* and *Cosmo* is similar to that of *FHM* and *Maxim*, then: the opposite sex is great for sex, and we are aware that they are thoughtful, emotional beings that we will make some effort to understand too.

Sex and sexuality

The magazines for young women like *Cosmo, Glamour* and *More* include numerous features on different sexual positions and techniques, 'sex tricks', 'driving your man wild', 'the best sex ever', and so on. (There are so many of these articles, in every imaginable permutation, that there's no point giving particular examples here, but several appear as sample cover stories in the list of magazines above.) Unsurprisingly, this aspect of the magazines has its critics. On the one hand, the conservative US organisation Morality in Media has an on-going campaign, launched in 1999, to stop the 'open display' of 'overly sexualised magazines, notably *Cosmopolitan* and *Glamour*, in [supermarket] checkout aisles', arguing that these 'porno-graphic' magazines should not be placed 'where even children old enough to read are exposed day after day' (MiM, 2000). Quoting cover lines such as '*Cosmo*'s Kama Sutra' and *Glamour*'s '30–Day Climax Class', they note that 'Naturally, those of us offended by such trash would prefer that it not be sold at all' (MiM, 1999). This is the conservative objection: that the magazines are much too open about sex (and they even seem to go further, suggesting that material about sexual pleasure should not really be available to anyone).

There is also a feminist objection: that the magazines are too *limited* in their coverage of sex, because their articles are almost always heterosexual. Stevi Jackson (1996), in an article based on looking at a handful of maga-zines, asserts that they are 'relentlessly heterosexual' and observes that lesbian sexuality is not regularly and routinely celebrated in the way that heterosexuality is. This is true, of course, although the magazines are more positive about lesbianism and bisexuality than Jackson thinks.

Angela McRobbie is not impressed with Jackson's approach; she seems to see it as a monolithic, determinedly grumpy form of feminism crashing into a slice of popular youth culture and dismissing it out of hand. McRob-bie agrees that lesbianism is not covered in great detail, or in every issue:

> There is no explicit information about the finer details of lesbian sex, no position of the fortnight for lesbian lovers. This point then marks the limits of permissible sexualities within the field of the magazines ... But does this mean we turn away from the magazines, dismissing them entirely on these grounds? Surely this ... is an issue that has to be thought through more seriously.
>
> (1999: 57)

McRobbie points out that the magazines are not only read, but also written and edited, by young women who want to have exciting and interesting lives, and who should have no desire to perpetuate patriarchy. Although it is regrettable that lesbian sexuality is not routinely included within the magazines' celebration of sexuality – which could cause misery and even psychological trauma to young women trying to come to terms with their excluded desires – McRobbie notes that the magazines show the clear impact of feminism in their coverage of (heterosexual) sex:

> The idea that sexual pleasure is learnt, not automatically discovered with the right partner, the importance of being able to identify and articulate what you want sexually and what you do not want, the importance of learning about the body and being able to make the right decisions about abortion and contraception, the different ways of getting pleasure and so on, each one of these figured high in the early feminist agenda. This was the sort of material found in books like *Our Bodies, Our Selves* (Boston Women's Health Collective, 1973), the volume which started as a feminist handbook and went on to sell millions of copies across the world.
>
> (ibid.)

This leads McRobbie to pose interesting questions about how feminist critics might now develop a dialogue with the producers and consumers of women's magazines, which we will come back to at the end of this chapter.

Relationships

A common assumption about women's magazines is that they are all about 'How to get a man'. The magazines are accused of suggesting that a man is the route to happiness, and the implication is that the magazines are simply reproducing a smartened-up version of the old-fashioned idea that if women manage to be sufficiently lovely and fragrant, then they will be fortunate enough to have a man come along and sweep them off their feet – ideally into wedded bliss. For example, in a *Washington Monthly* article, Alexandra Starr (1999) writes that, 'For the most part . . . women's magazines are pushing the same message they were half a century ago: women's existence revolves around landing the right guy' – although, she adds, today's technique is great sex rather than great cooking. She goes on to say that 'while these [sex] articles are packaged under the "liberated woman" motif, they're really just another variation on the "snagging and keeping a guy" theme'.

But the woman of today's magazines is not waiting for any man to come and pick her up; instead she is tracking down partner perfection like a heat-seeking missile. We have already seen, in the 'Men as sex objects' section, that the magazines like to rate men on their status as 'eye candy'. Cover stories such as *Cosmo*'s 'Man overload! How to reel in bunches of boys' and *Company*'s 'Will this be your summer of lust?' hardly suggest the image of a woman waiting for a nice husband to come along; and the advice for those in relationships – such as *B*'s 'Six love ultimatums and how to use them', and *New Woman*'s 'Make him a slave to your rhythms' – show that women should be in control. The advice pages of all of the magazines consistently argue that if a man is a serious disappointment, in any sense, then he should be ditched. Any reader who had taken all of these messages to heart would be the very *opposite* of the desperate-for-marriage wallflower. (In a further twist, though, other liberal critics are unhappy about this message as well. On the occasion of *Cosmopolitan*'s 30th birthday in February 2002, broadcaster Jenni Murray complained in the UK's *Daily Mail* that the magazine's emphasis on 'sex, sex and sex' fails to help women to cultivate real-life loving relationships – which, of course, may be true too).

Transformation and empowerment

Another common criticism of women's magazines is that they make women feel bad about themselves. Their repetitive celebration of a beauty 'ideal' which most women will not be able to match, but which will eat up readers' time and money – and perhaps good health – if they try, as well as the many pages of advice on how readers can improve their looks, sex skills or personalities, are likely to make some readers feel somewhat inadequate. This argument is made, for example, in Alexandra Starr's article, 'You've got a long way to go, baby: Women's magazines continue to create – and exploit – women's anxiety' (1999). As well as saying that magazines emphasise 'landing the right guy', Starr is also critical of the emphasis on physical perfection. '[Most] importantly,' she asserts, 'there isn't an acknowledgment that a solid sense of self-worth is a prerequisite to being in a successful relationship – or, for that matter, leading a healthy life.' Here Starr's argument wanders off the rails, because women's magazines contain an unavoidable stream of feel-good advice about having a positive self-image and being confident.

But the magazines are full of beauty ideals too, and this can certainly seem *contradictory*. Pamela Fraker (2001), in a similar article, is closer to the mark when she says: '*Elle* is going to share with their readers the criteria for emotional and physical health, and then encourage them to disregard it all in the name of beauty? Does this seem a little twisted to anybody else?' You could just as easily say it the other way round – that the magazines spell out the secrets of beauty, but then encourage readers to disregard it all in the name of emotional and physical health; but, in any case, it's true that these elements don't sit comfortably together.

Since the 'feelbad' element of women's magazines is so often discussed, it seems worthwhile to list a few examples of the more positive and empowering parts. Again, to keep things simple, most of the following examples are from issues dated August 2001:

- *Glamour* (UK) has a major article entitled, 'Your summer of self-discovery'. It begins: 'This summer, find some time to think – and we mean *really* think. Are you doing what you want in life? Are you in the right job, with the right man and truly living up to all your potential?' The piece offers advice on how to change these things for the better – with expert advice from Fiona Harrold, author of *Be Your Own Life Coach*.
- *Glamour* (USA) offers a 'Foolproof Recovery Plan' for various negative situations, plus a 'Wow! Women' feature on inspirational, successful women.
- Career advancement: *New Woman* has 'Are your bad work habits holding you back?', with advice on how to fix them; *Glamour* (UK) offers 'Bluff your way to the top', which advises things like 'Fake inner confidence' and 'Sit at the front'; and *She* reveals 'Six secrets of success: Forget sucking up to your boss – if you want your career to take off, just follow these six ultra-simple rules' which include 'Disagree with your boss' and 'Speak your mind'.
- *O – The Oprah Magazine* is full of life-affirming material encouraging women to get the most out of life, even if it means making difficult or unpopular choices. Indeed, *O*'s editor, Amy Gross, said recently, 'We are telling women what they need to know about themselves, not what they need to fix about themselves', claiming that the magazine was successful because it refused to fuel women's insecurities (Krum, 2001).
- *Cosmo* (UK) offers 'Unlock your secret self', a quiz to help readers work out some of their character traits, with advice on how to 'Be your best'. It also has a box of encouraging 'Gender Facts' such as: 'The number of female police sergeants in the UK has doubled over the past five years and the number of female solicitors has trebled.'
- *Cosmo* (UK) also meets 'the real-life Lara Croft', an independent, adventuring treasure-seeker. And *Rosie* (July 2001) has a profile of a courageous globe-trotting female photojournalist.
- *Marie Claire* challenges stereotypes with a positive article on fathers who stay at home to look after their children.

- The problem pages (such as 'Lovelife QandA' in *New Woman*) encourage women to be assertive in relationships, and to drop them if things aren't going right.
- Positive thinking: *Glamour* (USA) features 'Cut it out! You can remove negativity from your life!': '*Glamour* asked five upbeat women how they keep a positive outlook on life despite their highly stressful jobs'.
- *CosmoGirl* (July 2001) includes the article 'I'm not a toy! Females shouldn't be considered sex objects'. This magazine, like *J-17* and all the others, encourages confidence in being yourself.
- *YM* has a quiz called, 'Are you a yes girl? – Find out if you stick up for yourself', encouraging girls not to say 'yes' to anything they are not happy with.

There are, then, lots of 'girl power' messages in today's magazines aimed at more-or-less young women. This doesn't quite apply across the board: it's disappointing to note that even *Red* – perhaps the most 'youthful' of the magazines for more settled-down women – seems to assume that once readers have developed an interest in interior decorating, they won't be wanting to radically change their lives again. And the American *Redbook*, despite its youthful and sexy outlook, seems to assume that women will be doing the cooking in a relationship. In general, though, women's magazines speak the language of 'popular feminism' – assertive, seeking success in work and relationships, demanding the right to both equality and pleasure.

WHAT THE READERS SAY

As in the previous chapter, email interviews were conducted with readers of the magazines, mostly from across the USA and UK, but also from Australia, Hong Kong, Poland, Germany and India. Although this sample of readers – who were able and willing to email their thoughts about women's magazines – will not be exactly representative of the average reader profile, they *are* all examples of magazine readers, talking about the magazines which they actually routinely read in their everyday lives. The interviewees were encouraged to say what they *really* thought, rather than to make 'clever' critical points just for the sake of it. The following sections represent an overview of what the readers said.

DO WOMEN'S MAGAZINES AFFECT BODY IMAGE?

There is an on-going debate about the influence of women's magazines and, in particular, images of skinny fashion models and celebrities, upon the body image of women. It is even an issue discussed in the pages of women's magazines themselves: in an article entitled 'Why models got so skinny', for example, *Cosmopolitan* (US edition, August 2001) finds that designers, fashion editors and casting agents were picking ever-more waif-like models through the 1990s; already-thin models were losing work to even skinnier women and had to become even more willowy to keep working with top-rated designers. The increasingly close links between Hollywood and the fashion industry has led female movie stars in the same direction. Despite seeming unhappy about the unrealistic 'skinny trend', the *Cosmo* article offers little hope of a change, except from some quotes from men saying that they prefer a fuller figure. Elsewhere it has been suggested that the women's magazines – particularly at the 'high fashion' end of the market represented by *Vogue* and *Elle* – have no desire to change. Liz Jones, when editor of *Marie Claire* during the year 2000, tried to introduce initiatives to encourage magazine editors to feature a greater diversity of women – models of different sizes, and also more Black and Asian women. Her suggestions were pointedly and explicitly rejected by the industry. Jones resigned in April 2001 because, she said, 'I had simply had enough of working in an industry that pretends to support women while it bombards them with impossible images of perfection day after day, undermining their self-confidence, their health and hard-earned cash' (Jones, 2001b).

In scientific terms, the evidence for the negative impact of these images is mixed. A report by the British Medical Association, *Eating Disorders, Body Image and the Media* (BMA Board of Science and Education, 2000) noted that eating disorders such as anorexia and bulimia have one of the highest mortality rates of all psychiatric illnesses, and that 'the degree of thinness exhibited by [fashion models] is both unachievable and also biologically inappropriate, and provide unhelpful role models for young women' (2000: 36). Media influences could not be said to directly *cause* eating disorders, however. 'Eating disorders are caused by a complex interplay between genetics, family history, and the cultural environment,' the report notes. The point remains that, for those who are psychologically predisposed to anxiety about the body, or control of the self, media images can play an unhelpful role.

In her book *Body Image*, Sarah Grogan (1999) finds that body dissatisfaction can affect both women and men, but is most common in women. Surveying the mass of literature in this area, she concludes: 'The factors that seem to predict body dissatisfaction most accurately are social experiences, self-esteem and perceptions of control over one's life (including perceived control over the body)' (1999: 167). This perception of control is particularly important, Grogan suggests – anorexia is an extreme way of demonstrating control over the body, of showing self-discipline and raising self-esteem in the short term by denying one's own needs (ibid.: 173) – a finding which is 'well documented' (ibid.: 181). Media images of slenderness – or, for men, the combination of a slender but muscular body – may prompt feelings of dissatisfaction, but at the same time 'interview work suggests that women in particular are cynical about media portrayal of the "ideal body", and want to see more realistic images of women in the media' (ibid.: 189). Grogan also notes that, ironically, the empowering notion that individuals can change themselves, in modern society – which we discussed in Chapter 5 and elsewhere – can lead a person to feel a sense of failure if they cannot achieve the body of their dreams (ibid.: 191).

Overall, then, we have a slightly contradictory set of findings:

- Media images are likely to have *some* impact on how people view their own bodies. It would obviously be better if unhealthily skinny models were not promoted as icons of beauty by fashion magazines.
- However, media images are definitely *not* the main cause of extreme conditions such as anorexia or bulimia. These are potentially grave illnesses which should be taken seriously.
- Audiences view the culture of 'ideal bodies' critically, and say that they would like to see more diversity.
- However, the industry notes that, regardless of what readers say, images of thin models are 'popular' and will sell magazines. ('If you stick a beautiful skinny girl on the cover of a magazine you sell more copies', as model agency Premier told reporters (BBC Online, 2000c)).

Further reading

Orbach (1993); Davis (1995); Benson (1997); Grogan (1999);. (See also 'Selling beauty', in Chapter 4, pp. 77–81).

The 'pick and mix' reader

Analysis of the interviews suggests that female readers of women's magazines, from various developed countries, tend to share a feeling of ambivalent pleasure about these publications. They *enjoy* the magazines, and may at times learn bits and pieces – ideas for how to look or behave, as well as more straightforward information about health, popular culture or social issues. At the same time, these readers would not often argue that the magazines are 'perfect' or 'ideal' in terms of how they address women. This young German clearly articulates the 'pick and mix' approach to the magazines which many respondents shared:

> [The magazines] give an overview of what's 'hot' and celebrate consumption in every way, which is fun. *Elle*, and really all of the women's magazines I know, make it look so easy to become the sort of woman they idealise. That's not the point of reading these magazines. You get something to compare yourself with but you don't have to accept the ideal or follow it, that depends on the reader. They tell you how to dress, to do your make-up and how to behave in relationships. Still it's up to you, you can take up these things or leave them. What I regard as valuable is getting an idea of style and that can help you in the development of individual taste. So the influence of these magazines on me is mainly in the area of fashion. Still, I am not a fashion victim! The psychological tests and hints on solving problems with your significant other are pure fast food for me, fun for the moment but to take it seriously – no way.
>
> (24-year-old female from Berlin, Germany)

The magazines are not taken literally, then, even though they may suggest some good ideas; and some parts – such as the 'tests and hints' – are pure entertainment. This woman goes on to say:

> I can't identify with the '*Elle* woman' because I don't have the money, the perfect figure of a supermodel and I don't belong to any hip young group of people (as *Elle* defines them). It is a bit easier to identify with the [German magazine] *Allegra* ideal reader because she is a bit more down to earth but still one of the in crowd. I think my problem identifying with any group or ideal is that I never believed in such things. So I always take

the bits I like and discard the rest of the identity. I certainly
don't care if I fit into the target group of a magazine or not, if I
like it.

(as above)

Interestingly, those respondents who picked the more 'girly' interests –
beauty and fashion – as high points of the magazines were also successful
career women, who in their working lives might have to work *against*
stereotypes of femininity, but nevertheless seemed to enjoy the fantasy-
world of women's magazines when they had time to relax. For example, this
reader was an information architect, specialising in website organisation and
management:

[I like the magazines because] I like fashion and beauty. I have a
really stressful job and enjoy the alternative reality of 'fashion
books.' In addition, I take fashion seriously as a minor art form.
They are sensual as physical objects: glossy paper, heavy weight
of the magazine, super-saturated colors, etc.

(38-year-old female from Chicago, USA)

This woman, a producer in the competitive world of television, has similar
preferences:

[I like the magazines because] they offer the latest news on cosmetics and facial products. But at the end of the day, they are
just easy to read magazines which help to kill time when one is
at the hair-dresser's or waiting at restaurants for friends to show
up. *Cosmo*: The presentation and style makes reading easy. It's
an easy magazine to pick up and put down. *Her World*: Good
articles on tried and tested beauty products, good tips on where
to dine.

(26-year-old female from Hong Kong)

This woman works for a Polish government agency:

[I like the magazines because] I am interested in fashion. I like
professional pictures of it. That is the main reason, I think. Also
I like to know what's new in the cosmetics market ... and
some other things (news, fitness, etc.). It is good for 'casual'
relaxation.

(25-year-old female from Gdansk, Poland)

And a graduate student in Hong Kong said:

> They give me the most updated fashion news and what designers
> are doing. Some designers that I used to like may be shifting to
> things that I hate. And I can find out new favourites too. I can
> also check out new make-up or skincare products. And as
> fashion trends are like cycles, flipping through the magazines can
> give me ideas or inspirations – how to make my old clothes look
> fashionable by way of adding new accessories or new
> coordination.
>
> (35-year-old female from Hong Kong)

Nevertheless, she didn't take the magazines' fashion advice too literally:

> To be frank, I don't like to identify myself with the ideal reader.
> I want to be more critical, otherwise I have to spend much more
> money on those clothes and beauty things than I am doing now.
>
> (as above)

The respondents were well able to analyse their own enjoyment of the magazines. This woman, for example, gave an incisive and open account:

> [The magazines] provide an imaginary space of self-indulgence
> [where] I can play at being a different, more glamourous, shal-
> lower, richer version of myself. I love the sensuality of them –
> the heavy shiny pages, high production values, the scented
> sachets, silly free gifts (I'm a real sucker for the free gift). I also
> enjoy the polymorphous perversity of lots of images of gor-
> geous, naked or half dressed or fantastically clad young women
> who present themselves for a gaze that is somewhere between
> objectification and identification but clearly can't be reduced to
> either. I enjoy the engagement with consumerism – I love the
> fashion and beauty product information – that Creme de la Mer
> is the face cream of the moment, the Fendi Baguette the bag to
> have – even though I've no intention of actually purchasing
> either.
>
> (36-year-old female from London, England)

Thinking through identity

When asked about whether, and how, the magazines helped them to think about their own identity, respondents gave a range of answers. Some were straightforwardly aspirational:

> You kind of look at the images in the mags of attractive, success-ful, well dressed and healthy women, and I like to think of myself as perhaps nearing this type of image – and hopefully in the future – be a successful person.
>
> (21-year-old female from Bristol, England)

> I think the magazine you buy or read can say a lot about you as a person in the sense that it can be what the person aspires to be. For example, when I was in my teens I always bought the maga-zine *More* which I bought because it is very open on sexual issues, although not always in a entirely factual way. And I used to use this information to share with my friends, to appear grown up and knowledgeable about sex although still a virgin.
>
> (21-year-old female from Lincoln, England)

> [Reading magazines like *Cosmopolitan*] usually makes me feel pretty good about myself. When I read about the features of some women and how they are trapped in 'office politics/affairs', 'love affairs they can't get out of', 'addiction to alcohol/violence/sex', I feel that I'm in control of my own life. It also helps to establish that I'm in the know with the latest modern (female) gadgets, beauty stuff, etc. Helps establish a [certain young, upwardly-mobile] lifestyle.
>
> (26-year-old female from Hong Kong)

Some used the magazines for negative identification – feeling pleased that they did *not* share the same approach to life as the magazines:

> When I say that I don't identify with this 'type of magazine' [*Elle* (Polish edition) and *Vogue*] it could mean that I define myself as a person who is not so superficial, who is more 'intel-lectual', or something like that.
>
> (25-year-old female from Gdansk, Poland)

And some said that the magazines had little to do with their sense of self:

I don't think either of these magazines [*Allure* and *Seventeen*] help me establish my identity. They are 2 hours of entertainment each month. I sometimes buy some of the make up they feature, but that's about it.

(28-year-old female from New York, USA)

The analytical Londoner quoted previously had an interesting response to this – asserting that the pleasure of the magazines was to do with fantasy, but not in the straightforward sense of wanting to have the looks or lifestyles put forward by the magazines:

The pleasure (and perhaps sometimes a certain sadness) of consuming these publications is the gap between the fantasy of self indulgent vapid luxury [in the magazines], and the more complex, grittier reality of my life. Not only is the image on offer impractical and unattainable, but it's not even one I particularly desire – this might not make sense, but the fantasy [indulged in while reading the magazines] is not a straightforward relation of aspiration or of role models at all.

(36-year-old female from London, England)

The ideal woman

When asked about the nature of the 'ideal woman' promoted by the magazines, responses were quite consistent – centred around being *independent* in attitude and *attractive* in looks. These are typical comments:

[These magazines suggest that a woman should be] an attractive, well dressed and independent woman, who most often than not is very career minded. Also intelligent, and likes all modern types of things, for example, modern interior house decor and furnishings, types of clothes, books etc.

(21-year-old female from Bristol, England)

Clear skin ... Good (thin) figure ... Attractiveness. However the magazines do provide tips and ideas which suggest that anyone can look this way if they try. Also they promote healthiness and regular exercise, but then these are not all bad qualities to promote to women. And they give the idea that if you are single then it is okay to flirt and that you should be looking for men – they often provide tips on how to attract men when you go out, implying that it is an important quality.

> (20-year-old female from Bristol, England)

Someone who is active and independent. I guess they also believe that taking pride in one's appearance is a good quality – one can only agree with this in the world we live in where appearance is very important for success.

> (21-year-old female from Warwick, England)

Sexy, beautiful, intelligent, superwoman.

> (18-year-old female from Mumbai, India)

Independence, strength, competence, ability in many different realms, compassion, martyrdom, Hollywood 'knowledge', sexual appeal . . . fashion sense, sexual confidence, intelligence, craftiness (like a fox, as well as the ability to sculpt in soap ends).

> (34-year-old female from Melbourne, Australia)

The following interviewee had subscriptions to *Marie Claire*, *Jane*, *Vogue*, *In Style* and *Glamour*, and she would read all of these 'pretty much cover to cover while working out at the gym'. Identifying herself as a feminist, she felt that three of these magazines did a reasonable job politically:

> I think the good magazines (*Marie Claire*, *Vogue*, parts of *Jane*) hit the political content within the genre of women's magazines pretty well. They're not [feminist magazine] *Ms.*, obviously, but they suggest a sort of 70s liberal, sisterhood-is-powerful kind of feminism by focusing on women's issues around the globe and in the US. Their take on these issues is that these women, though different from 'me' (the ideal reader who wants make-up tips and has the money to spend on new fashion fads), are worthy of my attention, concern, letters to Congress and charitable donations. I think they promote a kind of informed, politically conscious perspective. All are explicitly pro-choice, and all have run articles about lesbians (two of my lightning rod issues for how much I like a magazine). Also, they suggest that while it's fine for women to want to look good, there are a variety of ways to look good (okay, [this doesn't apply to] *Vogue*) – and that looking good isn't the be-all and end-all. *Marie Claire* and *Jane* promote a kind of low key feminism that

while it's not as 'radical' as I think of myself as being, is pretty
solid within the genre. [On the other hand,] *In Style* and
Glamour are embarassing.

I don't like *Glamour*. I'm cancelling my subscription when it
comes up. The articles are too focused on sex tips for pleasing
men, and the magazine seems aimed at young (early 20s)
women who are insecure about their jobs, their sexuality, and
their body. The tips are all about being 'better,' but I think the
tips are either too dumb . . . or too self-explanatory. *In Style* is all
about celebrities . . . very fluffy . . . so I'm a little embarrassed
by it.

(33-year-old female from Wisconsin-Madison, USA)

The downside

Few, if any, of the interviewees were entirely happy with the women's magazines that they read, but some were much more critical than others. This
young woman, a manager at an IT training company, and a regular reader
of *Elle* and *Marie Claire* ('I probably buy one of them every month, sometimes both') had interesting thoughts on the possible negative impact of
women's magazines which are worth quoting at some length here:

The most harmful thing about [women's magazines] – and I do
think that they can be harmful – is that they encourage you to
question your life and your happiness and tell you what you
ought to be doing and feeling. I realise that women are perfectly
intelligent human beings but it's like being attacked from all
sides sometimes. You ought to be doing this or that, you ought
to look like this or that. I still think John Berger's *Ways of Seeing*
[which I read at university] describes fashion magazines perfectly. Men watch women, and women watch men watching
women. That's exactly how it feels. The thing is that you want
to think that it's just the men in society that make us think we
should all be blonde and thin with big breasts but in reality it
isn't. We pretty much know that men like us whatever, and it's
other women that the pressure originates from – which is mad,
and we shouldn't accept it but we do, and it's fashion magazines
where it's women telling other women all this harmful stuff, yet
claiming that they are part of some kind of 'sisterhood'. Basically
they say one thing and do another – you'll have an article at the
front of the magazine about how wonderful [large comedian]

Dawn French is – 'and so pretty!' – and then 'How to be as thin as Kate Moss'.

(23-year-old female from Leeds, England)

This woman is also frustrated by the way the magazines promote the idea that women and men are fundamentally different, which, she suggests, is a fiction invented for entertainment and 'self-help' purposes which even the journalists writing the articles are unlikely to believe in:

> In the magazines aimed at women in their twenties (*Cosmo*, *Elle*, *Marie Claire*, *More*), lots and lots of articles are about how different we are, how we communicate differently, how we see sex differently, how we want different things . . . I personally notice this specifically because my view is so totally opposite . . . In articles in magazines aimed at older women, e.g. *Red*, they're more obviously in line with my view – that we're fundamentally very similar. I think the disparity comes from the fact that men and women in their 20s in the 21st century are portrayed in certain ways – [the idea is that] men are immature and only concerned with pulling birds, and women are pretty much grown-up. Letting these hackneyed stereotypes inform their articles is just bloody lazy. I bet if you asked the women that write these articles about the men they actually know they'd be far nicer about them than they are about men in general in print.
>
> (as above)

It is worth noting that the same respondent saw the magazines for teenagers and younger women as being more responsible and less flippant about sex and society:

> I think the girl power thing has really helped young girls, and magazines can provide a sort of role model whether by showing them or tacitly expressing the sort of woman they think the reader should/could be. I was teaching at a secondary girls' school in London where 90% of the pupils are black or Asian, and groups like Destiny's Child are fantastic role models and can be accessed through these magazines. 'Independent women, honeys making money.' I certainly learned a lot from magazines such as *Just 17*, when they are aiming at younger readers they can be more basic and honest – they're more responsible because they're thinking about the readership. It all gets more

covert, complicated and hidden, and therefore sneaky, in magazines aimed at older teenagers and women.

(as above)

Interviewees also made the point that the magazines could also be alienating
to lesbian readers, or people wondering about their sexuality – as we noted
above in the discussion of sex and sexuality in the magazines (pp. 189–190).
The following lesbian respondent said that she occasionally 'felt the urge' or
'needed a fix' of 'glossy paper and seductive imagery' and so would purchase
Red, *Nova*, *She* or *Elle* – or she would read those magazines when her
partner had succumbed to the same impulse. Although she asserts that she
doesn't look to the magazines for lifestyle guidance, she notes that they can
nevertheless make her feel like an outsider at the (heterosexual) party. She
explains that she doesn't want to be like the women in the magazines, but:

> [Despite] saying that, I am seduced by 'cool.' I think I used to
> be very influenced by [style magazines] *i-D* and *The Face* when I
> was in my 20's. Now I don't feel I have so much to prove. I feel
> more comfortable with who I am. I don't need a glossy mag to
> tell me I am on the right track anymore. [But on the other
> hand] I can feel so left out and marginalised. These women's
> mags can make me feel so depressed and isolated – accentuating
> my otherness. I don't like to admit to this as I feel that most of
> the time I don't feel this way, but sometimes the attraction of
> the 'normals' is very compelling.
>
> (40-year-old female from London, England)

Although the magazines would be positive and encouraging on the occasions when they addressed homosexuality, the continuous emphasis on heterosexuality in the vast majority of features – which is also the case in men's
magazines – might make anyone considering their attraction to the same
sex think twice before stepping outside the attractive and popular world of
the 'normals' (as this interviewee put it).

The readers' conclusion – women win?

One respondent, when asked whether the magazines suggested that women
and men are fundamentally similar or different, replied:

> Fundamentally different. I think these magazines often, for
> example, give the impression that women are secretly *better* than

men, but feel strongly the need to protect [men] from this knowledge so that their delicate egos are not damaged. Women are also
represented as more emotionally competent, more able to cope
with life changes, better able, maybe even 'naturally' adept at,
child rearing, of higher endurance, possessing better fashion sense
and – well, lots of other things – I could go on. Suffice to say I
think that they pump women up to believe they are better than
men, and must care for them in ways the men do not understand.

(34-year-old female from Melbourne, Australia)

She felt that the magazines for women, like those for men, were not really
helping people (female or male) to get on with each other. At the same
time, though, we can appreciate that the view of women as competent and
powerful, projected by women's magazines, should be good for female
readers. However, others of course would point to the emphasis on conventional ideas of attractiveness, and in particular thin or skinny bodies, as a
very negative aspect of the magazines.

A slightly uncertain but generally optimistic assessment of the ideas
communicated by women's magazines is offered by the young German
interviewee:

So, the way I understand [what the magazines say overall] is:
stay who you are, don't let others get you down, and take risks.
It's then good for a woman to be a 'bad girl', but from time to
time it works as well for her to try out the traditional 'good girl'
behaviour. Especially when it comes to getting what you want,
everything seems to be appropriate. In a way [this message is]
liberating . . .?

(24 year old female from Berlin, Germany)

A less upbeat general feeling was that the magazines were good or enjoyable
in some respects, but that the repetition of messages about 'looking great'
was rather annoying – although readers could try to ignore or skip over
those parts.

SUMMARY AND CONCLUSION

Women's magazines, then – like men's magazines, but for different reasons
– offer a confusing and contradictory set of ideas. Many of their messages
are positive – most readers agreed that the magazines communicated a
picture of assertive, independent women – although the emphasis on

looking beautiful, too, was generally inescapable. But the readers also agreed that they didn't take all of the magazines' messages seriously anyway – favouring a pick'n'mix attitude to the various ideas in the magazines – which might suggest that those who fear for the reader–victims of these publications are overemphasising the power of the texts and underestimating the ability of readers to be selective and critical. On the other hand, one could fear that even readers who think they read the magazines very unseriously are still absorbing lots of messages about what society (as seen through the magazines) thinks is important – such as beauty and sex – and what readers can be less bothered about – such as serious political issues.

In terms of the theories discussed in previous chapters, then, we find that women's magazines – like men's magazines – suggest ways of thinking about the self, and propose certain kinds of lifestyle, which are then actively processed by the readers as they establish their personal biography, sense of identity and technologies of the self (see Chapters 5 and 6). The magazines for young women are clearly anti-traditional, emphatically rejecting older models of how women should behave and encouraging women to embody *a certain kind of* 'liberated' identity instead. Femininity is exposed as artifice and performance in the magazines, which celebrate women's opportunities to play with different types of imagery, which is in line with queer theory's proposition that gender is always a performance (Chapter 7). *However* – and this is a big 'however' – although women's magazines encourage a degree of playfulness in terms of clothing and make-up, they would never encourage women to step outside their carefully imagined boundaries of the 'sexy', the 'stylish' and the 'fashionable'.

Criticisms of women's magazines often come from a 'feminist' perspective, but as Angela McRobbie points out, the magazines themselves have incorporated – or at least respond to – many feminist ideas. Commenting on the publications for teenagers, she says:

> The place of feminism inside the magazines remains ambiguous. It has presence mostly in the advice columns and in the overall message to girls to be assertive, confident, and supportive of each other. It is also present in how girls are encouraged to insist on being treated as equals by men and boyfriends, and on being able to say no when they want to.
>
> (1999: 55)

We can add that in the magazines for older teenagers and young women, the encouragement of women to be sexual actors – even predators – rather than sexual objects or victims, reflects a 'feminist' turning of the tables.

Feminists never really suggested that having sex with lots of men was a goal in itself, but the rejection of passive femininity, and the *freedom* to openly desire others, is feminist progress. McRobbie goes on:

> For writers like Stevi Jackson the magazines only provide girls with the same old staples of heterosexual sex, body anxieties and 'the old idea that girls' sexuality is being attractive and alluring' (Jackson, 1997: 57). So she is saying that there are no great advances here. What I would say in contrast is that feminism exists as a productive tension in these pages.
>
> (ibid.)

Since feminism 'has become both common sense and a sign of female adult authority', McRobbie suggests, the young female readers and writers have 'a desire to be provocative to feminism' – which we have to accept is fair enough although, McRobbie notes, this tension between female generations comes as rather a surprise to feminists. She observes, 'Young women want to prove that they can do without feminism as a political movement, while enjoying the rewards of its success in culture and in everyday life' (ibid.: 56).

McRobbie therefore puts some new questions on the table. If we accept that women's magazines carry one kind of feminist argument – to be assertive, confident, sexual, 'true to yourself', demanding rights and pleasures – then how can this view and the more 'traditional' feminist view (which is unhappy about the magazines for other reasons) talk to each other? Does the more critical, radical (and perhaps only 'academic') feminism know what it would like 'popular feminism' to say to young women today? McRobbie suggests that by merely criticising the existing popular magazines as 'not good enough', the critical feminists escape the responsibility of saying what they would really like to see in a magazine for young women that would actually be popular. In some ways it's obvious – a better magazine would be wholly accepting of bisexual and lesbian sexualities, treating them just the same as heterosexuality, and would use images of a broad range of women instead of just conventionally beautiful, thin models. McRobbie seems to suspect – perhaps unfairly – that this simple formula still wouldn't satisfy the critics of the magazines. But she rightly suggests that since ' "ordinary women" are themselves set upon improving, often against the odds, their own lives and those of their daughters' (ibid.: 128), the critics of women's magazines would do well to escape the simplistic view that the women who write and edit the magazines are evil, and that their readers are victims. The debate needs to be more sophisticated, productive and sympathetic.

MAGAZINES FOR LESBIANS AND GAY MEN

Whilst gathering data about responses to men's and women's magazines, I was also able to conduct several email interviews with lesbians and gay men about the magazines aimed specifically at them. Lesbian titles include *Curve*, *Girlfriends* and *On Our Backs* in the US, *Women on Women* and *Lesbians on the Loose* in Australia, and *Diva* in the UK. Gay men's magazines include *Out*, *XY*, *Hero* and *Genre* in the US, and *Attitude*, *Gay Times*, *Fluid* and *Boyz* in the UK. In the US there is also a current affairs magazine for both gay men and lesbians, *The Advocate*.

It was clear from these interviews that gay magazines can help a person feel comfortable about their sexuality, and feel part of a broader queer community or identity:

> They provide me with a sense of a large queer community. Many times it is hard to identify with the heterosexual world. My issues are reflected in these magazines [*The Advocate* and *Out*]. They help me understand what it means to be queer. I feel more in touch with the queer world when I read these magazines.
>
> (24-year-old man from Chicago, USA)

> By just recognising and catering for a gay audience, [the magazines] help. There is, I think, an implied ideal reader in the shape of a 'cool, young, slightly outrageous, sexual person', but there's also something in it that celebrates difference and acceptance. So you *want* to identify with it, but it lets you bend the image to suit yourself.
>
> (22-year-old man from Leeds, UK)

> They help me feel a part of a queer community.
>
> (28-year-old woman from California, USA)

> What the magazine [*Lesbians on the Loose*] does for me is reduce the 'othering' – I feel like I actually belong – that my relationship with a woman is not an aberration and is not as uncommon as dominant ideologies would have me believe. So the magazines help me feel 'included'.
>
> (33-year-old woman from Adelaide, Australia)

> I like looking at other dykes! That's why I read these mags.
> I blush as I write this but it's true. It's like an "imagined
> community". I only have half a dozen lesbian friends so this
> creates a sense of community.
>
> > (38-year-old woman from New York, USA)

A minority of respondents, however, did not identify with the kind of
gay person shown in the magazines:

> [The magazines] don't help me with my identity today —
> they once did, when I was a 'gay girl' in the seventies
> looking for some idea about how to live. Then I read
> *Gay Sunshine* and loved Allen Ginsburg's words about being
> an artist, a faggot, what I could be — different and still
> alive.
>
> > (43-year-old woman from Chicago, USA)

> I am not like any of the lesbians and gay men portrayed in
> many senses — my sex life, physicality, economic status,
> occupation, mentality. I define myself in opposition to what
> is depicted.
>
> > (40-year-old woman from London, UK)

> [The magazines give me a sense of identity] only in the
> sense that they give me something to react to. If people
> know who they are by what they're not, I often look at these
> mags and think to myself 'not that, not that, not that'.
>
> > (38-year-old woman from New York, USA)

The magazines were not seen as being very flexible about the gay
identity; several readers pointed out that rather than seeing sexuality
as fluid, gay magazines seemed to see homosexuality as a fixed identity:

> There seems to be a tight line drawn around this area, actu-
> ally. Your sexuality is changeable until you realise you are
> gay and then it is absolutely fixed. Going back to heterosex-
> uality is a major sin. I can see that the reason for this is
> that so many people are hurt and defensive, but it's an
> interesting paradox. The magazines definitely push the
> idea that gay is good and if you are gay there's no getting

out of it, buster. *But* if you are heteosexual, then your sexuality is a fluid thing that you haven't bothered to explore – (laughs).

(34-year-old woman from Melbourne, Australia)

Another lesbian from Australia explained that, although she did not agree with the view, she could see why magazines should see gay identities as innate, for 'political' reasons, so that others could not suggest that this condition, if cultural, could be changed or 'cured'.

Asked whether the magazines reinforced stereotypes of gayness, one woman replied that the publications promoted an image of readers as 'Thin, fit, economically independent – rich even, white, sexually active, sociable, popular'; but a different female reader suggested the opposite of this narrow view, saying that the magazines promoted 'A sense of pride in one's sexuality, a sense of community, and a sense of open mindedness and inclusivity'. A gay man responded that although certain stereotypes were evident, in the British magazine *Boyz*,

There's something in the gay image they project that suggests it's very much a performance and you can do what you want with the identity-options available to you. It suggests that it's okay to be gay and you can do what you want with it. Which is good. It knows what the commercial gay world (i.e. of clubs and music and stuff) is like, and it both provides for and criticises it. It lets me, as a reader, be camp if I want to be, serious the next minute, sleazy . . . anything. And I carry that over into real life.

(22-year-old man from Leeds, UK)

Chapter 10

DIRECTIONS FOR LIVING
Role models, pop music and self-help discourses

THIS CHAPTER CONSIDERS further kinds of media messages which suggest 'ways of living'. Pop stars and other celebrities are often considered to be 'role models', and so we will discuss the meaning of this rather loose concept. We will then consider the rise of 'girl power' bands like the Spice Girls and Destiny's Child; note the more and less macho aspects of male pop icons; and discuss the popularity of Britney Spears, based on interviews with her fans. This is followed by an analysis of successful self-help books, ideas from which tend to 'trickle down' into popular culture more generally. What do they tell women and men about constructing a comfortable identity and lifestyle? And what can the popularity of these messages tell us about changing cultural ideas of masculinity, womanhood and the acceptable modern sense of self?

WHO IS A ROLE MODEL?

The idea of 'role models' comes up often in public discourse, but it's not always clear what the term means. A 'role model' seems to be popularly understood as 'someone to look up to,' and someone to base your character, values or aspirations upon. To begin our discussion of what people are talking about when they propose (or oppose) supposedly influential figures, here is a collection of examples of public talk about various 'role models'.

- In November 1998, the British government announced plans to set up a panel of 'role models' to inspire teenage girls. Newspapers reported that they had considered asking the pop star Geri Halliwell, posh actress Emma Thompson and therapist Susie Orbach. The idea was apparently dropped after the papers made fun of it: 'No youngster would be seen dead with a Government-approved role model,' noted one journalist (Phillips, 1998).

- In December 1999, as Victoria Beckham (Posh Spice) showed young women that motherhood was cool, and Cherie Booth (wife of the Prime Minister) demonstrated the joys of pregnancy in her mid-forties, there was concern that 'celebrity mum' role models would encourage teenage pregnancy – or put pressure on ordinary mothers who do not enjoy such highly-resourced lifestyles (Phillips, 1999).

- In September 2000, the British news media reported that researchers had suggested that the government's 'Playing for Success' scheme, which promoted (male) professional footballers as role models, was a bad idea because it alienated many girls and some boys, and reinforced masculine stereotypes (BBC Online, 2000b).

- In the US, however, the professional footballers who were described in one *San Francisco Chronicle* story as classroom 'role models' were all female – the stars of the American women's soccer league were said to be very proud to serve as an inspiration to young women (28 April 2001). Women's World Cup champion Brandi Chastain had been helping to train promising Bay Area girls. 'Brandi is bigger than a movie star at our school,' said one.

- In November 1997, a child welfare supervisor in Dallas, Texas, ordered the emergency removal of a baby boy from foster parents, because the couple were lesbians and therefore did not, in her view, serve as decent 'role models'. The state's social services department quickly overruled the decision, and demoted the supervisor. These events sparked much controversy and debate (Verhovek, 1997).

- In July 2001, the Australian media went crazy for *Big Brother* contestant Sara-Marie, described in celebrity magazine *NW* as 'the best ever female role model on TV'. She is celebrated for being highly entertaining, intelligent, and larger than the skinny norm of other TV stars. 'She proves that bigger certainly can be better,' *NW* enthuses, 'living proof that curvy girls are sexy' (*NW*, 2001: 14). The magazine even gave away a free cut-out Sara-Marie face mask, so that all Australians can look like their idol.

- In the USA, the *New York Times* often debates the value of various role models. On 28 December 1997 and again on 7 April 2000 it discussed whether the Barbie doll was a good role model for girls; on 27 September 1998 the status of the Miss America Pageant as a 'proper role model for girls and young women' came under scrutiny; and on 29 May 2001, the paper interviewed biological scientist Dr Jill Bargonetti whose position as 'one of the few [prominent] black women in science' made her 'a role model and mentor for many minority students'.

- The *New York Times* doesn't forget men, either: an article on 9 April 2000, for example, noted the number of comically dumb male characters on TV, such as Homer Simpson, and worried about men's lack of intelligent role models; a piece on 30 December 1999 discussed, with Bronx teenagers, whether Puff Daddy was a good role model, after the successful performer and producer had been arrested on a firearms charge; and on 6 December 2000 profiled Stanley Williams, an 'anti-gang role model' who spreads a message against violent gangs to young people, from his cell on death row – he is 'up for both a Nobel Peace Prize, and execution' the newspaper notes.

- Film reviewers frequently bring up the idea of 'role models', particularly if there is a female character who may be of interest to girls or young women. For example, the *Dallas Observer*'s Michael Sragow was impressed with the title character in Disney's *Mulan* (1998): 'Mulan's virtues as a female role model are manifold. She's smart and independent; just as important, she's comely yet no bombshell' (Sragow, 1998). The title character in *Lara Croft: Tomb Raider* (2001) was called a 'really great positive role model' by the star herself, Angelina Jolie, who even told magazines that Lara was 'the perfect woman'. *Heat* magazine agreed, saying that Jolie 'kicks ass and is a good role model for teenage girls'. (More movie examples appear in Chapter 4, pp. 65–75.)

- Numerous obituaries for pioneering journalist Katharine Graham, ex-head of the *Washington Post*, described her as an inspiration to women. 'Graham is widely credited with serving as a role model for women, especially women in journalism, because her life entailed an extraordinary transformation,' noted the *Los Angeles Times* (18 July 2001), from conventional housewife, to defiant and powerful reporter and editor.

- A few days earlier in the *Los Angeles Times*, members of Backstreet Boys were discussing bandmate A. J. McLean's spell in a rehabilitation centre (14 July 2001). 'It's important for us to be honest about it and not push it under the rug,' said Kevin Richardson. 'We have a lot of young fans, and it's important to be a good role model'.

- The website 'Role Models on the Web' (www.rolemodel.net) suggests several people whom young people may wish to take as their inspiration, including:
  - Diane Sawyer, who overcame her shyness to become 'one of the finest investigative reporters on television'.

- Bill Koch, an entrepreneur who 'pioneered' new forms of environment-friendly energy, and winner of the America's Cup sailing race.
- Jehan Sadat, Egyptian feminist and 'powerful decision-maker', 'a devoted activist for peace and women's rights'.
- Steven Spielberg, who 'has given us a legacy of films and dreams, to encourage the dreamer in each of us'.
- Rosie O'Donnell, the actress, comedian and talk-show host who 'challenges the social order of things with her honest, straightforward style'.
- Tiger Woods, the star golfer who 'thinks his golf is just a vehicle for him to influence people'.

SO WHAT IS A ROLE MODEL?

From the examples above we can see that role models can be divided into six slightly different types.

1 **The 'straightforward success' role model**: people who have been successful in their chosen field, such as any popular film star or leader – Brad Pitt, Cameron Diaz, Tony Blair or Mary Robinson. This category, when used by authority figures, excludes people who have done well but have tarnished their reputation by being associated with inappropriate or 'immoral' practices – although cult status as an 'outsider' role model (see number 5) may well depend on the latter.
2 **The 'triumph over difficult circumstances' role model**: people who have overcome adversity to achieve success often become the most popular role models. For example, Tiger Woods surmounted the racism of the golf world to become its youngest-ever champion; Maya Angelou escaped from the abuse and poverty of her childhood to become an inspirational, best-selling writer; Nelson Mandela remained strong through 27 years of imprisonment and became a leader of huge international standing; Katharine Graham overcame the sexism of the newspaper world to become one of the most influential reporters; and the 'Role Models on the Web' site is very excited about Christopher Reeve, 'fighting back' after being paralysed. This type of role model is sometimes inappropriately used to argue against those who complain about injustice – as in 'You can't say that Hollywood is racist – look at the success of Eddie Murphy'.
3 **The 'challenging stereotypes' role model**: female action heroes like Lara Croft counter the idea of 'feminine' women, and the idea that only men can fill tough leading roles. Madonna was famously a confi-

dent and assertive sexual icon in the late 1980s and 1990s, challenging traditional assumptions about female sexuality. (Men with unusually 'feminine' traits, though, are rarely seen as role models.) Disabled people who succeed in jobs where some might be surprised to see them also fill this role. Because of the difficulty of challenging oppressive ideas, this category is linked to 'triumph over difficult circumstances'.

4   The 'wholesome' role model: these are the 'role models' which older generations are comfortable showing to their children, such as 'clean-living' pop bands, the better-behaved sports stars and stars who say 'no' to sex before marriage. Supporting such figures is 'risky' for conservatives because there is always the possibility that the icon will become a public disappointment, as in the Backstreet Boys case. And in 1999, Angela Phillips reported: 'Last year Emma Thompson was held up by the government as the role model every young woman should aspire to, as an antidote to teenage pregnancy. This year – whoops – as the unmarried mother of a baby girl, she's slipped from that particular pedestal'.

5   The 'outsider' role model: rejected by mainstream culture, the outsider role model is a hero to those who reject conventional social expectations, such as Marilyn Manson, Eminem and even dead stars like Kurt Cobain and River Phoenix. There seem to be fewer well-known women in this category – suggesting that popular culture is less kind to very transgressive females – but possible recent nominees include hip hop star Lil' Kim and the artist Tracey Emin, for their sexual frankness, and other strong independent free-thinkers from the music world such as Sinead O'Connor, Mary J. Blige and Shirley Manson.

6   The family role model: this category includes looking up to members of your own family, and other popular celebrity parents such as Victoria Adams and David Beckham; as well as being negatively defined by those who label certain parents as 'inappropriate role models' (as in the Texan lesbian foster parenting controversy mentioned above, p. 212).

These categories broadly summarise the kinds of people, and positions they represent, that become talked about as 'role models'. It remains unclear, though, in a psychological sense, how 'role modelling' might actually work. Social psychology books usually have little to say about 'role models', although they do trot out the shallow 'social learning theory' which suggests that people learn behaviour by observing it in others – such as role models – and will repeat the behaviour if it is reinforced – in other words, if it seems to have a positive outcome, or other people appear to appreciate it (Burr, 1998; Malim and Birch, 1998; Pennington, Gillen and Hill, 1999;

Brannon, 2001). This 'theory' is very simple – more of a thought than a theory – but it could, of course, still be correct, even though we currently lack an understanding of the processes involved.

In a recent discussion of the psychological literature on 'role models' specifically, Nauta and Kokaly concur that 'the defining characteristics of role models and exactly how they influence various aspects of the career [and, we might add, aspirational] development process remains somewhat unclear' (2001: 81). Although there are different definitions of 'role models', there is general agreement that:

> role models are other persons who, either by exerting some influence or simply by being admirable in one or more ways, have an impact on another.
>
> (2001: 82)

Fair enough. As Nauta and Kokaly assess the few theoretical discussions of how 'role models' might have an impact, it becomes clear that social learning theory is indeed as deep as it gets, although the idea of 'people learning behaviour through observation' has been expanded, in the obvious way, to accommodate the loose modelling of whole lifestyles. In other words, watching *Tomb Raider* or *Charlie's Angels* might encourage girls to become somewhat more independent and feisty, without them needing to directly *copy* an extensive fight sequence or to go on a perilous quest for ancient artefacts. In their preliminary survey research, Nauta and Kokaly found that 81 per cent of respondents could name a famous person who was a 'role model' for them, and could describe some reasons or attributes to explain this (2001: 84–86). Since the respondents were responding to a *request* to name a famous role model, however, it would be inappropriate to infer that the majority of these people felt that famous role models were deeply important to them; and we can note that when asked to name their greatest overall role model, 63 per cent of respondents chose one of their own parents.

GIRL POWER

The field of pop music offers many icons and potential role models. Pop music today is not only the sounds on the recordings we buy, or hear on the radio or played in shops, cafés, bars and clubs, but is also the carefully packaged set of images we see through television and magazines. In gender terms, the 1990s took an interesting turn when the Spice Girls burst onto the scene in 1996, shouting (literally) about 'girl power' at every opportunity. Mixing conventional glamour with a feisty, ultra-confident, 'in your face' approach, the Spices – driven by Geri Halliwell – really did push the 'girl power' agenda for a while. (After Geri's departure in 1998, they became just another girl band.) In her autobiography, *If Only*, Geri recalls a point in 1994 where she wondered whether the band was going to work or not:

> I asked a DJ friend what I should do. 'Girl bands don't work,' he said bluntly.
>
> I disagreed with him. The music scene *needed* young, positive female recording artists. At twelve years old I had Madonna to look up to. The teenagers today needed someone like that.
>
> (Halliwell, 1999: 221)

Outlining the characteristics of each Spice Girl to a journalist from *The Face* in 1997, Geri explained, 'We've all got balls, but I've got quite big balls, basically' (March 1997: 78). In the same year, British newspaper the *Guardian* thought it might be amusing to send along a well-known older feminist, Kathy Acker, to interview the group. Whilst rather overwhelmed by their noise and energy, Acker was relatively impressed. She confesses to being a little concerned about the individualism of their 'do what you want' message, but Geri tells her that the Spice Girls between themselves, and with their fans, are a community which is more powerful than the sum of its parts. She says:

> Normally, when you get fans of groups, they want to act like you, they copy what you're wearing, for instance. Whereas our fans, they might have pigtails and they might wear sweatclothes, but they are so individual, it's unbelievable. When you speak to them, they've got so much balls! It's like we've collected a whole group of our people together! ... I can remember someone coming up to us and going, 'Do you know what? I've just finished with my boyfriend! And you've given me the incentive to go "Fuck this!"'.
>
> (Acker, 1997: 14)

Acker asks whether the Spice Girls want boyfriends. Mel B replies:

> I think whoever we would choose to be with should respect the way we are – and our job as well. The way we are together. None of us would be interested in a man that wanted to

dominate, wanted to pull you down, and wanted you to do what
he wanted you to do.

(ibid.)

The Spice Girls, in this interview as in many others, said many other things
about fulfilling your dreams, going against expectations and creating your
own opportunities for success. Acker notes that in the 1980s, feminism was
represented in Britain and America by intellectual, middle-class women and
was popularly seen as elitist and anti-sex. She notes with pleasure that in the
1990s, the Spice Girls were able to confidently represent 'the voices, not
really the voice, of young women and, just as important, of women not
from the educated classes' (1997: 19). She continues:

It isn't only the lads sitting behind babe culture, bless them,
who think that babes or beautiful lower and lower-middle class
girls are dumb. It's also educated women who look down on
girls like the Spice Girls, who think that because, for instance,
girls like the Spice Girls take their clothes off, there can't be anything 'up there' [in their brains].

(ibid.)

The 'girl power' concept was a celebration of self-belief, independence and
female friendship, and whilst cynics muttered that it was an empty ideology
– sneering that its goals were only the right to shout 'girl power' a lot – it
nevertheless did seem to be empowering for young girls. Pop music expert
Sheila Whiteley notes that the Spice Girls were 'a challenge to the dominance of lad culture . . . they introduced the language of independence to a
willing audience of pre- and teenage girls' (2000: 215). Putting forward a
thesis similar to Acker's, Whiteley notes that although the discourses of
feminism were well-known in the 1990s, they were assigned a negative
image in tabloid newspapers and other popular media, and presented as
'heavy' and opposed to men and sex. She says the Spice Girls changed that:

The impact of the Spice Girls . . . was to provide a new twist to
the feminist discourse of power and subjectivity. By telling their
fans that feminism is necessary and fun, that it is part of every-
dayness, and that girls should challenge rather than accept traditional constraints – 'What you looking at boy? Can you handle a
Spice Girl?' – they sold the 1990s as 'a girl's world' and presented the 'future as female'.

(ibid.: 216–217)

Whilst it was easy for cynics to criticise the 'girl power' idea as a bunch of banal statements about 'believing in yourself' and 'doing whatever you want to do', it was still an encouraging confidence boost to young women and should not be dismissed too readily. At the time, TV programmes and magazine articles – as well as letters written to pop magazines and the anecdote everyone had about the super-confidence of their little sister or daughter – suggested that 'girl power' was more than a phenomenon imagined within the media and did indeed have an impact in the real world.

Other female stars and groups inherited this inspirational mantle, although without the clear hook of the Spice's 'girl power' slogan. Geri went on to be a slightly lesser star, and gay icon, in her own right. Interviewed by *Attitude* magazine in 2001, she was still saying life-affirming and liberal things like, 'I believe that anything is possible for anyone – shutting down possibilities is a waste of living', and, 'Last week I was entertaining the idea of becoming a lesbian' (Flynn, 2001). In the same month she told *Marie Claire*: 'I'm a tomboy who likes to dress as Barbie,' and 'I do get comments about how I look, but I have to try and let that go ... What matters is how I feel about myself' (Forrest, 2001).

In 2001, Destiny's Child were the most clearly defined 'girl power' icons, and conveyed the message in their actual *songs* more clearly than the Spice Girls ever did. And they were a massive international success: the album *Survivor* (2001) sold five million copies within five weeks. Previous album *The Writing's On the Wall* sold over nine million worldwide. Almost all of the songs on *Survivor* were both written and produced by key band member Beyoncé Knowles. An MTV documentary celebrated their ' "take no mess" attitude' and gushed that the group communicated a 'message of self-reliance and personal strength in the most *alluring* of packages'. It also noted that this was 'a new kind of act: fierce, foxy and frankly intelligent, proudly shouting out their self-sufficiency' (*All Eyes on Destiny's Child*, MTV, June 2001). Their big 1999 hit 'Bills, Bills, Bills' was a goodbye note to a boyfriend who didn't pay his way and was always borrowing money from the richer female protagonist. 'Independent Women Part 1' (2000) continued the emphasis on women having their own money and paying their own bills – financial independence – celebrating 'All the honeys makin' money', and asserting 'I depend on me'. In 'Independent Women Part 2' (2001) the women insist that they will never be controlled, and will offer no love or commitment.

These words are notable simply because they are so different to the typical loving or 'I want you' lyrics common in pop music. Destiny's Child have made 'I *don't* want you' lyrics unusually popular. And it goes down well with the audience. One fan comment posted at online store

Amazon.co.uk says that Beyoncé is 'truly inspirational' and notes that the group are 'promoting a more sophisticated "Girl Power" message that the Spice Girls failed to carry' (12 May 2001). Another user seems slightly more jaded: 'We've heard the "girl-power" lark time and time before, but Destiny's Child are acutely aware of its selling power and the appeal it has to the "Jerry Springer generation"' (30 May 2001). This comment contains two points – one, that the 'girl power' discourse is actually a commercial tool (and therefore, by implication, not actually very challenging) and two, that there is a generation brought up on shouty daytime TV shows for whom the idea of criticising and dumping inadequate partners is a source of *pleasure*.

In an online interview, Beyoncé said that the group's central message is 'for women to be independent, strong women, and for women to demand respect' (Yahoo! Chat Event, July 2000). A fan from Florida agrees, at Amazon.com, 'Survivor is a good CD for young women to listen to compared to some of the other artists out there' (11 May 2001). And another American fan comments:

> 'Independent Women' and 'Survivor' are unforgettable ... Beyoncé's writing is exceptional, she speaks to our generation – delivering messages in unique ways. The girl is tough. I hope she keeps going going going.
>
> (2 May 2001)

As with the Spice Girls, Destiny's Child use sex appeal to sell their music, and critics would assert that the promotion of a particular image of thin, attractive women is not a pro-feminist thing to be doing. On the other hand, of course, it could be argued that these are positive, attractive images of black women which might counteract the emphasis on beautiful *white* women in the mass media. We should also note that mainstream *male* pop stars are required to be thin and conventionally good-looking too.

MUSIC FOR BOYS

Away from the world of (possibly) empowering girl groups, pop stars are, of course, a mixed bunch. Male artists range from the machismo of many rap artists – including Eminem, DMX and the Wu Tang Clan – to the squeaky-clean, super-groomed image of boy bands such as *Nsync, Backstreet Boys and Westlife. The world of DJs and dance music is still very male dominated, although female DJs such as Lottie and Lisa Lashes have appeared on the scene. Leading rock bands – in particular the 'nu metal' school such as

Limp Bizkit and Linkin Park – remain male in terms of line-up and masculine in terms of attitude. The more gentle UK rock bands like Travis and Coldplay do, however, remind us that all-male groups can produce emotional and sensitive songs. (Which is not to say that a melancholic 'indie' song is *necessarily* better than an assertive rock anthem.)

There has also been a significant stream of effeminate or androgynous men in pop, from David Bowie, Marc Bolan and the New York Dolls in the 1970s, to several 1980s bands – Japan, Culture Club, Duran Duran, The Human League, The Cure and Depeche Mode for example – through to 1990s artists such as Placebo, Jarvis Cocker of Pulp, Richey Edwards in the early Manic Street Preachers and even Marilyn Manson. Modern boy bands such as *Nsync and 911 typically have a line-up of more-or-less effeminate 'lads' – an odd mix – who are eager to show their caring and sensitive sides in teen pop mags. This considerable number of male pop stars who are not conventionally macho, or who do not dress in a traditional masculine style and who wear make-up and discuss affairs of the heart in pop songs, must send out some kind of message to their adolescent fans. One place where such a message becomes more explicit is in the pages of pop magazines. One of my email interviewees (found via a message board on a music website) told me:

> I still remember reading an interview with Martin Gore from Depeche Mode in a mid-1980s *Smash Hits*, where he was asked about his effeminate clothing and make-up, and he said that he personally enjoyed expressing himself in that way, and had found that *women tended to prefer* a man who was in touch with his 'feminine' side too. I wasn't a Depeche Mode fan, but this made a big impression on me and encouraged me to disregard some of the masculine conventions of school life, and so actually in the long run helped me to be a better and more interesting person.
>
> (30-year-old male from Leicester, England)

A more recent example comes from UK *Top of the Pops* magazine's regular 'Pop Therapy' page from May 2001, headed 'People said I was effeminate'. Here, Darren Hayes from pop duo Savage Garden confessed that he was picked on at school:

> People made fun of me because . . . I could sing and I was interested in things and did things that weren't considered manly, tough or cool . . . I would sit and read, write poems and lyrics and try to sing as much as I could . . . People thought I was really effeminate cos in their eyes what I was doing was girls' stuff.

He explains that he 'stuck to it and never gave up', and rose above the taunts, although these experiences led to a later period of insecurity. Eventually the bullying stopped – 'I was who I was and they could see I was strong enough to know that.' Asked what advice he would give to someone going through a similar situation, he replies:

> My advice for anyone would be – and I know it sounds like a cliché – to be true to yourself and stick to your guns. Believe me, you *will* beat them!

The magazine adds its own advice in a helpful box:

> Be proud of who you are, you're one of a kind! No matter what you look like, sound like, how you dress or what you do, you are what you are and no one has the right to try to change that.

Messages of empowerment and self-belief such as this may be ignored, overlooked, or laughed at by some young readers, but nevertheless will convey a comforting or inspiring message to others.

A concrete example of the impact of male popular music icons comes in the personal account of another of my email interviewees, Jon, a 20-year-old male from Philadelphia, USA. At school Jon had been confused about his sexuality, as he was attracted to men, but no one else seemed to feel this way, or discuss such things. In his teens, he dated girls to 'fit in', but was profoundly troubled:

> It got very scary for me towards the end of 9th grade, I would cry so hard in the shower trying to figure out why I felt this way and why no one else did. I came very close to trying to kill myself because I just felt so different.
>
> Then in 10th grade [age 16] something amazing happened that would end up changing my life for ever, I bought my first David Bowie CD, *The Rise and Fall of Ziggy Stardust and the Spiders From Mars*. Let me just say it blew my mind away! I saw for the first time in my life a man who was a little bit like me! He had homoerotic lyrics all through that CD and I realized for the first time that I was not alone . . . After that I started to get into other artists who were open about their sexuality, Erasure, Pet Shop Boys, and Placebo. I listened to them religiously, and they gave me the strength to tell people that I was gay for the first time.

I was the only openly gay male at my school and that became very hard for me. But I just continued to sit in my room and listen to these openly gay men singing about love, sex and the hardships of growing up gay. I am not sure if bands like Erasure, Pet Shop Boys and Placebo know how much effect their music has on younger gay teenagers, but all I know is that through their music they saved my life, helped me figure out who I am, made me feel like I belonged somewhere, and gave me the strength and courage to be proud of who I am.

Today, Jon is at college, has a steady boyfriend and several gay friends and is very comfortable with his sexuality. Whilst this case may not be typical, it provides one illustration of the power of role models in popular culture, and the way in which they can sometimes provide support or inspiration which may not be available from family and friends in everyday life.

EMINEM: ROLE MODEL

'OK, I'm going to attempt to drown myself – You can try this at home – You can be just like me!' So begins white rapper Eminem's 1999 song 'Role model', an obviously sarcastic rant against those people who say he's not a good role model, when he never intended to be one. Explaining the song in his book *Angry Blonde*, he says: 'I wanted to be clear: Don't look at me like I'm a fucking role model' (2000: 48).

Nevertheless, that is how many people look at the highly successful star. Numerous journalists, politicians, parents and campaigners have denounced him for his total failure to be a 'good role model'. In February 2001, a member of the House of Lords in Britain called upon the Home Secretary to bar Eminem from entering the country as this 'icon of the drug culture' would be a bad influence upon children; and in July 2001, members of the House of Congress Telecommunications Subcommittee in the US were adamant that Eminem's lyrics were so dangerous to children that further steps should be taken to protect them and warn parents (Boliek, 2001). Hundreds of newspaper and magazine articles in 2000–2001 discussed whether Eminem was a 'bad role model', or a brilliant but misunderstood artist. The idea that he was playing a 'character', and/or mirroring the 'dark side' of American society, was not a satisfactory defence for those who felt that many young fans would take the misogynist and homophobic lyrics at face value.

BRITNEY SPEARS: ROLE MODEL?

Pop superstar Britney Spears shot to international fame in the late 1990s. By her twentieth birthday in December 2001, she had sold over 40 million albums (*Rolling Stone*, December 2001). *Money* magazine (April 2001) reported that Britney had album and concert sales in excess of 200 million US dollars within the year 2000 alone. Her early smash hit, 'Baby One More Time', raised eyebrows with its schoolgirl video and ambiguous lyrics (did 'Hit me baby one more time' refer to sex, violence, or neither?). Nevertheless, Britney became a 'girl power' icon of sorts, helped along by her assertive dancing, sometimes-independent lyrics and general success story. The second album, *Oops! I Did It Again* (2000), was less 'fluffy' than the first and contained several messages of self-reliance and inner strength, and not needing a man to be happy. Spring 2001 saw the publication of a novel, *A Mother's Gift*, written by Britney and her mother, Lynne Spears, telling the not entirely surprising story of a girl who has a close relationship with her mother and who wants to be a pop star. The book was much too 'sugary' for the critics, but was nevertheless lapped up by younger fans. Britney's creativity was seen to continue on the slightly more 'grown up' third album, *Britney* (2001), for which she had co-written several songs.

A poll by Mori for the BBC in January 2001, which asked a sample of the British public to name the person they found to be 'most inspirational', saw Britney come in seventh place. Although less inspirational than figures such as Nelson Mandela, Margaret Thatcher and Tony Blair, Britney scored higher than such well-known icons as Jesus and Mother Theresa (Ananova, 2001). On the other side of the world, thousands of viewers of MTV Asia voted Britney Spears as their 'biggest' female role model (MTVAsia.com, 5 February 2001).

Figure 10.1   Drawing of Britney Spears, posted on the Web by her fan, Carolina Repiso Toquero

The question of whether or not Britney is a good 'role model' has been played out in the media several times already. Her well-publicised vow of chastity before marriage has meant that politicians and health campaigners have found it useful to refer to Britney in their campaigns against teen pregnancy (although the star has been noticeably less emphatic about this in interviews since mid-2001). But some public moralists have still felt that Britney is too provocative in her clothing and dancing. In February 2001, Myrna Shure, a developmental psychologist and author of *Raising A Thinking Child*, was quoted in the press, asserting, 'She's corrupting our kids. It's not just teenagers we're talking about. Little girls are emulating Britney too. I believe she's an awful role model.' Organisations such as the American Family Association have warned parents that Britney may not be as 'wholesome' as she might seem. At the more extreme end of the scale, evangelical Christians on the 'Dial-the-Truth Ministries' website assert that Britney's music and performances are intended to provoke 'youthful lusts', and they even call her a 'whorish woman' (see Watkins, 2000) – not really a remark filled with Christian generosity. (The same group says that parents who do not stop their children from listening to the Spice Girls are 'co-conspirators in this cultural rape of their daughters' (Thomas, 2000)).

The judgements of young pop fans often seem to be quite moralistic anyway. In summer 2001, hundreds of young people posted replies on an Internet message board which asked, 'Putting your opinion on who is a better performer aside, who do you think is a better role model for young people, Britney Spears or Christina Aguilera?' (www.dotvsdot.com). The posted comments typically point to the virtues of whichever is the preferred star, and attack the other one for dressing or acting in a way which is seen as being too sexually provocative, sometimes even calling that star a 'slut' or a 'bitch'. A couple of representative comments:

> I don't see how anyone can see that skank Christina as a role model to young people! Britney talks about how she attends church as much as possible, and speaks out about her strong morals. Christina's latest music video consists of her touching herself, other people touching her, and vulgar lyrics. Ya, she's really a saint!
>
> ('Peach', at Dot vs Dot message board)

> To tell you the truth, I think that both of them are pretty good role models. I think that Christina might be a better one because she doesn't dress like Britney as much – but she does sometimes. If you think about it, there are little kids that look up to these

girls and if you look at the way they dress – then, well they have a good chance of growing up to dress like that. I think that both girls are very talented and they should be proud of it. But I just think that they should cover up a little more.

('Jessica', at Dot vs Dot message board)

Of course there is much sexism in the amount of criticism these women receive for supposedly 'sexual' dress or behaviour, whilst numerous male performers are just as provocative in their videos – or more so – but are not attacked in the same way.

Britney herself has struggled with the 'role model' image. In various interviews she has conceded that she is a role model to girls, and feels, in some ways, obliged to act accordingly. At the same time, she has defended her 'sexy' image, saying in June 2000: 'I don't understand [what the problem is]. I'm 18, I'm a girl, it's nice to feel sexy . . . I feel comfortable doing it and it's not like I walk around in hot pants' (Ananova, 2000). In December 2001 she told *Glamour* magazine, 'I don't see anything wrong with being sexy. I think that's a beautiful thing.' However, she told *US Weekly* magazine that she didn't want to be considered a role model in terms of sex and relationships, saying, 'I just want to live my life' (4 June 2001). Soon afterwards, though, *Arena* magazine asked Britney how she would like to be remembered, and she replied: 'As somebody who was a good role model to young people' (August 2001).

Such contradictions run through the whole Britney package, and no doubt add to her appeal – there's something for everyone. For the moralists, there's the church-going all-American girl who said she wouldn't sleep with her boyfriend; but for those unimpressed by such wholesomeness, there's the writhing sex kitten who refuses to be told to tone down her performances. For those who don't like manufactured pop mannequins, there is the control freak who exercises a growing amount of control over her image and music. For those worried about her conservatism, there's the independent-minded pop queen who says of her gay dancers, 'I love them – they're my best friends . . . I think it's very cool' (*Smash Hits*, 28 November 2001). This slippery identity means that some potentially offensive bit of the Spears persona is usually counteracted by another bit; and perhaps adds to the enticing sense of mystery – who *is* the real Britney? – which kept Madonna going for so long.

BRITNEY SPEARS: WHAT THE FANS SAID

In March, April and May 2001, I conducted several interviews, by email, with female Britney Spears fans from around the world. (I also did some follow-up interviews after the third album, *Britney*, was released in November 2001). I contacted these fans by writing directly to young women who had created their own Britney fan sites, or to those who had posted messages on message boards within Britney fan sites. Others contacted me after I posted notices saying that I wanted to ask 'a few questions' to Britney Spears fans, for my research, on those website message boards. I interviewed girls rather than boys, because of the (perhaps rather simplistic) notion that Britney would be a role model to girls specifically – because young women face slightly different expectations and judgements in society. Of course, Britney's songs of self-belief, and love, as well as her successful career, could well be inspirational to boys too. My small number of email exchanges with male Britney fans would suggest that this question would be more difficult to explore, however – the boys (stereotypically enough) indicated that Britney inspired feelings of *desire* rather than feelings of inner confidence. This is confirmed by the sharp difference between what males and females say about Britney on websites and Internet message boards: for every girl who finds Britney 'cool', there is a boy who finds her 'hot'.

My interviews with female fans showed a real depth of passion and commitment to their idol. (For the sake of clarity, I have added some punctuation and corrected some spellings in the quotations below, but

Figure 10.2   Just four of the many Britney Spears fan websites

otherwise the respondent's sentences remain unchanged.) To almost all of the fans, Britney was much more than a performer who made music and videos which they enjoyed. She was an icon, and, more particularly, an *inspiration* to these young women:

> I like Britney because of the way she thinks. [...] Really she is just comfortable with who she is and that is really cool. [...] Sometimes I pretend I am her just to boost up my confidence like as if I am acting, and this really helps me out when I meet new people. Like a mask in a way. Really if you pretend to be like Britney you can have more fun, but I like to be myself with more edge and 'coolness' if you get my drift. [...] I do believe that Britney sends out good messages to girls. She shows self esteem which makes girls believe that they can achieve anything, and she shows us that there is another Britney behind all the hair and makeup that is just average which shows us girls that we can be anything we want.
>
> (15-year-old female from Sydney, Australia)

> I think that Britney sends out the message for us girls to have self-confidence. I have a great amount of confidence in myself. [...] It's definitely a good thing to have self-confidence in what you do, wear, etc. If you don't have confidence in yourself how do you expect anyone else to. [...] With all these girl power songs coming out, saying how we don't need guys, I have so much confidence – it definitely helped me out. Like 'look at me now, you can't have me, too bad, you lost'.
>
> (17-year-old female from Mississippi, USA)

> [Britney] makes me feel confident inside, her words are just there saying, you know, I am who I am, like it – or leave, I don't need to depend on someone! [...] I know that there are a lot of people who say she is a bad influence, but I honestly feel as if she's a real girl ... who deserves to be treated like every other 19 year old girl. She sends out the most important message – 'Be happy with yourself, and love yourself'. My favorite quote I have ever heard from Brit is 'You can't love anyone until you learn to love yourself'.
>
> (16-year-old female from California, USA)

Britney gives me a message of accepting yourself, and not letting boys push you around. She also advocates 'Girl Power' for instance in one of her songs ['What You See (Is What You Get)'] she says, '[...] You should never try to change me, I can be nobody else and I like the way I am ... I can promise you baby what you see is what you get.' Here she is basically saying that [...] if a boy wants to change her than he better leave. That shows girls not to let their boyfriends boss them around. To be their own woman. Also in 'Stronger': 'I am stronger than yesterday, now it's nothing but my way, my loneliness ain't killing me no more ... I'm stronger.' Here her boyfriend just dumped her but she is stronger because of it. If a girl ever broke up with her boyfriend she could listen to these songs and get empowered.

Britney is such a good role model. [...] For her to advocate abstinence, and still have guys pining after her shows a lot about her. It shows you don't have to have sex to be sexy. I don't really know why I would want to copy Britney as a person. I mean wouldn't my mom seem like a better person, or Princess Diana, or Mother Theresa. There is just a spark that Britney shows that attracts everyone to her. Britney is the best thing to ever happen to me I think. I make it seem like my life is really horrible or something, which it isn't, I just wish that Brit was my older sister or something. That is how I look up to her. Like a younger sister looks up to an older sister.

She always makes me happy, and happiness is confidence. [...] Oh also in her book she explains about her troubles, how long it took her to get where she is, and all of her hardships. I realize that if I work hard I could be where I want to be and Britney helps me see that.

(15-year-old female from Pennsylvania, USA)

Several others also mentioned the songs 'Stronger' and 'What You See (Is What You Get)' – from the album *Oops! ... I Did It Again* (2000) – as particularly inspiring ones. ('Stronger' was also an international hit single in 2000–2001). These songs were brought up by young women from all over the world (specific song titles were not mentioned in the questions):

I think that 'What You See Is What You Get' is the song I can relate to the most. In the song she sings about how her boyfriend should like her for who she is, and not try to change her, or there will be consequences.

(15-year-old female from Texas, USA)

'What You See Is What You Get' – it's just great and it lets every girl out there know that it's good to let the guy know that you're not gonna change your whole life style for him. He should accept you, and that's nice to know [that Britney is] preaching that.

(14-year-old female from Florida, USA)

[The lyrics to 'Stronger' and 'What You See (Is What You Get)'] mean so much to me, because for so long in my life, I did everything I could to try and please everyone else, and it got me nowhere but heartache. But Britney came along, and she's shown me that I don't have to put up with shit!

(16-year-old female from California, USA)

['What You See (Is What You Get)'] is very important. It sums up Britney's personality. She always says how she's just herself and can't change her attitudes/habits for anyone else. I model myself after her quotes. I am very self conscious, and strive to like myself more, as most teenage girls do.

(16-year-old female from Massachusetts, USA)

'Stronger' ('Stronger than yesterday, now it's nothing but my way, my loneliness ain't killing me no more') shows that I need nobody to live my life and I will be OK if I am alone.

(11-year-old female from Athens, Greece)

Britney Spears is a role model to me for her honesty and kind-ness. Her song 'Stronger' makes me feel as if I am a girl in that position. I think a lot of people think that too.

(9-year-old female from Georgia, USA)

Britney is so cool. [...] If somebody is horrible to me then I always get quite upset, but I then made 'Stronger' my new theme tune. It plays inside my head every time somebody says something that hurts my feelings and at times like that.

(13-year-old female from Bristol, UK)

Following the release of 'Britney' the latter correspondent added:

Britney still inspires me. As she gets older I'm also getting older with her. So, I kind of grow up with her music. So, as her music gets more sophisticated I am also getting more sophisticated. I love the line 'Say hello to the girl that I am' in 'Overprotected'.

(as above)

Another fan found 'Oops' to be particularly meaningful:

Singing 'Oops! I Did It Again' makes me feel sexy and confident. In this song the girl is in charge of the relationship and the guy is just infatuated with her, but she's just playing with him – which is a relief from all those stupid rap songs where the girls are just there to please the guy. This song empowers me to be me and guys will soon follow! [Videos like the one for 'Oops' are] just good clean happy fun, and since all guys like Britney, it shows girls that they don't have to be a slut to get guys to like them.

(15-year-old female from New Jersey, USA)

Some fans were wary of calling Britney a 'role model' as such:

I'd prefer not to copy a 'role model', because every person must have their own taste.

(11-year-old female from Astana, Republic of Kazakhstan)

Does Britney help me feel more confident? Not really. I like being my self but if I didn't, a singer wouldn't help me.

(11-year-old female from Athens, Greece)

Britney shouldn't be looked at as a role model, she didn't ask to be looked up to, she simply had talent and made it shown. [...] Many parents say she is a bad role model for their children but that's their job, not hers. [...] I think she is a good influence because she grew up ordinary but she became something extraordinary. A normal girl, when she was my age she wasn't extremely popular, wasn't the smartest or most beautiful, but she was herself and she liked who she was, and is. It gives me the strength to think 'Wow, she was just a normal girl with an abnormal future.' It makes me think 'If she can be successful, so can I.'

(14-year-old female from Lansing, Michigan, USA)

I do not look to Britney Spears as a 'role model'. No celebrity should be considered a role model, in my opinion. Teachers,

parents, siblings, and coaches have accessible personalities and
should be the real role models.

(19-year-old female from Washington, DC, USA)

Nevertheless, this 19-year-old fan goes on to explain that Britney is certainly
a powerful *inspiration* to her:

> But I admire Britney very much. I admire her ambition, her
> positive attitude, and her relentless work ethic. I admire the way
> she does not take herself too seriously, and openly
> admits/makes mistakes. She feels real. [...] She does send out a
> good message to girls – be secure in yourself and your body, no
> matter what anyone says, you'll pull through if you exude confi-
> dence. Britney has worked very hard for what she wants and she
> got it all, and makes it clear to her fans that we can achieve what
> we dream of, too. So many girls, myself included, have no one
> to tell them that nowadays. [...] I would not say that Britney,
> or any celebrity, should be a role model, because when you take
> on a role model with a calculated image, there's going to be a
> conflict of identities; girls need to be themselves, not a celebrity,
> and Britney herself makes that clear. Britney makes my friends
> and myself feel confident because she is a girl our age who has so
> many great talents, yet is seemingly grounded. That makes us
> feel as though we can excel without giving in to so many pres-
> sures. She [...] has power and beauty, and that makes girls
> proud to be girls (smile).
>
> (19-year-old female from Washington DC, USA)

Similarly, some fans were sensibly cautious about the idea that a pop star
would turn you into a better person (an assumption perhaps contained in
questions of mine such as, 'Does Britney help you feel confident about
being yourself?'). The respondents were nevertheless still eager to assert
how inspiring Britney could be:

> Confidence really comes from within, I don't think that an artist
> like Britney can really make you be confident, [but] they help
> you. I believe Britney's music has helped me be more secure
> about myself and be less afraid of what guys think about me.
> Her songs are very inspiring to me. [...] I think Britney sends
> out a positive message to not just girls but guys as well. Her
> lyrics are never negative and she also tries to get girls to be who

they are. 'Just be yourself' as I've heard her say many times, which is true, and 'Never give up, cause you can do anything you want, you really can,' as she has said in Britney TV specials. [...] I enjoy 'What You See (Is What You Get)' – it's an inspiring song that basically tells girls to be themselves.

(16-year-old female from Saskatchewan, Canada)

After the release of 'Britney' this respondent added:

I still think Britney is very inspiring and even more so now that she's actually co-written some of the songs she sings in her new album. She's got a lot of talent.

(as above)

As mentioned above, Britney Spears has been the target of complaints from church leaders and parents, who have asserted that Britney is a bad role model because of her revealing clothing and (arguably) provocative dancing. Almost all of the fans were aware of these criticisms and brought up the issue (without being prompted by any direct questions on this matter). A few of them could see the argument against Britney's clothing:

I don't think Britney is a good role model. I like her music, it's just the way she dresses sometimes. I don't think it's good for young girls to see that, because they might think it's OK to dress like that.

(15-year old female from Texas, USA)

Just because she dresses sexy, doesn't mean she is a slut. I could see why people might think it is a wrong message. [...] I don't think there is anything wrong with girls wanting to look sexy. I do think there is something wrong with 6 year olds dressing like Britney, but the parents should be responsible for that. And the clothes companies that distribute those clothes should be held responsible.

(15-year-old female from Pennsylvania, USA)

Other fans, less surprisingly, defended Britney and admired her self-confidence:

I think Britney does send out good messages. She tells you to believe in yourself and that everything you want to do, if you try hard enough, you will get it. I think her sexy dressing can be a positive message if you look at it that way. By showing off skin she shows she is confident about herself and isn't scared to show everyone how she is.

(13-year-old female from New Jersey, USA)

Some detected sexism in the complaints about their idol:

Why is it okay for guys to get on TV and rap and sing while they grab themselves, [but] it's not alright for a girl to get on stage and do a dance while showing bare midriff, and shaking her stuff a little. I don't get it.

(17-year-old female from Mississippi, USA)

After all of this discussion of Britney Spears as a 'role model', it is also worth mentioning that fans would often say that Britney just makes them *happy*. To give just one example:

She has songs on her albums that are upbeat and fun to sing to and that I can relate to. I don't know why I first started to like her. I think it was when I saw a special on MTV about her. She was so positive about things, and had all the guys after her, and she seemed like a good person with good morals. Whenever I see a picture with her (they are all over my wall) or a commercial, or something with her in it, it makes me happy. [...] Whenever I have a rough day, or am tired, or sad, or just want to have fun I pop in my Britney albums and everything is ok.

(15-year-old female from Pennsylvania, USA)

This set of email interviews with Britney Spears fans around the world, then, shows that these young women were inspired, first and foremost, by Britney's self-confidence. The message that you should 'love yourself' and not worry too much what others think of you – as long as you are doing your best, being a teenager – seemed to have had quite an impact on these respondents. Britney's 'no sex before marriage' message was seen as important by some, irrelevant by others. Although the pro-marriage position is rather conservative, the message that girls should not have sex until they feel ready for it is one that would be seen as positive by many groups, including most feminists, educators, parents and politicians, as well as the more predictable church leaders.

Although some of her critics portray Britney as a rather doll-like male fantasy – and earlier singles such as the execrably-titled 'Born To Make You Happy' ('I don't know how to live without your love/I was born to make you happy') didn't exactly challenge this idea – Britney's fans see her as assertive, strong and confident, and an example that young women can make it on their own. The independent, self-assured message of songs like 'Stronger', 'What You See (Is What You Get)' and 'What It's Like To Be Me' seemed to be favoured over the more slushy lyrics of songs like 'From The Bottom Of My Broken Heart' and 'One Kiss From You', which were seen as less interesting and relevant, although the fans clearly enjoyed them too. Even the more recent single with the not-entirely-empowering title 'I'm a Slave 4 U' (2001) was not seen as subservient – fans knew that the song was meant to be *about music* and saw it as a celebration of Britney growing up, citing lyrics such as, 'All you people look at me like I'm a little girl, well did you ever think it'd be OK for me to step into this world?'. The fans were also very keen on 'Overprotected' (released as a single in 2002), which is another assertion of independence and self-reliance. (It might be said that the interviewees were perhaps reacting affirmatively to my questions about whether Britney was a good role model, and so produced more thoughts about Britney's positive influence than they otherwise might; nevertheless, it would seem unlikely – and rather patronising – to suggest that these girls and young women dreamt up their elaborate tributes to the power of Britney without really meaning them.)

Of course, although Britney Spears is hugely popular, the majority of young people are not big Britney fans. Indeed, some teenagers don't like her at all. On one 'Anti-Britney Spears' webpage, part of 'Felicia and Randeen's Music Site', these two American teenagers comment:

> Ugh! Britney Spears. [. . .] She's untalented, a bad role model, [. . .] and she dresses like a cheap hooker. [. . .] Britney is teaching young girls that in order to be popular, you need to show off as much skin as you can. For all those young girls who are reading this, that think Britney is their role model, well all I have to say is you need someone better to look up to. You need to idolize someone who actually does something good in this world. Sure you may think Britney is pretty and she gets all the guys to drool over her, but what does it get you in the end. Guys only look at you as a sex object. They don't care if you have a brain [. . .] You can ask almost any guy why they love Britney and they will all say the same thing. They like her because she's hot and she has a nice body. They will hardly ever say they like her because she sings good or they love her mind.

Is that what you young girls really want? To be thought of as nothing more then a body? If that's what you want then you can go on idolizing your precious Britney. But as for me, I want people to like me for how intelligent I am, not for how much skin I'm showing.

(Felicia and Randeen's Music Site, 2001)

Although different people will account for the Britney phenomenon in varying ways, then, it seems clear that to Britney's fans, she offers a message of empowerment, confidence and independence. This is not just an 'idea' but something which the fans seem to carry forward into their lives. Although critics are concerned with the amount of sultry pouting and skin display which Britney has employed to achieve success, she nevertheless 'works' as an icon who shows that young women can be provocative but remain in control, and can run relationships on their own terms, or simply exist as a happy independent being.

ROLE MODELS: SUMMARY

The idea of 'role models' remains a little vague, in academic terms, and psychologists don't seem to have found any very clever way of describing the process by which individuals may employ role models in their self-development. That's okay, though, as it leaves the way clear for a straightforward understanding of how role models might work: that as people grow up, and indeed advance into their twenties and later years, they look for inspiring or comforting figures who offer positive-looking examples of how life can be lived. These identities are not 'copied' in any big or direct sense, but they feed into our on-going calculations about how we see life and where we would like to fit into society. As we construct our narratives of the self – see Chapter 5 – we are able to appropriate (borrow) the positive bits of other people's attitudes or lives that we fancy for ourselves. This means that media stars can be seen as an inspiration for one aspect of their character but not for another – Britney Spears, for example, can be seen as an icon due to her apparent independence and success, whilst other aspects of her persona, such as her religious beliefs or provocative clothing, may be ignored. Because of this selectivity, it is perhaps unnecessary for authority figures to feel that 'role models' should be flawless.

SELF-HELP BOOKS AND THE PURSUIT OF A HAPPY IDENTITY

In Chapters 5 to 7, on the ideas of Giddens, Foucault and queer theory, we saw the emergence of an approach to personal identities which suggests that in modern societies, individuals feel relatively unconstrained by traditional views of their place in the world and carve out new roles for themselves instead. As a person grows and develops, they typically continue to work upon their sense of 'self' – their self-identity – and gradually modify their attitudes and self-expression to accommodate a mix of social expectations and also, importantly, *what they themselves are most comfortable with*. (It is during this thinking-through of self-identity that role models may be of significance.)

In the future, it is anticipated that this role freedom will become even greater. The media, as we've said before, gives us ideas about gender, and relationships, and ways of living. These ideas come over in TV, movies, magazines and pop music, all of which we have discussed. The most explicit carriers of advice about gender, lifestyle and relationships, though, are self-help books – also known as 'popular psychology' and in some cases 'recovery' texts – which we turn to now.

It may not be obvious why we'd be looking at self-help books here: they may be popular as non-fiction books go – even a 'publishing phenomenon' – but a lot of people don't read them. If they count as 'popular mass media' at all, they are on the margins. But there are two reasons for taking a look at self-help texts:

1   The ideas in self-help books 'trickle down' into popular culture. Note the rise of 'therapy speak' in movies as diverse as *The Mexican* and *HeartBreakers*, as well as obvious places like *Analyze This* and any Woody Allen film. When Bette Midler says in *What Women Want* that men are from Mars, we all know what she's talking about. In TV too, from the relationship-obsessed women in *Ally McBeal* to the trying-to-be-tough guys in *NYPD Blue* and obviously *The Sopranos*, the language of therapy and self-help can't be avoided. Women's magazines, in particular, both dissipate and assume a working knowledge of today's self-help clichés. And Elayne Rapping (1996) observes that there are numerous successful TV shows, in the mould of *Oprah* in the US and *Tricia* in the UK, which have a very strong relationship with self-help publishing, using self-help authors as star experts and directing viewers to their books for solutions.

2   As well as noting that ideas from self-help books go forth into everyday

culture, we can assume that the approach of the books – and the most successful ones in particular – is in itself a *reflection* of the changes in society and the needs of (some) readers. Giddens has described self-help books as 'a kind of on-the-ground literature of our reflexive engagement with our everyday lives' (Giddens and Pierson, 1998: 141), and whilst we should be cautious about reading them as accounts of a universal reality, these popular publications must tell us something about life today.

The books aimed specifically at either women or men are of additional interest because they describe aspirational but reasonably realistic (as opposed to utopian) models of how we might expect women and men to present themselves in today's society. Where academic texts on feminism or masculinities fail to actually assert how women and men should act in modern society, these books step in and spell it out – a role which they share, incidentally, with lifestyle magazines (see Chapters 8–9).

EXTENDED ANALYSIS AVAILABLE

This short discussion of self-help books is based on a much more substantial on-going analysis of these texts, which I will publish in the future. Meanwhile a much extended version of the present discussion of self-help books appears on this book's website at www.theoryhead.com (Gauntlett, 2002).

Personal narratives and lifestyles

As we saw in Chapter 5, Giddens (1991, 1992) argues that in modern societies, individuals have to construct a 'narrative of the self' – a personal biography and understanding of one's own identity. Self-help books typically incorporate the same kind of idea, and I would argue that they typically suggest one of three challenges to the readers' own narrative:

1   Many self-help books suggest ways in which readers can make their narrative of self more strong, coherent and resilient, so that they can acquire a greater sense of personal power, confidence and self-direction. These are books for people who lack self-belief and many of them are marketed at women.

2   Other self-help books are about *transforming* the self – rewriting the previous narrative, or ditching it altogether, in order to become a new,

strong, positive person. These are books for people who want to overcome character flaws which prevent them from feeling fulfilled, and
most of the titles for men fall into this category, as do many more for
women.

3   A different kind of self-help book encourages the reader to amend their
narrative of themselves and their view of others, so that the world 'as it
is' can be accepted more happily. This approach is less common, but
includes the super-successful *Men Are from Mars, Women Are from
Venus,* which (as we will see) argues that men and women can get along
really well as long as they accept that they are from totally different
planets.

As we saw in Chapter 6, Michel Foucault became interested in 'techniques
of the self' and 'the care of the self' – questions of lifestyle which today are
tackled by self-help books. In the introduction to *The History of Sexuality
Volume Two, The Use of Pleasure,* Foucault helpfully proposes a methodology for this kind of study:

> A history of the way individuals are urged to constitute them-
> selves as subjects of moral conduct would be concerned with the
> models proposed for setting up and developing relationships
> with   the   self,   for   self-reflection,   self-knowledge,   self-
> examination, for the decipherment of the self by oneself, for the
> transformations that one seeks to accomplish with oneself as
> object. This last is what might be called a history of 'ethics' and
> 'ascetics,' understood as a history of the forms of moral subjecti-
> vation and of the practices of the self that are meant to ensure it.
>
> (1992: 29)

Foucault, then, lends support to the idea that we can learn about our
culture by looking at its self-help books; he was interested in the ways in
which a society enabled or encouraged individuals to perceive or modify
their self-identity.

Solutions to every problem

Self-help books cannot easily be pigeon-holed or stereotyped with any accu-
racy. Literally thousands of new self-help titles are published every year
(Stine, 1997), and during the 1990s sales of self-help, popular psychology
and 'recovery' books grew to over 60 million per year in the USA (American Booksellers Association, 2001). The shelves of any major bookstore will

offer many titles on being confident, being positive, being successful and loving yourself. There are also numerous titles on relationships, covering issues such as how to find a partner, how to keep a partner, how to have better sex, how to communicate with your partner, how to escape your abusive partner, and how to begin a new life afterwards. There are subdivisions of each category – books on each of the above areas aimed at larger people, older people and black people, for example. Many self-help books are explicitly aimed at women, many others are not gender-specific and a smaller number are for men in particular. When asked about the relative numbers of women and men reading self-help books, some booksellers specialising in this genre indicated that a growing number of men were joining women in seeking advice from these texts on how to improve and transform their lives (see Gauntlett (2002), on website).

Self-help for men

My study of a number of recent self-help books for men (again, see Gauntlett (2002)) took in volumes such as *Understanding the Tin Man: Why So Many Men Avoid Intimacy* by William July II (2001), *Ordinary Heroes: A Future for Men* by Michael Hardiman (2000), *If Men Could Talk, This is What They Would Say* by Alon Gratch (2001), *Ten Stupid Things Men Do To Mess Up Their Lives* by Laura Schlessinger (1998) and *Success for Dummies* by Zig Ziglar (1998). Although they varied considerably in approach and style, it was found that these books shared the following messages:

- Men are not monolithic and unchangeable. Men can change for the better.
- Men are not good at intimacy, expressing their more vulnerable or loving feelings, connecting with others, or admitting pain or failure. They can and should improve in all of these respects.
- Men generally place too much emphasis on work and fail to develop a fulfilling personal and home life. But nobody on their deathbed regrets that they spent too little time at the office.
- You may be able to 'do what you like' in modern society, but you won't be happy without a mixture of love and responsibility.
- Men cultivate a tough outer appearance, distinguishing themselves from women, but inside they have a complex emotional life and needs that are remarkably similar to women's.

The books are generally built on the same assumptions that underlie theories of late modernity (or postmodernity, as some would call it), such as we saw in the work of Giddens: relationships have become more fluid; traditional ties have broken down; identities are flexible; and there are increasingly loose and 'free' choices of lifestyle and sexual activity available. The self-help authors do not want to be academic observers or theorists, though – their approach is, of course, much more proactive: they tell readers how they can lay a stable path through the quagmire of modern living, making firm (and usually very *responsible*) choices in order to gain happiness and fulfilment.

Self-help for women

My study of books aimed at women included *The Go-Girl Guide: Surviving your 20s with Savvy, Soul and Style* by Julia Bourland (2000), *Sisters of the Yam: Black Women and Self-Recovery*, an excursion into self-help territory by renowned black feminist and cultural critic bell hooks (1993) and Laura Schlessinger's *Ten Stupid Things Women Do To Mess Up Their Lives* (1995). (See Gauntlett (2002), on website, for a more detailed discussion). These diverse texts were all agreed on the following messages:

- Modern living can be difficult and stressful. The solutions include posit-ive thinking and a planned approach, in which you tackle problems in an assertive but not reckless way. Thinking about your needs, with the help of a self-help book, is a good idea.
- You should absolutely *do what you want to do*. Doing things in life just because others expect you to, or because of habit or tradition, is a very bad idea.
- Self-esteem is very important. You have to feel good about yourself.
- Don't make excuses. Take control of your life.

It can be noted that unlike the books for men, which focused on men's emotional tardiness, insecurity and screwed-up inner life, the successful books for women generally encourage readers to feel that they have no problems inside, as long as they can be confident; with self-assurance and a positive approach, they suggest, anything can be achieved.

More self-help for everyone

There are, of course, many self-help books which are not aimed at either sex in particular, because their advice about life-planning, relationships or over-coming problems is intended to benefit everybody. Here we'll briefly look at two rather different examples. (Again, longer discussions appear on this book's website).

Men Are From Mars, Women Are From Venus by John Gray (1993) is one of the best-known self-help books today, often referenced (whether in admiring or mocking tones) in movies, TV shows and magazines. It has sold 'more than seven million copies in the United States and millions more in 40 different languages around the world' (www.marsvenus.com). In fact the book has been turned into a publishing 'franchise', with the same basic ideas being reworked into many more books by the same author (including *Mars and Venus in the Bedroom, Mars and Venus in Love, Practical Miracles for Mars and Venus* and several others), plus cassettes, CDs, videos, computer software, courses, workshops, a syndicated newspaper column, a radio show, a TV show (www.marsvenustv.com), a musical stage play (!) and even a board game, all bearing the *Mars and Venus* brand.

Unlike most self-help books, which encourage readers to change their circumstances when they are not happy with them, *Men Are From Mars* is all about changing one's *perception* of reality so that it can be accepted more happily. 'When men and women are able to respect and accept their differences,' Gray explains, 'then love has a chance to blossom' (1993: 14). The book is built on the explicit assumption that women and men are 'completely different' (ibid.: 5), illustrated by the metaphor of the book's title, which suggests that the problem with (heterosexual) relationships today is that men and women have 'forgotten' that they originally came from different planets. This is, in short, a way of asserting that traditional sex stereotypes were right all along – men are rational and analytic, whilst women are emotional and talk a lot (ibid.: 36). Gray says that when women and men don't get along perfectly in today's world, it is because they have made the modern mistake of assuming that men and women are fundamentally similar, which leads to misunderstandings, tension and frustration. The solution lies in appreciating these 'natural' differences and taking the time to communicate more clearly based on these principles.

Although it is common to see the success of *Men Are From Mars* as a modern, liberal 'touchy-feely' phenomenon, then, this is quite inappropriate, as the book proposes a return to 1950s-style gender roles within relationships. The aim of *Men Are From Mars* is to foster relationships where a heterosexual couple are equally 'understanding' of each other – which sounds nice – but are not actually equals. The Mars–Venus programme may bring happiness and reconciliation to couples who were previously insufficiently sympathetic to each others' character traits – as many satisfied couples now apparently attest – but it remains problematic. If a Mars-Venus couple were to procreate, for example, they would seem to be destined to bring up children whose ridiculously outdated views of gender would cripple them in the modern world.

The main problem with *Men Are From Mars, Women Are From Venus*, though, is its failure to recommend real, root-and-branch change. Many of the men described in Gray's relationship anecdotes are emotionally retarded shells, unable to connect or communicate on any deep level. These cases could be read as a disturbing indictment of our culture which produces such men; but Gray's idea is that we should just accept it. He knows that change is difficult – and so he tells women to love and respect their male partners' strange behaviour. He tells men to change a little – by listening to their partners more, without responding with hurt or hostility – but it's not enough to break society's cycle of producing men and women who feel that they are from different planets (as the book's success shows). Whenever the book edges towards suggesting real change for its male or female users, it consistently shies away and seeks refuge in the idiotic mantra of its title. If a woman is frustrated that her man will not change, 'she is forgetting that men are from Mars!' (ibid.: 104), Gray writes gleefully, but not all readers (one hopes) will find this glib explanation to be entirely helpful.

An entirely different approach is proposed in *Life Strategies* by Phillip C. McGraw (2001) – 'Dr Phil' from TV's *Oprah*. This book is another hit, having sold over one million copies within two years of its first publication in 1999. Unlike Gray, McGraw does not think that one should learn to accommodate unhappy situations. If something isn't working, says Dr Phil, change it. The words 'Stop Making Excuses!' are plastered across the book's front cover. The back summarises the content well:

> Whether it's a bad relationship, a dead-end career, or a harmful habit, Dr McGraw helps you wake up and get out of your rut. It is never too late to take charge of, and be responsible for, your life.

McGraw asserts that you have to be your own 'life manager', and make the same assertive demands of yourself that you would make if you had been hired to 'manage' someone else (2001: 169, 226). McGraw asks his readers to consider whether they are doing what they *really* want in life, or if it is just the result of habit or compromise (ibid.: 14). You have to be 'accountable for your own life' (ibid.: 15), and accepting an unhappy deal is not recommended. McGraw suggests strategies and planning techniques to achieve this.

Readers who had posted their views of the book at Amazon.com seemed to appreciate the emphasis on personal accountability, the 'realism' and drive for solutions – as opposed to over-optimistic or victimisation perspectives – and the author's 'straight talking' approach. On the other hand, one reader suggested that the advice is all common sense and that Dr Phil fails to recognise that life is about the *journey*, not planning its conquest.

SELF-HELP: SUMMARY AND CONCLUSION

On the whole, the self-help literature proposes a quite consistent set of messages, centred around the acquisition of self-belief, self-esteem and the confidence to change things and seek a better life. All of them emphasise success in personal relationships above achievement at work, although several of them stress that *happiness* in one's work is important too.

With the exception of John Gray's compassionately worded but disturbingly stereotyped *Men Are From Mars* thesis, self-help books typically assert that personal change is *necessary* and *essential*. They are usually very clear on this point – indeed, the tough-talking Laura Schlessinger would say that the failure to pursue fundamental change is 'pathetic'.

To summarise the most common self-help messages:

- believe in yourself and you can achieve anything. Social 'barriers' can generally be disregarded if you have the will to overcome them.
- you can't let the world 'happen' to you; instead you must take control of your life.
- it may not be obvious what would make you happy in life, and what is available to you. These things have to be worked out; and then you can to strive to get them. ('You have to name it to claim it,' as McGraw says).
- women and men are fundamentally similar on the 'inside', although men may have learned to be overly insular, emotionally withdrawn and bad at communicating, whilst women may not be confident or recognise the full range of their capabilities. But in any case, both women and men can adopt new ways of thinking and behaving so that they can become fully-functioning, balanced, self-assured, emotionally intelligent people.
- change is always possible.

As I have noted already in this chapter, these approaches and ideas are very much in line with Anthony Giddens's view of modernity – a world of fluid relationships, where identities and personal connections have to be worked on and negotiated, and where we continually have to make choices about who we are, how we will present ourselves, and who we want to associate with. The book of tradition has been (more or less) ripped up, to be replaced with a bookstore bulging with new lifestyle manuals – some of which, like *Mars and Venus* and *The Surrendered Wife* (Doyle, 2000), offer a return to tradition for those who want it, whilst others, like *Life Strategies* and *Feel the Fear and Do It Anyway* (Jeffers, 1997) and thousands more, propose an assertive new approach where social forces are to be pummelled into submission by the independent, feisty individual.

Whilst commentators upon the self-help scene such as Elayne Rapping (1996) and Wendy Simonds (1996) are concerned that the desire for inner healing may have replaced the quest for bigger changes in society – which is a reasonable concern – I think the two are not mutually exclusive, but can go hand-in-hand. Rapping, to be fair, recognises that this might be a possibility, but she is further concerned about the tendency of self-help and the 'recovery' movement to lead people towards 'shelter from the storm of modern life', which she suggests is a weak ambition; 'staying dry, while important for survival, is not really our ultimate goal', she says (1996: 185), meaning of course that modern life is something to be encountered and challenged, not hidden away from. This would be a good point, but I have found that most of today's self-help bestsellers promote a forceful engagement with the world, not a retirement from it. They are very individualistic, of course – they are about finding empowerment, success and happiness for yourself, not your community or social group – but they promote values of compassion and emotional sensitivity too, so we can hope that those individuals who reach a happy, self-actualised state will then go on to spread their good fortune, and try to help others. (That may be optimistic, but not necessarily wrong.) Self-help books generally ignore social constraints – they do not tell readers that they will most likely not get on well in life because of sexism, racism, or other forms of discrimination and oppression – which makes them bad as social analyses; but they are not intended as sociological studies, they are meant to encourage and empower individuals to believe in themselves regardless of their social category or background, so the books cannot really be criticised on that basis.

EMOTIONAL LITERACY

I have considered self-help books here because they offer the most explicit expression of an outlook and approach which is becoming increasingly widespread in modern societies: the rise of emotion and communication skills; the drive for equality in all areas; and in particular the need for fulfilment and to be 'your own person', which is a goal at the heart of many movies, pop songs and magazines. This ethos has taken hold in the more austere corners of public life too: in the past, political leaders could be relatively aloof and unapproachable, as long as the people had faith in their abilities. Today, it is 'emotional intelligence' which is seen as the heart of impressive leadership. Tony Blair is said to have mastered it and so maintains an enviable popularity in modern politics where an ability to 'connect' with the people has become essential, and where the public fascination is with the 'emotions and ambitions' that drive government, not the policies themselves (Rawnsley, 2001). Furthermore, in January 2001 the British government launched the manifesto of Antidote, the 'Campaign for Emotional Literacy' (www.antidote.org.uk) which aims 'to create an emotionally literate culture, where the facility to handle the complexities of emotional life is as widespread as the capacity to read, write and do arithmetic'. So we can note that self-help, formerly a kind of popular resistance to 'establishment' norms of emotional conservatism, restraint and self-control (in British terms, the 'stiff upper lip'), is now being recommended by governments – hoping that self-help discourses will penetrate culture from the 'top down' – as well.

FEARLESS AND ASPIRATIONAL DISCOURSES

In this chapter we have looked at the 'girl power' slogans of the Spice Girls, the assertions of independence in hit singles from Britney Spears and Destiny's Child, the positive and negative aspects of male pop idols and the promotion of self-reliance and inner strength in popular self-help books. In each of these examples, as in the lifestyle magazines considered in the previous chapters, we see possible insecurities within modern self-identities being addressed through fearless, confident discourses, generally in a glamorous and aspirational form. In the final chapter I will seek to draw together the theories and the media examples to suggest some conclusions about the interaction between media, gender and identity today.

Chapter 11

CONCLUSIONS

A NUMBER OF themes have emerged in this book, which we will set out and briefly discuss in this final chapter. The themes are:

- fluidity of identities and the decline of tradition
- the knowing construction of identity
- generational differences
- role models
- masculinity in crisis?
- girl power
- popular feminism, women and men
- diversity of sexualities
- gender trouble
- media power versus audience power
- contradictory elements
- change.

FLUIDITY OF IDENTITIES AND THE DECLINE OF TRADITION

We have seen various ways in which popular ideas about the self in society have changed, so that identity is today seen as more fluid and transformable than ever before. Twenty or thirty years ago, analysis of popular media often told researchers that mainstream culture was a backwards-looking force, resistant to social change and trying to push people back into traditional categories. Today, it seems more appropriate to emphasise that, *within limits*, the mass media is a force for change. The traditional view of a woman as a housewife or low-status worker has been kick-boxed out of the picture by the feisty, successful 'girl power' icons. Meanwhile the masculine ideals of absolute toughness, stubborn self-reliance and emotional silence have been shaken by a new emphasis on men's emotions, need for advice and the problems of masculinity. Although gender categories have not been shattered, these alternative ideas and images have at least created space for a greater diversity of identities.

Modern media has little time or respect for tradition. The whole idea of traditions comes to seem quite strange. Why would we want to do the same as previous generations? What's so great about the past? Popular media fosters the desire to create *new* modes of life – within the context of capitalism. Whether one is happy with capitalism, or seeks its demise, it must surely be considered good if modern media is encouraging the overthrow of traditions which kept people within limiting compartments.

THE KNOWING CONSTRUCTION OF IDENTITY

Not only is there more *room* for a greater variety of identities to emerge; it is also the case that the construction of identity has become a *known requirement*. Modern Western societies do not leave individuals in any doubt that they need to make choices of identity and lifestyle – even if their preferred options are rather obvious and conventional ones, or are limited due to lack of financial (or cultural) resources. As the sociologist Ulrich Beck has noted, in late modern societies everyone wants to 'live their own life', but this is, at the same time, 'an experimental life' (2002: 26). Since the social world is no longer confident in its traditions, every approach to life, whether seemingly radical or conventional, is somewhat risky and needs to be worked upon – nurtured, considered and maintained, or amended. Because 'inherited recipes for living and role stereotypes fail to function' (ibid.), we have to make our own new patterns of being, and – although this is not one of Beck's emphases – it seems clear that the media plays an important role here. Magazines, bought on one level for a quick fix of glossy entertainment, promote self-confidence (even if they partly undermine it, for some readers, at the same time) and provide information about sex, relationships and lifestyles which can be put to a variety of uses. Television programmes, pop songs, adverts, movies and the Internet all also provide numerous kinds of 'guidance' – not necessarily in the obvious form of advice-giving, but in the myriad suggestions of ways of living which they imply. We lap up this material because the social construction of identity today is the *knowing* social construction of identity. Your life is your project – there is no escape. The media provides some of the tools which can be used in this work. Like many toolkits, however, it contains some good utensils and some useless ones; some that might give beauty to the project, and some that might spoil it. (People find different uses for different materials, too, so one person's 'bad' tool might be a gift to another.)

GENERATIONAL DIFFERENCES

There are some generational differences which tend to cut across these discussions. Surveys have found that people born in the first half of the twentieth century are less tolerant of homosexuality, and less sympathetic to unmarried couples living together, than their younger counterparts, for example (see Chapters 1 and 4). Traditional attitudes may be scarce amongst the under-30s, but still thrive in the hearts of some over-65s. We cannot help but notice, of course, that older people are also unlikely to be consumers of magazines like *Cosmopolitan*, *More* or *FHM* and are not a key audience for today's pop music sensations. In this book's discussions of popular media which appear to be eroding traditions, I have focused on generally young audiences with the implicit assumption that anti-traditional (or liberal, or post-traditional) attitudes established in the young will be carried into later life. This may not be so, however: maybe conservative attitudes, rather than literally 'dying out' with the older generations, tend to develop throughout the population as we get older. There is evidence that people's attitudes become somewhat less liberal as they get older, but at the same time the 'generation gap' in attitudes is closing (Smith, 2000). We can note that those people who were 25 in the 'swinging' times of the late 1960s are now entering their sixties themselves. Nevertheless, as I have argued throughout this book, the mass media has become more liberal and considerably more challenging to traditional standards since then, and this has been a *reflection* of changing attitudes, but also involves the media actively *disseminating* modern values. It therefore remains to be seen whether the post-traditional young women and men of today will grow up to be the narrow-minded traditionalists of the future.

ROLE MODELS

We have noted that the term 'role models' is bandied about in the public sphere with little regard for what the term might really mean, or how we might expect role models to have an impact on individuals. Nevertheless, in this book I have suggested that by thinking about their own identity, attitudes, behaviour and lifestyle in relation to those of media figures – some of whom may be potential 'role models', others just the opposite – individuals make decisions and judgements about their own way of living (and that of others). It is for this reason that the 'role model' remains an important concept, although it should not be taken to mean someone that a person wants to *copy*. Instead, role models serve as *navigation points* as individuals steer their own personal routes through life. (A person's general direction, we should note, however, is more likely to be shaped by parents, friends, teachers, colleagues and other people encountered in everyday life.)

MASCULINITY IN CRISIS?

We saw in Chapter 1 that contemporary masculinity is often said to be 'in crisis'; as women become increasingly assertive and successful, apparently triumphing in all roles, men are said to be anxious and confused about what their role is today. In the analysis of men's magazines (Chapter 8) we found a lot of signs that the magazines were about men finding a place for themselves in the modern world. These lifestyle publications were perpetually concerned with how to treat women, have a good relationship and live an enjoyable life. Rather than being a return to essentialism – i.e. the idea of a traditional 'real' man, as biology and destiny 'intended' – I argued that men's magazines have an almost obsessive relationship with the socially constructed nature of manhood. Gaps in a person's attempt to generate a masculine image are a source of humour in these magazines, because those breaches reveal what we all know – but some choose to hide – that masculinity is a socially constructed performance anyway. The continuous flow of lifestyle, health, relationship and sex advice, and the repetitive curiosity about what the featured females look for in a partner, point to a clear view that the performance of masculinity can and should be practised and perfected. This may not appear ideal – it sounds as if men's magazines are geared to turning out a stream of identical men. But the masculinity put forward by the biggest-seller, *FHM*, we saw to be fundamentally caring, generous and good-humoured, even though the sarcastic humour sometimes threatened to smother this. Individual quirks are tolerated, and in any case we saw from the reader responses that the audience disregards messages that seem inappropriate, irrelevant or offensive. Although the magazines reflected a concern for men to find an enjoyable approach to modern living, then, there was no sign of a 'crisis' in either the magazines or their readers. Rather than tearing their hair out, everybody seemed to be coping with this 'crisis' perfectly well.

The self-help books for men (discussed in Chapter 10) also refuted the idea that changing gender roles had thrown men into crisis. The problem for men was not seen as being their *new* role – or lack of one; instead, men's troubles stemmed from their exaggerated and pointless commitment to men's *old* role, the traditional role of provider and strong, emotionless rock. Where men had a problem, then, it was not so much because society had changed, but because they as individual men had failed to modernise and keep up. Happily, the books took the view that people can change, and that troubled men would be able to create a satisfying and more relaxed life for themselves if they put in a bit of effort.

It's not all a world of transformed masculinities, though. Images of the conventionally rugged, super-independent, extra-strong macho man still circulate in popular culture. As incitements for women to fulfil any role proliferate, conventional masculinity is increasingly exposed as tediously monolithic. In contrast with women's 'you can be anything' ethos, the identities promoted to men are relatively constrained. We noted evidence in Chapter 1 that, whilst young females are taking to the full spectrum of school subjects and jobs, their male counterparts still generally avoid subjects and work that they see as 'female'. These things are continually crumbling, though. It is worth remembering, as we noted in Chapter 4, that even that archetype of masculine strength and independence, James Bond, cannot be too hard and self-reliant in today's Bond movies without being criticised for it by another character.

GIRL POWER

One of the most obvious developments in recent pop culture has been the emergence of the icons and rhetoric of 'girl power', a phrase slapped into mainstream culture by the Spice Girls and subsequently incorporated into the language of government bodies as well as journalists, educationalists, culture critics and pop fans themselves. Magazines for young women are emphatic in their determination that women must do their own thing, be themselves and/or be as outrageously sassy and sexy as possible (see Chapter 9). Several recent movies have featured self-confident, tough, intelligent female lead characters (Chapter 4). Female pop stars sing about financial and emotional independence, inner strength and how they don't need a man; while the popular mantra of self-help books is that women can become just as powerful as these icons, if they cultivate their confidence and self-belief, and draw up a plan of self-development (Chapter 10).

This set of reasonably coherent messages from a range of sources – their clarity only disturbed by the idea that women can be extremely tough and independent whilst also maintaining perfect make-up and wearing impossible shoes – seems to have had some impact on the identities of young women (as the Britney Spears and Destiny's Child fans quoted in Chapter 10 would attest), as well as being very successful within pop culture as an image/lifestyle idea.

POPULAR FEMINISM, WOMEN AND MEN

The discourses of 'girl power' are today's most prominent expressions of what Angela McRobbie calls 'popular feminism' – the mainstream interpretation of feminism which is a strong element of modern pop culture even though it might not actually answer to the 'feminist' label. Popular feminism is like a radio-friendly remix of a multi-layered song, with the most exciting bits sampled and some of the denser stuff left out. As McRobbie notes:

> To [many] young women official feminism is something that belongs to their mothers' generation. They have to develop their own language for dealing with sexual inequality, and if they do this through a raunchy language of 'shagging, snogging and having a good time', then perhaps the role this plays is not unlike the sexually explicit manifestoes found in the early writing of figures like [feminist pioneers] Germaine Greer and Sheila Rowbotham. The key difference is that this language is now found in the mainstream of commercial culture – not out there in the margins of the 'political underground'.
>
> (1999: 126)

McRobbie further argues that 'This dynamic of generational antagonism has been overlooked by professional feminists, particularly those in the academy, with the result that the political effectivity of young women is more or less ignored' (ibid.). There is an interesting parallel here with the scholarship on men and masculinity – the texts on masculinity are largely focused on the difficulties of middle-aged or older men who find it hard to shake off traditional masculine archetypes. Perhaps predictably, these studies are apparently *written* by middle-aged or older men who also cannot help bringing in the older tropes of masculinity. Meanwhile there is a generation of younger men who have adapted to the modern world (in a range of ways), who have grown up with women as their equals and who do not feel threatened or emasculated by these social changes. These men and their cultures are largely ignored by the problem-centred discourse of masculinity studies. This is perhaps a relief, though, because they would almost certainly

Figure 11.1 The popularity of feisty female icons, such as the ultra-confident pop
star Pink – as reflected in these fan websites – suggests that
passionately assertive women have become a regular part of culture

fail to understand the playful, humorous discourse about gender that circulates in men's magazines. (These magazines are not wholly anti-sexist, and there is a legitimate concern that dim readers will take 'joke sexism' literally, of course, but the more significant observation should perhaps be that sexism has shifted from being the expression of a meaningful and serious ideology in former times, to being a resource for use in silly jokes today.) As we found in Chapter 8, the magazines are often centred on helping men to be considerate lovers, useful around the home, healthy, fashionable and funny – in particular, being able to laugh at themselves. To be obsessed about the bits which superficially look like 'a reinscription of masculinity' is to miss the point. Men's magazines are not perfect vehicles for the transformation of gender roles, by any means, but they play a more important, complex and broadly positive role than most critics suggest.

DIVERSITY OF SEXUALITIES

Lesbian, gay, bisexual and transgendered people are still under-represented in much of the mainstream media, but things are slowly changing. In particular, television is offering prime-time audiences the chance to 'get to know' nice lesbian and gay characters in soap operas, drama series and sit-coms (see Chapter 4). Tolerance of sexual diversity is slowly growing in society (Chapter 1), and by bringing into people's homes images of sexual identities which they might not be familiar with, the media can play a role in making the population more – or less – comfortable with these ways of living.

GENDER TROUBLE

In Chapter 7, we discussed Judith Butler's manifesto for 'gender trouble' – the idea that the existing notions of sex, gender and sexuality should be challenged by the 'subversive confusion and proliferation' of the categories which we use to understand them. The binary division of 'male' and 'female' identities should be shattered, Butler suggested, and replaced with multiple forms of identity – not a new range of restrictive categories, but an abundance of modes of self-expression. This joyful excess of liberated forms of identity would be a fundamental challenge to the traditional understandings of gender which we largely continue to hold onto today.

Butler, as we noted, did not make direct reference to the mass media, but it seems obvious that if there is to be a major proliferation of images in the public eye, then the media must play a central role. To date, there have only been a relatively small amount of media representations fitting the Butler bill. Some advertising – such as the sexually charged but androgynous imagery promoting the *CK One* fragrance 'for a man or a woman' – had reminded viewers of the similarity of genders, hinting that it wouldn't matter which of the attractive male or female models you chose to desire. Other ads (such as ones for *Impulse* deodorant and *Kronenbourg* lager) playfully teased heterosexual desires only to reveal that the lust object was more interested in their own sex, pointing audiences to the unpredictability of sexualities. In this book we have discussed further cases of films, TV shows and magazines which have also celebrated non-traditional visions of gender and sexuality. Nevertheless, there remains a great deal of scope for the mass media to be much more challenging in these areas.

MEDIA POWER VERSUS AUDIENCE POWER

In Chapter 2 we set out the background debate over whether the mass media has a powerful influence upon its audience, or if it is the audience of viewing and reading consumers who wield the most power, so we should return to that question here. During the discussions in this book we have found, unsurprisingly, that the power relationship between media and the audience involves 'a bit of both', or to be more precise, *a lot* of both. The media disseminates a huge number of messages about identity and acceptable forms of self-expression, gender, sexuality and lifestyle. At the same time, the public have their own even more robust set of diverse feelings on these issues. The media's suggestions may be seductive, but can never simply overpower contrary feelings in the audience. Fiske talked in terms of semiotic 'guerrilla warfare', with the audience metaphorically involved in 'smash and grab' raids on media meanings, but this imagery inaccurately sees change as a fast and noisy process. It seems more appropriate to speak of a slow but engaged dialogue between media and media consumers, or a rather plodding war of attrition against the forces of tradition and conservatism: the power of new ideas (which the media conveys) versus the ground-in power of the old ways of doing things (which other parts of the media still like to foster). Neither the media nor the audience are powerful in themselves, but both have powerful arguments.

CONTRADICTORY ELEMENTS

We cannot bring this discussion towards a close without noting the inescapable levels of *contradiction* within popular culture. Although we may occasionally find ourselves saying that 'the mass media suggests' a particular perspective or point of view, the truth is that not only is 'the mass media' wildly diverse, but that even quite specific parts of media culture put out a whole spectrum of messages which cannot be reconciled. It is impossible to say that women's magazines, for example, always carry a particular message, because the enormous range of titles target an equally diverse set of female audiences. Furthermore, even one magazine will contain an array of viewpoints. As we saw in Chapter 3 via the account of one *Cosmo* editor, magazine staff – like almost all media producers – are far more interested in generating 'surprise' than in maintaining coherence and consistency. Contradictions are an inevitable by-product of the drive for multiple points of excitement, so they rarely bother today's media makers, or indeed their audiences.

The contradictions are important, however, because the multiple messages contribute to the perception of an open realm of possibilities. In contrast with the past – or the modern popular view of the past – we no longer get singular, straightforward messages about ideal types of male and female identities (although certain groups of features are clearly promoted as more desirable than others). Instead, popular culture offers a range of stars, icons and characters from whom we can acceptably borrow bits and pieces of their public persona for use in our own. In addition, of course – and slightly contradictorily – individuals are encouraged to 'be yourself', and to be creative – within limits – about the presentation of self. This opens the possibilities for gender trouble, as discussed above. Today, nothing about identity is clear-cut, and the contradictory messages of popular culture make the 'ideal' model for the self even more indistinct – which is probably a good thing.

CHANGE

As we have noted numerous times, things change and are changing. Media formats and contents change all the time. Audiences change too, albeit more slowly. Views of gender and sexuality, masculinity and femininity, identity and selfhood, are all in slow but steady processes of change and transformation. Even our views of change itself, and the possibilities for personal change and 'growth', have altered over the years. Although we should be careful not to overestimate the extent or speed of transformations in society and the media, it is worth reasserting the obvious fact that things do change, because some authorities within the disciplines of media studies and gender studies tend to act as though things do not really change over periods of ten or twenty years – filling textbooks with mixed-together studies from the 1970s, 1980s and 1990s as if they were providing accounts of fixed phenomena. These things are not stationary. To discuss gender and media is to aim arguments at moving targets – which, again, is just as well.

FINALLY

In this book I have sought to argue, and demonstrate, that popular media has a significant but not entirely straightforward relationship with people's sense of gender and identity. Media messages are diverse, diffuse and contradictory. Rather than being zapped straight into people's brains, ideas about lifestyle and identity that appear in the media are *resources* which individuals use to think through their sense of self and modes of expression. In addition to this conscious (or not particularly conscious) use of media, a wealth of other messages may breeze through the awareness of individuals every day. Furthermore, people are changing, building new identities founded not on the certainties of the past, but organised around the new order of modern living, where the meanings of gender, sexuality and identity are increasingly open. Different aspects of popular media can aid or disturb these processes of contemporary reorientation. Some critics say that the media should offer traditional role models and reassuring certainties, but this view is unlikely to survive. Radical uncertainties and exciting contradictions are what contemporary media, like modern life, is all about.

REFERENCES

Note about website addresses (URLs): Because the specific URL for articles within media websites often change over time – as well as being long and difficult to type in – I have in many cases provided the main URL for each website, and the corresponding article can be found by searching at that site for the author or title given.

Acker, Kathy (1997) 'All girls together', *Guardian Weekend*, 3 May, 12–19.

Adorno, Theodor W. (1991) *The Culture Industry: Selected Essays on Mass Culture*, London: Routledge.

Althusser, Louis (1971) *Lenin and Philosophy and Other Essays*, London: New Left Books.

Altman, Dennis (2000) *Global Sex*, Chicago: University of Chicago Press.

American Booksellers Association (2001) 'Category share of consumer purchases of adult books: The U.S., Calendar 1991–1998', Report by ABA Research Department, http://www.bookweb.org/research/stats/387.html

Ananova (2000) 'It's good to feel sexy, says Britney', 28 June, http://www.ananova.com/entertainment/story/sm_8635.html

Ananova (2001) 'Thatcher is more popular than Jesus – poll', 14 January 2001, http://www.ananova.com/news/story/sm_172697.html

Apter, Terri (2000) 'Bland ambition', *Guardian*, 6 April, http://www.guardian.co.uk

Arbuthnot, L. and Seneca, G. (1982) 'Pretext and text in *Gentlemen Prefer Blondes*', reprinted in Erens, Patricia (ed.) (1991) *Issues in Feminist Film Criticism*, Bloomington: Indiana University Press.

Arlidge, John (2001) 'Straights and gays take to same lifestyle', the *Guardian*, 27 May, http://www.guardian.co.uk

Baehr, Helen and Dyer, Gillian (eds) (1987) *Boxed In: Women and Television*, London: Pandora.

Bailey, Susan McGee and Campbell, Patricia B. (2000) 'It shouldn't be girls vs. boys in getting a good education', *San Francisco Chronicle*, 13 January, http://www.sfgate.com

Bartlett, Nancy H., Vasey, Paul L. and Bukowski, William M. (2000) 'Is gender identity disorder in children a mental disorder?', *Sex Roles*, 43, 11–12, 753–785.

Bartsch, Robert A., Burnett, Teresa, Diller, Tommye R. and Rankin-Williams, Elizabeth (2000) 'Gender representation in television commercials: updating an update', *Sex Roles*, 43, 9–10, 735–743.

BBC Online (2000a) 'Blair to take "paternity holiday"', 8 April, http://www.bbc.co.uk/news

BBC Online (2000b) 'Football role models "alienate girls"', 27 September, http://www.bbc.co.uk/news

BBC Online (2000c) 'Models link to teenage anorexia', 30 May, http://www.bbc.co.uk/news.

BBC Online (2001a) 'Cambridge's "macho" culture', 30 January, http://www.bbc.co.uk/news

BBC Online (2001b) 'Poor body image plagues women', 9 May, http://www.bbc.co.uk/news.

Beck, Ulrich (2002) 'A life of one's own in a runaway world: individualization, globalization and politics', in Beck, Ulrich and Beck-Gernsheim, Elisabeth *Individualization*, London: Sage.

Beck, Ulrich and Beck-Gernsheim, Elisabeth (2002) *Individualization*, London: Sage.

Beezer, A., Grimshaw, J. and Barker, M. (1986) 'Methods for cultural studies students', in Punter, D. (ed.) *Introduction to Contemporary Cultural Studies*, London: Longman.

Bell, Vikki (ed.) (1999) *Performativity and Belonging*, London: Sage.

Benson, Susan (1997) 'The body, health, and eating disorders', in Woodward, Kathryn (ed.), *Identity and Difference*, London: Sage.

Berger, John (1972) *Ways of Seeing*, London: Penguin.

BMA Board of Science and Education (2000) *Eating Disorders, Body Image and the Media*, London: British Medical Association.

Boliek, Brooks (2001) 'Eminem irks House panel', *The Hollywood Reporter*, 22 July, http://www.hollywoodreporter.com

Borden, Richard J. (1975) 'Witnessed aggression: influence of an observer's sex and values on aggressive responding', *Journal of Personality and Social Psychology*, 31, 3, 567–573.

Bourland, Julia (2000) *The Go-Girl Guide: Surviving Your 20s With Savvy, Soul and Style*, Lincolnwood, Chicago: Contemporary Books.

Brannon, Linda (2001) *Gender: Psychological Perspectives – Third Edition*, Boston: Allyn and Bacon.

Bristow, Joseph (1997) 'Discursive desires' in *Sexuality*, London: Routledge.

Brooke, Jill (1997) 'Gay characters don't always cost TV ad dollars', *CNN.com*, 9 April, http://www.cnn.com/showbiz/9704/09/ellen/index.html

Brooks, Ann (1997) *Postfeminisms: Feminism, Cultural Theory and Cultural Forms*, London: Routledge.

Bryant, Christopher G. A. and Jary, David (eds) (2001) *The Contemporary Giddens: Social Theory in a Globalizing Age*, Basingstoke: Palgrave.

Buckingham, David (1993) *Children Talking Television: The Making of Television Literacy*, London: Falmer.

Buckingham, David (1996) *Moving Images: Understanding Children's Emotional Responses to Television*, Manchester: Manchester University Press.

Bunting, Madeleine (2001) 'Loadsasex and shopping: a woman's lot', 9 February, the *Guardian*, http://www.guardian.co.uk

Bureau of Labor Statistics (2001) all statistics available from website at http://www.bls.gov

Burr, Vivien (1998) *Gender and Social Psychology*, London: Routledge.

Butler, Judith (1990) *Gender Trouble: Feminism and the Subversion of Identity*, London: Routledge.

Butler, Judith (1999) 'Revisiting bodies and pleasures', in Bell, Vikki (ed.) *Performativity and Belonging*, London: Sage.

Carter, Hannah (1996) 'New man, old myth?' *20:20 Media Magazine*, winter, 14–15.

Carver, Charles S. and Scheier, Michael F. (2000) *Perspectives on Personality – 4th Edition*, Boston: Allyn and Bacon.

Cassidy, Sarah (2001) 'Gap between girls and boys widens in GCSE performance', the *Independent*, 28 July, http://www.independent.co.uk

Chauncey, George (1994) *Gay New York: Gender, Urban Culture, and the Making of the Gay Male World 1890–1940*, New York: Basic Books.

Clare, Anthony (2000) *On Men: Masculinity in Crisis*, London: Arrow.

Cohan, Steven and Hark, Ina Rae (eds) (1993) *Screening the Male: Exploring Masculinities in Hollywood Cinema*, London: Routledge.

Coleman, Robin R. Means, (ed.) (2002) *Say It Loud!: African–American Audiences, Media, and Identity*, London: Routledge.

Coltrane, Scott and Messineo, Melinda (2000) 'The perpetuation of subtle prejudice: race and gender imagery in 1990s television advertising', *Sex Roles*, 42, 5–6, 363–389.

Cortese, Anthony J. (1999) *Provocateur: Images of Women and Minorities in Advertising*, Lanham, Maryland: Rowman & Littlefield.

Crabtree, Shona (2000) 'They have a hungry audience', *The Eagle-Tribune*, 9 April, http://www.eagletribune.com/news/stories/20000409/LI_001.htm

Cronin, Anne M. (2000) 'Consumerism and "compulsory individuality": women, will and potential', in Ahmed, Sara, Kilby, Jane, Lury, Celia, McNeil, Maureen and Skeggs, Beverley (eds) *Transformations: Thinking Through Feminism*, London: Routledge.

Curran, James and Park, Myung-Jin (eds) (1999) *De-Westernizing Media Studies*, London: Routledge.

Currie, Dawn H. (1999) *Girl Talk: Adolescent Magazines and their Readers*, Toronto: University of Toronto Press.

Davies, Bob (2001) 'Seven things I wish pro-gay people would admit', national association for research and therapy of homosexuality website, http://www.narth.com/docs/7things.html.

Davis, D. M. (1990) 'Portrayals of women in prime-time network television: some demographic characteristics', *Sex Roles*, 23, 5–6, 325–332.

Davis, Kathy (1995) *Reshaping the Female Body: The Dilemma of Cosmetic Surgery*, London: Routledge.

De Certeau, Michel (1984) *The Practice of Everyday Life*, Berkeley: University of California Press.

Deveaux, Monique (1994) 'Feminism and empowerment: a critical reading of Foucault', *Feminist Studies*, 20, 2, 223–247.

DeWolf, Rose (1997) 'ABC, others don't see advertisers fleeing from a lesbian-themed Ellen', 6 March, *Philadelphia Daily News*, http://www3.newstimes.com/archive97/mar0697/tvc.htm

Dittmar, Helga, Lloyd, Barbara, Dugan, Shaun, Halliwell, Emma, Jacobs, Neil and Cramer, Helen (2000) 'The "body beautiful": English adolescents' images of ideal bodies', *Sex Roles*, 42, 9–10, 887–915.

Douglas, Susan J. (1995) *Where the Girls Are: Growing Up Female with the Mass Media*, London: Penguin.

Doyle, Laura (2000) *The Surrendered Wife: A Practical Guide to Finding Intimacy, Passion, and Peace with a Man*, New York: Simon and Schuster.

Dyer, Gillian (1987) 'Introduction', in Baehr, Helen and Dyer, Gillian, (eds), *Boxed In: Women and Television*, London: Pandora.

Easton Ellis, Bret (1991) *American Psycho*, London: Picador.

Edwards, Tim (1997) *Men in the Mirror: Men's Fashion, Masculinity and Consumer Society*, London: Cassell.

Edwards, Tim (1998) 'Queer fears: against the cultural turn', *Sexualities*, 1, 4, 471–484.

Elasmar, Michael; Hasegawa, Kazumi and Brain, Mary (1999) 'The portrayal of women in US prime time television', *Journal of Broadcasting and Electronic Media*, 44, 1, 20–34.

Elliot, Gregory (ed.) (1994) *Althusser: A Critical Reader*, Oxford: Blackwell.

Emap (2001) Press release: 'Sale of Emap USA', 2 July, http://www.emap.com

Eminem (2000) *Angry Blonde*, New York: HarperCollins.

EU Commission (2001) *Annual Report on Equal Opportunities for Women and Men in the European Union 2000*, Brussels: Commission of the European Communities.

Faith, Karlene (1997) *Madonna: Bawdy and Soul*, Toronto: University of Toronto Press.

Faludi, Susan (1991) *Backlash: The Undeclared War Against Women*, London: Vintage.

Faludi, Susan (1999) *Stiffed: The Betrayal of the Modern Man*, London: Chatto & Windus.

Farrell, Warren (2001) *The Myth of Male Power*, New York: Penguin.

Felicia and Randeen's Music Site (2001) http://www.gurlpages.com/musicmania1

Ferguson, Robert (1998) *Representing 'Race': Ideology and the Media*, London: Arnold.

Ferree, Myra Marx, Lorber, Judith and Hess, Beth B. (eds) (1999) *Revisioning Gender*, London: Sage.

Fiske, John (1989a) *Understanding Popular Culture*, London: Unwin Hyman.

Fiske, John (1989b) *Reading the Popular*, London: Unwin Hyman.

Fiske, John (1989c) 'Moments of television: neither the text nor the audience', in Seiter, Ellen, *et al.* (eds) *Remote Control: Television, Audiences and Cultural Power*, London: Routledge.

Flynn, Paul (2001) 'Geri: a glove story', *Attitude*, April, 36–48.

Forrest, Emma (2001) 'Sugar & spice', *Marie Claire*, May, 38–44.

Foucault, Michel (1980) *Power/Knowledge: Selected Interviews and Other Writings 1972–1977*, Colin Gordon (ed.), New York: Pantheon.

Foucault, Michel (1990) *The Care of the Self: The History of Sexuality Volume Three*, translated by Robert Hurley, London: Penguin.

Foucault, Michel (1992) *The Use of Pleasure: The History of Sexuality Volume Two*, translated by Robert Hurley, London: Penguin.

Foucault, Michel (1996) *Foucault Live: Collected Interviews, 1961–1984*, edited by Sylvère Lotringer (eds), New York: Semiotext(e).

Foucault, Michel (1998) *The Will To Knowledge: The History of Sexuality, Volume One*, translated by Robert Hurley, London: Penguin.

Foucault, Michel (2000) *Essential Works of Foucault 1954–1984: Ethics*, Paul Rabinow (ed.), London: Penguin.

Fraker, Pamela (2001) 'The hypocrisy of so-called women's magazines', *Voices: The Women's College Magazine at Santa Monica College*, 2, 1, Spring, http://www.smc.edu/voices/volume2_1/politics/Women's%20Magazines.htm

Frank, Lisa and Smith, Paul (eds) (1993) *Madonnarama: Essays on Sex and Popular Culture*, Pittsburgh, Pennsylvania: Cleis Press.

Frazer, Elizabeth (1987) 'Teenage girls reading *Jackie*', *Media, Culture and Society*, 9, 407–425.

Friedan, Betty (1963) *The Feminine Mystique*, Penguin: London.

Garfinkel, Harold (1984) *Studies in Ethnomethodology*, Cambridge: Polity.

Garratt, Sheryl (1997) 'Funny, useful and selling', the *Guardian: Media Guardian*, 17 February, 6.

Gateward, Frances K. and Pomerance, Murray (eds) (2002) *Sugar, Spice, and Everything Nice: Cinemas of Girlhood*, Detroit: Wayne State University Press.

Gauntlett, David (1995) *Moving Experiences: Understanding Television's Influences and Effects*, London: John Libbey.

Gauntlett, David (1997) *Video Critical: Children, the Environment and Media Power*, Luton: John Libbey Media.

Gauntlett, David (1998) 'Ten things wrong with the "effects model"', in Dickinson, Roger, Harindranath, Ramaswani and Linné, Olga (eds) *Approaches to Audiences – A Reader*, London: Arnold.

Gauntlett, David (2000) *Web.Studies: Rewiring Media Studies for the Digital Age*, London: Arnold.

Gauntlett, David (2001) 'The worrying influence of "media effects" studies', in Barker, Martin and Petley, Julian (eds) *Ill Effects: The Media/Violence Debate – Second Edition*, Routledge: London.

Gauntlett, David (2002) 'Self-help books and the pursuit of a happy identity', considerably extended version of the material given here, available at www.theoryhead.com.

Gauntlett, David and Hill, Annette (1999) *TV Living: Television, Culture and Everyday Life*, London: Routledge.

Giddens, Anthony (1991) *Modernity and Self-Identity: Self and Society in the Late Modern Age*, Cambridge: Polity.

Giddens, Anthony (1992) *The Transformation of Intimacy*, Cambridge: Polity.

Giddens, Anthony (1998) *The Third Way: The Renewal of Social Democracy*, Cambridge: Polity.

Giddens, Anthony (1999) *Runaway World: How Globalisation is Reshaping Our Lives*, London: Profile Books.

Giddens, Anthony (2000) *The Third Way and its Critics*, Cambridge: Polity.

Giddens, Anthony and Pierson, Christopher (1998) *Conversations with Anthony Giddens: Making Sense of Modernity*, Cambridge: Polity.

Glenn, Gary (2001) 'Compassionate society should discourage deadly homosexual behavior', American Family Association website, http://www.afa.net/homosexual_agenda/ha031901.asp

Goffman, Erving (1959) *The Presentation of Self in Everyday Life*, London: Penguin.

Gratch, Alon (2001) *If Men Could Talk, This Is What They Would Say*, London: Arrow.

Gray, Ann (1992) *Video Playtime: The Gendering of a Leisure Technology*, London: Routledge.

Gray, Herman (1995) *Watching Race: Television and the Struggle for 'Blackness'*, Minnesota: University of Minnesota Press.

Gray, John (1993) *Men Are From Mars: Women Are From Venus*, London: Thorsons.

Greer, Germaine (1999) *The Whole Woman*, London: Doubleday.

Grogan, Sarah (1999) *Body Image: Understanding Body Dissatisfaction in Men, Women and Children*, London: Routledge.

Gunter, Barrie (1995) *Television and Gender Representation*, London: John Libbey.

Gutting, Gary (1994) 'Michel Foucault: a user's manual', in Gutting, Gary (ed.) *A Cambridge Companion to Foucault*, Cambridge: Cambridge University Press.

Hacking, Ian (1986) 'Self-improvement', in Couzens Hoy, David (ed.) *Foucault: A Critical Reader*, Oxford: Blackwell.

Hagell, Ann and Newburn, Tim (1994) *Young Offenders and the Media: Viewing Habits and Preferences*, London: Policy Studies Institute.

Hall, Stuart (1973) 'Encoding/decoding', reprinted in Hall, Stuart, Hobson, Dorothy, Lowe, Andrew and Willis, Paul (eds) (1980) *Culture, Media, Language*, London: Hutchinson.

Hall, Stuart (1983) 'The great moving Right show', in Stuart Hall and Martin Jacques (eds) *The Politics of Thatcherism*, London: Lawrence and Wishart.

Hall, Stuart (1988) *The Hard Road to Renewal*, London: Verso.

Hall, Stuart (1997) 'Cultural identity and diaspora', in Woodward, Kathryn (ed.) *Identity and Difference*, London: Sage.

Halliwell, Geri (1999) *If Only*, London: Bantam.

Halperin, David M. (1994) *Saint Foucault: Towards a Gay Hagiography*, New York: Oxford University Press.

Halpern, Sue (1999) 'Susan Faludi: the Mother Jones interview', *Mother Jones*, September/October, http://www.motherjones.com/mother_jones/SO99/faludi.html

Handy, Bruce (1999) 'Bosom buddies: today's men's magazines all share a common interest. Can you tell?', *Time* magazine, 153, 615, February.

Hardiman, Michael (2000) *Ordinary Heroes: A Future for Men*, Dublin: Newleaf.

Harding, Jennifer (1998) *Sex Acts: Practices of Femininity and Masculinity*, London: Sage.

Harris Interactive (2000) 'New Harris Interactive/Witeck-Combs Internet survey shows that 3 out of 4 gays and lesbians and 2 out of 5 heterosexuals are less likely to buy products advertised on shows with negative portrayals of gays and lesbians', Harris Interactive archive, 22 June, http://www.harrisinteractive.com/news

Harrold, Fiona (2000) *Be Your Own Life Coach*, London: Hodder and Stoughton.

Hart, Kylo-Patrick R. (2000) 'Representing gay men on American television', *The Journal of Men's Studies*, 9, 1, 59–79.

Helmore, Edward (2001) 'The Observer profile: Julia Roberts', 25 March, The *Observer*, http://www.guardian.co.uk

Hermes, Joke (1995) *Reading Women's Magazines: An Analysis of Everyday Media Use*, Cambridge: Polity.

Hill, Annette (1997) *Shocking Entertainment: Viewer Response to Violent Movies*, Luton: John Libbey Media.

Hodgson, Jessica (2001a), '*Loaded*'s acting editor resigns', the *Guardian*, 23 January, http://www.guardian.co.uk

Hodgson, Jessica (2001b), 'Meet the man who wants to turn *Loaded* into a woman-friendly read', the *Guardian*, 29 January, http://www.guardian.co.uk

Hodgson, Jessica (2001c), 'New editor's vision angers *Loaded* staff', the *Guardian*, 3 April, http://www.guardian.co.uk

Hollows, Joanne, Hutchings, Peter and Jancovich, Mark (eds) (2000) *The Film Studies Reader*, London: Arnold.

hooks, bell (1982) *Ain't I A Woman: Black Women and Feminism*, London: Pluto.

hooks, bell (1992) *Black Looks: Race and Representation*, Boston: South End Press.

hooks, bell (1993) *Sisters of the Yam: Black Women and Self-Recovery*, Boston: South End Press.

hooks, bell (1996) *Reel to Real: Race, Sex, and Class at the Movies*, London: Routledge.

hooks, bell (2000) *Feminist Theory: From Margin to Center – Second Edition*, London: Pluto.

Horkheimer, Max and Adorno, Theodor W. (1979) *Dialectic of Enlightenment*, London: Verso.

Huffman, Karen, Vernoy, Mark and Vernoy, Judy (2000) *Psychology in Action – 5th Edition*, New York: Wiley.

Humm, Maggie (1997) *Feminism and Film*, Edinburgh: Edinburgh University Press.

Jackson, Peter, Brooks, Kate and Stevenson, Nick (1999) 'Making sense of men's lifestyle magazines', *Environment and Planning D: Society and Space*, 17, 353–368.

Jackson, Peter, Stevenson, Nick and Brooks, Kate (2001) *Making Sense of Men's Lifestyle Magazines*, Cambridge: Polity.

Jackson, Stevi (1996) 'Ignorance is Bliss, when you're Just Seventeen', *Trouble and Strife*, 33.

Jeffers, Susan (1997) *Feel the Fear and Do It Anyway*, London: Rider.

Jeffords, Susan (1993) 'Can masculinity be terminated?', in Cohan, Steven, and Hark, Ina Rae (eds) *Screening the Male: Exploring Masculinities in Hollywood Cinema*, London: Routledge.

Jones, Liz (2001a) 'Why it's all over for Nova', the *Observer*, 6 May, http://www.guardian.co.uk

Jones, Liz (2001b) 'I expose the guilty fashion editors who drive young women to starve themselves', the *Mail on Sunday*, 15 April, 32–33.

July, William II (2001) *Understanding the Tin Man: Why So Many Men Avoid Intimacy*, New York: Broadway Books.

Kane, Pat (2000) 'Dispatches from the genderquake zone', the *Independent*, 14 August, http://www.independent.co.uk

Kaplan, E. Ann (1983) *Women and Film: Both Sides of the Camera*, London: Methuen.

Kaplan, E. Ann (1992) Review of *Gender Trouble, Signs*, 17, 4, 843–848.

Kaplan, E. Ann (1993) 'Madonna politics: perversion, repression, or subversion? Or masks and/as master-y', in Schwichtenberg, Cathy (ed.) *The Madonna Connection: Representational Politics, Subcultural Identities, and Cultural Theory*, Boulder, Colorado: Westview Press.

Kaspersen, Lars Bo (2000) *Anthony Giddens: An Introduction to a Social Theorist*, Oxford: Blackwell.

Kendall, Gavin and Wickham, Gary (1999) *Using Foucault's Methods*, London: Sage.

Kenny, Michael, and Stevenson, Nick (2000) 'Masculinity: a risky path to take?', in Rutherford, Jonathan (ed.) *The Art of Life: On Living, Love and Death*, London: Lawrence and Wishart.

Kirkham, Pat and Thumim, Janet (eds) (1993) *You Tarzan: Masculinity, Movies and Men*, London: Lawrence & Wishart.

Kirkham, Pat and Thumim, Janet (eds) (1995) *Me Jane: Masculinity, Movies and Women*, London: Lawrence & Wishart.

Kohlberg, L. (1966) 'A cognitive-developmental analysis of children's sex-role concepts and attitudes', in Maccoby, E. E., ed., *The Development of Sex Differences*, Stanford, California: Stanford University Press.

Krum, Sharon (2001) 'Stars in their eyes', the *Guardian*, 26 April, http://www.guardian.co.uk

Lauzen, Martha M. and Dozier, David M. (1999) 'Making a difference in prime time: women on screen and behind the scenes in the 1995–1996 television season', *Journal of Broadcasting and Electronic Media*, vol. 43, no. 1, pp. 1–19.

Lehman, Peter, (ed.) (2001) *Masculinity: Bodies, Movies, Culture*, London: Routledge.

Lentricchia, Frank (1982) 'Reading Foucault (punishment, labor, resistance)', *Raritan* 2.1, pp. 41–70.

Lloyd, Fran (ed.) (1993) *Deconstructing Madonna*, London: Batsford.

Macdonald, Myra (1995) *Representing Women: Myths of Femininity in the Popular Media*, London: Arnold.

McGraw, Phillip C. (2001) *Life Strategies: Doing What Works, Doing What Matters*, London: Vermilion.

McKee, Robert (1999) *Story*, London: Methuen.

McNair, Brian (2002) *Striptease Culture: Sex, Media, and the Democratisation of Desire*, London: Routledge.

McNeil, J. (1975) 'Feminism, femininity and the television shows: a content analysis', *Journal of Broadcasting*, 19, 259–269.

McRobbie, Angela (1999) *In the Culture Society: Art, Fashion and Popular Music*, London: Routledge.

Maio, Kathi (1991) *Popcorn and Sexual Politics*, Santa Cruz, California: Crossing Press.

Malik, Sarita (2002) *Representing Black Britain: Black and Asian Images on Television*, London: Sage.

Malim, Tony, and Birch, Ann (1998) *Introductory Psychology*, London: Macmillan.

Martin, C. L. (1991) The role of cognition in understanding gender effects, *Advances in Child Development and Behaviour*, 23, 113–149.

Martin, Rux (1988) 'Truth, power, self: an interview with Michel Foucault, October 25, 1982', in Martin, Luther H., Gutman, Huck and Hutton, Patrick H. (eds), *Technologies of the Self: A Seminar with Michel Foucault*, Amherst: University of Massachusetts Press.

Matlin, Margaret W. (2000) *The Psychology of Women – Fourth Edition*, Fort Worth: Harcourt College.

Meštrović, Stjepan G. (1998) *Anthony Giddens: The Last Modernist*, London: Routledge.

Miles, B. (1975) *Channelling Children: Sex Stereotyping as Primetime TV*, Princeton: Women on Words and Images.

Millar, Stuart (2000) 'Britons get "stress and spend" blues', the *Guardian*, 25 February.

Miller, John L. (2000) 'Gender Identity Disorder', http://www.athealth.com/Consumer/disorders/GenderIden.html

Miller, Stephen H. (2000) 'Just folks', *Independent Gay Forum*, 15 December, http://www.indegayforum.org/articles/miller32.html

MiM (1999) 'MiM campaign to shield children from prurient magazine covers at supermarket checkout counters', Morality in Media (New York), http://www.moralityinmedia.org/badcosmo2.html

MiM (2000) 'Supermarkets can refuse to allow their checkouts to be used for the open display of "pornographic or indecent talk"; "common decency requires nothing less"', Morality in Media (New York) Press Release, 9 October, http://www.moralityinmedia.org/storelet10.html

Moorhead, Joanna (2001) 'At 42, is Barbie past it?', the *Guardian*, 8 May, http://www.guardian.co.uk

MORI (2001) 'Poll shows prejudice rife as Stonewall launches new project to combat discrimination', MORI Polls and Surveys Archive, 19 June, http://www.mori.com/polls

Morley, David and Chen, Kuan-Hsing (eds) (1996) *Stuart Hall: Critical Dialogues in Cultural Studies*, London: Routledge.

Mulvey, Laura (1975) 'Visual pleasure and narrative cinema', *Screen*, 16, 3, 6–18.

Muncer, Steven, Campbell, Anne, Jervis, Victoria and Lewis, Rachel (2001) ' "Ladettes," Social Representations, and Aggression', *Sex Roles*, 44, 1–2, 33–44.

Murray, Jenni (2002) 'Cosmo's Curse', *Daily Mail*, 7 February, 56.

National Centre for Social Research (2000) 'British Social Attitudes: Focusing on diversity – the 17th report: 2000–01 edition', NCSR Press Release, 28 November, http://www.natcen.ac.uk

National Statistics (2001) *Population Trends: Spring 2001*, London: The Stationery Office.

Nauta, Margaret M. and Kokaly, Michelle L. (2001) 'Assessing role model influences on students' academic and vocational decisions', *Journal of Career Assessment*, 9, 1, 81–99.

Newport, Frank (2001) 'American attitudes toward homosexuality continue to become more tolerant', Gallup website, 4 June, http://www.gallup.com/poll/releases/pr010604.asp

Nixon, Sean (1996) *Hard Looks: Masculinities, Spectatorship and Contemporary Consumption*, London: UCL.

Nussbaum, Martha (1999) 'The Professor of Parody', *The New Republic*, 22 February. Accessed at *The New Republic Online*: http://www.tnr.com/archive/0299/022299/nussbaum022299.html

NW (2001) 'Sara-Marie rocks', *NW*, 9 July, 14–15.

O'Brien, Martin, Penna, Sue and Hay, Colin (eds) (1999) *Theorising Modernity: Reflexivity, Environment and Identity in Giddens' Social Theory*, Harlow: Addison Wesley Longman.

Orbach, Susie (1993) *Hunger Strike: The Anorectic's Struggle as a Metaphor for our Age*, London: Penguin.

Osborne, Peter and Segal, Lynne (1994) 'Gender as performance: an interview with Judith Butler', *Radical Philosophy* 67 (summer).

Palmer, Patricia (1986) *The Lively Audience: A Study of Children Around the TV Set*, Sydney: Allen and Unwin.

Pennington, Donald C., Gillen, Kate and Hill, Pam (1999) *Social Psychology*, London: Arnold.

Phares, E. Jerry and Chaplin, William F. (1998) *Introduction to Personality: Fourth Edition*, New York: Longman.

Phillips, Angela (1998) 'Which of these would you prefer your kids to follow?', the *Guardian: Saturday Review*, 14 November, 3.

Phillips, Angela (1999) 'Immaculate misconceptions', the *Guardian*, 14 December, http://www.guardian.co.uk

Phillips, E. Barbara (1978) 'Magazines' heroines: is *ms.* just another member of the family circle?', in Tuchman, Gaye, Kaplan Daniels, Arlene, and Benét, James (eds) *Hearth and Home: Images of Women in the Mass Media*, New York: Oxford University Press.

Posener, Jill (1982) *Spray it Loud*, London: Routledge & Kegan Paul (see also www.jillposener.com).

Queen, Carol and Schimel, Lawrence (eds) (1997) *PoMoSexuals: Challenging Assumptions about Gender and Sexuality*, San Francisco: Cleis Press.

Rapping, Elayne (1996) *The Culture of Recovery: Making Sense of the Self-Help Movement in Women's Lives*, Boston: Beacon Press.

Rawnsley, Andrew (2001) *Servants of the People: The Inside Story of New Labour*, London: Penguin.

Rekers, George A., (ed.) (1995) *Handbook of Child and Adolescent Sexual Problems*, New York: Lexington Books.

Richardson, Diane (2000) *Rethinking Sexuality*, London: Sage.

Rosen, Marjorie (1973) *Popcorn Venus*, New York: Avon Books.

Ross, Karen (1995) *Black and White Media*, Cambridge: Polity.

Said, Edward W. (1983) *The World, the Text, and the Critic*, Cambridge, Massachusetts: Harvard University Press.

Sarup, Madan (1996) 'Foucault: sex and the technologies of the self', in *Identity, Culture and the Postmodern World*, Edinburgh: Edinburgh University Press.

Scheibe, C. (1979) 'Sex roles in TV commercials', in *Journal of Advertising Research*, 19, 23–28.

Schirato, Tony, and Yell, Susan (1999) 'the "new" men's magazines and the performance of masculinity', *Media International Australia*, 92, August, 81–90.

Schlesinger, Philip, Dobash, R. Emerson, Dobash, Russell P., and Weaver, C. Kay (1992) *Women Viewing Violence*, London: British Film Institute Publishing.

Schlessinger, Laura (1995) *Ten Stupid Things Women Do To Mess Up Their Lives*, New York: Harper Perennial.

Schlessinger, Laura (1998) *Ten Stupid Things Men Do To Mess Up Their Lives*, New York: Harper Perennial.

Schwichtenberg, Cathy (ed.) (1993) *The Madonna Connection: Representational Politics, Subcultural Identities, and Cultural Theory*, Boulder, Colorado: Westview Press.

Segal, Lynne (1997) 'Sexualities', in Woodward, Kathryn (ed.) *Identity and Difference*, London: Sage.

Simonds, Wendy (1996) 'All consuming selves: self-help literature and women's identities', in Grodin, Debra and Lindlof, Thomas R. (eds) *Constructing the Self in a Mediated World*, London: Sage.

Skeggs, Beverley (1997) *Formations of Class and Gender: Becoming Respectable*, London: Sage.

Smith, Sharon (1972) 'The image of women in film: some suggestions for future research', *Women and Film*, 1, 13–21.

Smith, Tom W. (1999) 'Marriage wanes as American families enter new century', National Opinion Research Center at the University of Chicago, 24 November, http://www-news.uchicago.edu/releases/99/991124.family.shtml

Smith, Tom W. (2000) *Changes in the Generation Gap, 1972–1998*, GSS Social Change Report No. 43, Chicago: National Opinion Research Center, University of Chicago.

Social Trends (2001) *Social Trends*, London: Office for National Statistics (available free from http://www.statistics.gov.uk).

Soutar, Mike (2000) 'Hello boys!', The *Guardian*, 1 May, http://www.guardian.co.uk

Southwell, Tim (1998) *Getting Away With It: The Inside Story of Loaded*, London: Ebury.

Spicer, Andrew (2001) *Typical Men: The Representation of Masculinity in Popular British Culture*, London: I. B. Tauris.

Sragow, Michael (1998) 'This tomboy's life', *Dallas Observer*, 18 June, www. dallasobserver.com

Stacey, Jackie (1987) 'Desperately seeking difference', reprinted in Kaplan, E. Ann (ed.) (2000) *Feminism and Film*, Oxford: Oxford University Press.

Stald, Gitte, and Tufte, Thomas (eds) (2001) *Global Encounters: Media and Cultural Transformation*, Luton: University of Luton Press.

Starr, Alexandra (1999) 'You've got a long way to go, baby: women's magazines continue to create – and exploit – women's anxiety', *Washington Monthly*, 31, 10, http://www.washingtonmonthly.com

Stevenson, Nick, Jackson, Peter and Brooks, Kate (2000) 'The politics of "new" men's lifestyle magazines', *European Journal of Cultural Studies*, 3, 3, 369–388.

Stine, Jean Marie (1997) *Writing Successful Self-Help and How-To Books*, London: John Wiley and Sons.

Strinati, Dominic (1995) *An Introduction to Theories of Popular Culture*, London: Routledge.

Sullivan, Andrew (2000) 'Dumb and dumber', *The New Republic*, 15 June, http://www.thenewrepublic.com/062600/trb062600.html

Summerskill, Ben (2001) 'Shopping can make you depressed', the *Observer*, 6 May.

Tasker, Yvonne (1998) *Working Girls: Gender and Sexuality in Popular Cinema*, London: Routledge.

Thomas, Cal (2000) 'For the Spice Girls, there's nothing sugar or nice', Dial-the-Truth Ministries website, http://www.av1611.org/othpubls/spicegls.html

Tuchman, Gaye (1978) 'Introduction: the symbolic annihilation of women by the mass media', in Tuchman, Gaye, Kaplan Daniels, Arlene and Benét, James (eds) *Hearth and Home: Images of Women in the Mass Media*, New York: Oxford University Press.

Tucker, Kenneth H. Jr (1998) *Anthony Giddens and Modern Social Theory*, London: Sage.

UN (2000) *The World's Women: Trends and Statistics*, New York: United Nations Statistics Division. (Summary available at www.un.org/Depts/unsd)

Van Zoonen, Liesbet (1994) *Feminist Media Studies*, London: Sage.

Varley, Nick (1999) 'Away the lads', the *Guardian*, 12 April, http://www. guardian.co.uk

Verhovek, Sam Howe (1997) 'Homosexual foster parent sets off a debate in Texas', *The New York Times*, 30 November, http://www.nytimes.com

Vernon, Polly (1999) 'Girls at our best', 27 October, The *Guardian*, http://www. guardian.co.uk

Vogler, Christopher (1999) *The Writer's Journey: Second Revised Edition*, London: Pan.

Walter, Natasha (1998) *The New Feminism*, London: Little, Brown.

Watkins (2000) 'The dirty little secret about rock's teen idols: what are The Backstreet Boys, N'Sync and Britney Spears really saying?', Dial-the-Truth Ministries website, http://www.av1611.org/othpubls/teenidol.html

Whelehan, Imelda (2000) *OverLoaded: Popular Culture and the Future of Feminism*, London: Women's Press.

Whiteley, Sheila (2000) *Women and Popular Music: Sexuality, Identity and Subjectivity*, London: Routledge.

Wilke, Michael (2000) 'Advertisers battle Dr Laura', 29 May, *The Commercial Closet*, http://www.commercialcloset.org

Wilke, Michael (2001) 'CBS show heightens gay TV presence', 4 March, *The Commercial Closet*, http://www.commercialcloset.org

Williams, J. E. and Best, D. L. (1977) 'Sex stereotypes and trait favorability on the Adjective Check List', *Educational and Psychological Measurement*, 37, 101–110.

Williams, J. E. and Best, D. L. (1990) *Measuring Sex Stereotypes: A Multination Study (Revised Edition)*, Newbury Park, California: Sage.

Williams, Zoe (2002) 'Just Fancy . . .' (interview with Kim Cattrall), the *Guardian Weekend*, 5 January, pp. 14–19.

Wilson, Katherine (2001) 'GIDreform.org: challenging psychiatric stereotypes of gender diversity', http://www.gidreform.org

Winship, Janice (1987) *Inside Women's Magazines*, London: Pandora.

Woods, Tim (1999) *Beginning Postmodernism*, Manchester: Manchester University Press.

Woodward, Will (2000) 'Gender stereotypes still hamper young', the *Guardian*, 20 September, http://www.guardian.co.uk

WriteNews (2000) 'EMAP USA launches *FHM*', 15 February, http://writenews.com/2000/021500_fhmusa.htm

Ziglar, Zig (1998) *Success for Dummies*, Foster City, California: IDG Books.

INDEX

Acker, Kathy 217–218
action movies: representations of gender 38–40, 45–49, 64–69, 72–75
active audience 16–17, 23–26, 111, 196–198, 254–255; *see also* reflexive project of the self
Adorno, Theodor W. 19–25, 28, 41
advertising and gender roles 54–56, 75–81
Alien 46
Aliens 40, 46, 49
All My Children (TV series) 85
Allen, Woody 46
Ally McBeal (TV series) 59–60
Althusser, Louis 27
Altman, Dennis 18
American Beauty 74
American Psycho 103, 105–106
Arbuthnot, L. 40
Arena magazine 155, 165, 178, 226
autonomy *see* personal autonomy
axes of identity 13–14, 136–139

B magazine 185
backlash against feminism 48–49, 152–153, 159, 173–175, 180
Baehr, Helen 44
Barrymore, Drew 66–69
Bartlett, Nancy H. 36
Bartsch, Robert A. 76
Baudrillard, Jean 80

beauty 77–79; *see also* body image
Beck, Ulrich 114, 248–249
Beck-Gernsheim, Elisabeth 114
Bedelia, Bonnie 38
Beezer, Anne 182
Being John Malkovich 74
Bell, Vikki 151
Benson, Susan 195
Berger, John 38, 202
Beverley Hills 90210 (TV series) 85
Big Brother (TV series) 83
Billy Elliot 74
biography of the self *see* reflexive project of the self
biological determinism: definition 16
Birch, Ann 34, 215
bisexuality 13, 82, 84–85, 89, 128, 189, 207, 253; *see also* sexuality
Blair, Tony 6, 92–93, 214, 225, 246
body and identity (in Giddens) 104–106; *see also* Foucault, queer theory
body image 9, 77–81, 104–105, 178–179, 191, 194–195
Bond, James: movie series adapting to changing ideas about gender 49
Borden, Richard J. 31
Bourland, Julia 241
Bowie, David 222
boy bands 220–222
Boyz magazine 208, 210

Brannon, Linda 215
Bridget Jones's Diary 74
Bristow, Joseph 133, 151
Britney *see* Spears, Britney
Broken Arrow 40
Brooks, Ann 143
Brooks, Kate 159, 166–176
Brookside (TV series) 83
Bryant, Christopher G. A. 114
Buckingham, David 30, 32
Buffy the Vampire Slayer (TV series) 61, 84
Bunting, Madeleine 60–61
Burr, Vivien 216
But I'm a Cheerleader 86
Butler, Judith 134–151, 254; *see also* queer
    theory

Cambridge University: macho culture 5
Cameron, James 110
capitalism 17, 20–25, 52–56, 77, 96–97,
    101–102, 248
career choices 5
Carver, Charles S. 33
change: changing field of study 256;
    Foucault on personal change 115–116
Charlie's Angels (2000 movie version)
    66–69, 216
Chauncey, George 128
Chen, Kuan-Hsing 27
Christianity 87–90, 122, 126–127, 225
cinema and gender 38–40, 45–49, 64–75,
    86–90
Claire wearing 'girls are fab' slogan 11
Clare, Anthony 6–8
Cocker, Jarvis 221
cognitive-developmental theory 34–35
cohabitation 3
Cohan, Steven 17, 45
Coleman, Robin R. Means 14
Coltrane, Scott 76
Company magazine 54, 185, 188, 191
conformity 20–23
constraints, versus personal autonomy: *see*
    personal autonomy
construction of identity *see* reflexive project
    of the self; gender roles
consumerism and identity 9, 20–26, 95,
    101–102, 129, 179, 198; *see also* men's
    magazines, women's magazines
contradictions in media messages 53, 56,
    157, 169, 191–192, 205, 226, 255–256

Coronation Street (TV series), transsexual
    storyline 85–86
Cortese, Anthony J. 80–81
CosmoGirl magazine 187, 193
Cosmopolitan magazine 11, 51–54, 56,
    181, 184–205, 249
criticisms of this book addressed 16–18
Cronin, Anne M. 129
Crouching Tiger, Hidden Dragon 73
Crowe, Russell 39
culture industry, the *see* Adorno
Curran, James 18
Currie, Dawn H. 183

Dark Angel (TV series) 84
Davis, D. M. 43
Davis, Kathy 195
Dawson's Creek (TV series) 82, 85
Dead Calm 48
democratisation of emotions and
    relationships 3, 92, 96–108
Depeche Mode 221
Destiny's Child 219–220
Deveaux, Monique 143
Die Hard series 38
discourses: explained 16, 116; of sexuality
    120–132
Disney as target of homophobic
    campaigners 89–90
Dittmar, Helga 79
divorce *see* marriage and divorce
Doctor Who 26
Douglas, Susan J. 54
Doyle, Laura 245
Durkheim, Emile 92–93
Dyer, Gillian 44
Dynasty (TV series) 82–83

EastEnders (TV series) 83–84
Easton Ellis, Bret 103, 105–106
Edwards, Tim 146–151, 155
effects: study of female violence 69; ten
    things wrong with the media effects
    model 28–33; *see also* media influences
effeminate men in pop 220–222
Elasmar, Michael 43, 58, 59
Elle magazine 185–204
Ellen (TV series) 82, 90
Elliot, Gregory 27
email interviews *see* methodology
Emin, Tracey 215

Eminem 21, 215, 220, 223
Emmerdale (TV series) 83
emotional literacy 245–246
emotions: significance in Giddens's theory 112–113; *see also* intimate relationships
encoding/decoding model 23, 26
Enterprise (TV series) 64
Equal Opportunities Commission 5
Erin Brockovich 74
Esquire magazine 155, 161–165
ethnicity and 'race' 13–14, 63, 136, 149, 194, 203, 213, 214, 220, 245

Faith, Karlene 143
Faludi, Susan 6–9, 48–49
Farrell, Warren 3
Fatal Attraction 48–49, 65
female gaze *see* gaze
femininity 9–12; and Britney Spears 224–236; girl power 216–220; *see also* gender roles, representations of gender
feminism 3–10, 36–45, 52–56, 67–69, 76–78, 91, 117, 120, 136–151, 152–180, 181–193, 201, 206–207, 214, 216–220, 234, 238, 241, 247, 252–253
Ferguson, Robert 14
Ferree, Myra Marx 151
FHM magazine 152–180, 188, 249, 250; *FHM Bionic* spin-off 105, 158, 167
Fight Club 74
film and gender 38–40, 45–49, 64–75, 86–90
Final Destination 73
Final Fantasy: The Spirits Within 72
Fiske, John 19, 23–25, 28, 41, 255
fluid identities 247–248; *see also* Foucault; queer theory
Flynn, Paul 219
Forrest, Emma 219
Foucault, Michel 115–133, 239; on discourses 116; earlier vs later work 116; on emergence of 'homosexuality' 121–122; further reading 133; on gay lifestyles 131–132; Giddens on 101, 105–107; on life as a work of art 130–131; on lifestyles and ethics 124–132, 239; on magazines 132; model of power 117–122; Paris walking tour 117; on personal change 115–116; productive nature of power 121–122;

resistance to power 120–122; on sex and identity 122–128; technologies of the self 125–129
Fraker, Pamela 191
Frank, Lisa 10, 143
Frankfurt School *see* Adorno
Frazer, Elizabeth 182
Freud, Sigmund 36, 101, 122
Friedan, Betty 50–54
Friends (TV series) 59
Front magazine 156, 164, 168, 173–175
Full Monty, The 74

Garfinkel, Harold 94
Garratt, Sheryl 157
Gateward, Frances K. 17
Gauntlett, David: reference to analysis of self-help books 238–241; references to other works 28–32, 65, 111
gay and lesbian characters: on TV 82–86; in movies, 86–87
gay identities *see* sexuality
gay lifestyles (Foucault) 131–132
gay magazines 208–210
gaze 38–39
gender identity 'disorder' 36
gender roles 3–13, 33–40, 94–95, 134–143; *see also* Britney Spears; girl power; housewife role; men's magazines; representations of gender; women's magazines
gender trouble *see* Butler, Judith
gender: theories of psychologists 33–40
generational differences 249
Gibson, Mel 69–72, 75, 109
Giddens, Anthony 91–114; on the body and identity 104–106; on consumerism and identity 101–102; criticised by Meštrović 111–113; on democratisation of emotions and relationships 3, 92; further reading 114; on institutional reflexivity 106–108; and intimate relationships 97–98, 100, 106–108, 112–113; key themes listed 92; and 'late modernity' 92, 95–98; on lifestyles 102–104, 131–133; and post-traditional society 96, 103; and postmodernity 16, 95–96; on presentation of self 104–106; on reflexive project of the self 99–101, 109–111; on reproduction of gender roles 94–95; on self-help books and the

Giddens, Anthony *continued*.
　ideal self 108, 237–238, 241, 244; and
　self-identity 96–114; on sexuality and
　the self 101; structuration theory 92,
　93–94; and the 'third way' 92–93.
girl power 5, 10–11, 66–69, 72, 193, 203,
　211, 216–220, 224–236, 246, 248,
　251–253
Gladiator 39, 72
Glamour magazine 51, 54, 184–185, 189,
　192–193, 201–202, 226
glossary of terms 16
Goffman, Erving 104–106
Goldeneye 49
Gone in Sixty Seconds 73
GQ magazine 155, 161–165, 178
graffiti added to billboard adverts 56
Grange Hill (TV series) 84
Gratch, Alon 240
Gray, Ann 32
Gray, Herman 14
Gray, John 242–244
Greek ethics 126, 130
Greer, Germaine 77–78, 253
Grogan, Sarah 194–195
Gunter, Barrie 43, 55
Gutting, Gary 133

Hacking, Ian 124
Hagell, Ann 30
Hall, Stuart 23, 26–27, 41
Halliwell, Geri 212, 216–219
Halperin, David M. 119, 133
Handy, Bruce 162
Hannibal 74
Hardiman, Michael 240
Harding, Jennifer 151
Hark, Ina Rae 17, 45
Harrold, Fiona 192
Hart, Kylo-Patrick R. 85
Hayes, Darren 221–222
Heathers 48
Hermes, Joke 154, 167, 182–183
Hess, Beth B. 151
heterosexual matrix 137–139
High Art 87
Hill, Annette 28, 32, 111
Hitchcock, Alfred 38, 46
Hodgson, Jessica 160
Hollow Man 74
Hollows, Joanne 36

homophobia 87–90
homosexuality *see* gay and lesbian
　characters; magazines for lesbians and
　gay men; sexuality
hooks, bell 5, 14, 136, 241
Horkheimer, Max 20–23
horror films, 73–74
housewife role 4, 43, 46, 50–58, 75, 213,
　248
Huffman, Karen 33
Humm, Maggie 45, 64

identity: passim, but *see* axes of identity;
　femininity; masculinity; reflexive project
　of the self; self-identity
impression management 104–106
Indiana Jones movies 47, 67
influences *see* media influences
institutional reflexivity 106–108
internet: representations of gender 65;
　used for research 15, 154; *see also*
　website of this book
interpellation 27
intimate relationships 97–98, 100,
　106–108, 112–113, 122–132

J-17 magazine 186, 193
Jackie magazine 182
Jackson, Peter 159, 166–176
Jackson, Stevi 189, 207
Jary, David 114
Jeepers Creepers 73
Jeffers, Susan 245
Jeffords, Susan 64, 66
Jolie, Angelina 39, 66, 73, 213
Jones, Indiana 47, 67
Jones, Liz 187, 194
July, William II 240
Jurassic Park III 73

Kane, Pat 8
Kaplan, E. Ann 10, 45, 48, 143
Kaspersen, Lars Bo 114
Kendall, Gavin 133
Kirkham, Pat 45
Kohlberg, L. 35
Kokaly, Michelle L. 216
Kosofsky Sedgwick, Eve 135

LA Law (TV series) 83
lad culture *see* masculinity; men's magazines

'ladettes' 69; *see also* girl power; strong women
Lara Croft 39, 72, 192, 213, 214, 216
late modernity 92, 95–98
Later magazine 160
Lauzen, Martha M. 58
Lehman, Peter 17
Lentricchia, Frank 119
lesbian characters: in movies 86–87; on TV 82–86
lesbian identities *see* sexuality
lesbian magazines 208–210
life as a work of art 130–131
lifestyles 102–104, 124–132; *see also* men's magazines; reflexive project of the self; self-help books; women's magazines
Lil' Kim 215
Lloyd, Fran 10, 143
Loaded magazine 79, 152–180; refutes idea that men like very skinny women 79
Lois and Clark (TV series) 61
Long Kiss Goodnight, The 40
Lorber, Judith 151
Lord of the Rings 72
Lucas, George 110
Lucky Break 74
Lyotard, Jean-Francois 96; *see also* postmodernity

Macdonald, Myra 56, 76
Madonna and queer theory 143
Madonna 10, 25, 86, 139, 143, 214, 217, 226
magazines: for lesbians and gay men 208–210; for men *see* men's magazines; for women *see* Foucault on 132; women's magazines
Maio, Kathi 48
male gaze *see* gaze
Malik, Sarita 14
Malim, Tony 34, 215
Marie Claire magazine 185–187, 192–194, 201–203, 219
Manson, Marilyn 21, 215, 221
marriage and divorce 3, 97, 123–124; *see also* intimate relationships
Martin, C. L. 35
Marxism 20–22, 92–93, 101
masculinity 6–9, 250–251, 253; advertising 80–81; and men's magazines 152–180; in movies 38–40, 45–47,

64–66, 69–75; and *NYPD Blue* 61–62; on television 59–63; in outdated studies 253; *see also* gender roles; representations of gender
Matlin, Margaret W. 37
Matrix, The 68, 73
Maxim magazine 97, 152, 155, 161–163, 166, 172–173, 175, 188
McCall's magazine 50
McGraw, Phillip C. 243–244
McKee, Robert 109–110
McNair, Brian 13
McNeil, J. 43
McRobbie, Angela: earlier work on Jackie 182; on new women's magazines 183, 189–190, 206–207; on popular feminism 252–253
media influences: passim, but *see* 1–2, 19–28; media 'effects' studies 28–33, 69
Melrose Place (TV series) 84
men *see* gender roles; masculinity; men's magazines
men's magazines 152–180; backlash against feminism 152–153, 173–175; content and circulation 156–166; emergence of 154–155; and existential disappointment 177; fear of intimacy 172–173; irony 167–172; polarisation of gender identities 175–176; sexism 167–172, 173–175; showing men 'lost' 179; social construction of masculinity as their subject matter 170; women's views 179–180
Messineo, Melinda 76
Meštrović, Stjepan G. 111–113, 145
methodology 15, 154
Mexican, The 74
Miles, B. 43
Miller, John L. 36
Miller, Stephen H. 82, 84
Minogue, Dannii 97
modernity: definition 16; *see also* postmodernity
Moorhead, Joanna 10
Morality in Media 88, 189
More magazine 39, 54, 97, 173, 186, 188–189, 199, 203, 249
Morley, David 27
movies and gender 38–40, 45–49, 64–75, 86–90

Ms magazine 51–52
Mulvey, Laura 36–41
Mummy Returns, The 73
Muncer, Steven 69
Murray, Jenni, criticises *Cosmopolitan* 191

narrative of the self *see* reflexive project of the self
narrative structures 109–111
Nauta, Margaret M. 216
new media *see* internet
New Woman magazine 185, 188–193
Next Best Thing, The 86
Nixon, Sean 155
Normal, Ohio (TV series) 85
Northern Exposure (TV series) 84
Number 96 (TV series) 82
Nussbaum, Martha 143–146
NYPD Blue (TV series) and representations of masculinity 61–62

O – The Oprah Magazine 186, 192
objectification: of men in women's magazines 187–188; of women in men's magazines 152–180
O'Donnell, Rosie 186, 214
Oranges are Not the Only Fruit (TV series) 83
Orbach, Susie 195, 212
Osborne, Peter 134, 142
Out magazine 208
outline of the book 14

Palmer, Patricia 32
Panic Room 72
Park, Myung-Jin 18
Party of Five (TV series) 85
passive audience 20–23
paternity leave 6
Patriot, The 72
Pennington, Donald C. 215
Perfect Storm, The 73
performance *see* gender roles
personal autonomy 17; *see also* gender roles
Pet Shop Boys 222–223
Phares, E. Jerry 34
Philadelphia 87
Phillips, Angela 212, 215
Phillips, E. Barbara 51, 52
Pierson, Christopher 93, 95, 114, 238

Pink 253
Pomerance, Murray 17
pop music 216–236
popular feminism 252–253
postmodernity 95–96, 151; versus modernity 16
post-traditional society 96, 103, 247–248; *see also* consumerism and identity; gender roles; Giddens
power of the media 19–33, 254–255
power: Foucault's model 117–122
presentation of self 104–106
psychology research 28–37; reinforcing status quo 35–37; on role models 215–216
pure relationship 98, 106, 113

Queen, Carol 151
Queer as Folk (TV series) 62, 84, 87, 150
queer theory 134–151, 254; and advertising 254; attacked by Edwards 146–151; attacked by Nussbaum 143–146; challenge to feminism 136–139, 143–146; further reading 151; gender as a performance 139–141; heterosexual matrix 137–139; inclusivity 150–151; and Madonna 143; on subversion and parody 140–144; summary 135

race *see* ethnicity and 'race'
Raiders of the Lost Ark 47, 67
Ralph magazine 168
Rapping, Elayne 237, 245
Rawnsley, Andrew 246
Red magazine 184, 186, 193
Redbook magazine 184, 193
reflexive project of the self 99–101, 109–111, 170, 237–239, 248–250; *see also* men's magazines; self-help books; women's magazines
relationships *see* intimate relationships
representations of gender: in advertising 54–56, 75–81; in men's magazines 152–180; more recently (1990–2002) 56–90; in movies 38–40, 45–49, 64–75, 86–90; in new media 65; in the past (1940–1990) 42–56; in pop music 216–236; in self-help books 237–245; on television 43–45, 58–64; in women's magazines 50–54

resistance and power (Foucault) 120–122
respectability 11–12
Richards, Denise, as nuclear scientist 49
Richardson, Diane 151
role models: examples 211–214; types
    214–216; psychological research
    215–216; girl power 216–220; Spice
    Girls 216–219; Destiny's Child
    219–220; Britney Spears 224–236; as
    navigation points 249–250
roles *see* gender roles
romantic love, emergence of 100
Roseanne (TV series) 84, 85
Rosen, Marjorie 47
Rosie magazine 186, 192
Ross, Karen 14

Said, Edward W. 119
Sarup, Madan 133
Scheibe, C. 55
Schimel, Lawrence 151
Schirato, Tony 153, 168
Schlesinger, Philip 32
Schlessinger, Laura 82, 240–241, 244
school and gender 5, 10, 94, 178, 203,
    221–223, 251
Schwichtenberg, Cathy 10, 143
scopophilia 38
Scream movie trilogy 73
Sedgwick, Eve Kosofsky *see* Kosofsky
    Sedgwick, Eve
Segal, Lynne 134, 142, 151
self-help books 7, 108, 237–245,
    250–251; aimed at men 240–241;
    aimed at women 241; bad relationship
    advice 242–243; and emotional literacy
    245–246; and personal narratives and
    lifestyles 238–239; significance of
    237–238; summary of messages
    244–245
self-identity: concluding thoughts
    247–256; and fans of Britney Spears
    227–236; and Giddens 96–114; and
    men's magazines 166–180; as a
    performance 134–151; and self-help
    books 237–245; and women's
    magazines 199–200
self-restraint 130–131
sex and identity 101, 121–133
Sex and the City (TV series) 59–61
sex roles *see* gender roles

sexual assertiveness of women 53–54,
    76–77, 183–193
sexuality: acceptance of diversity 12–13,
    107, 253–254; anti-gay campaigners
    87–90; creation of the 'homosexual'
    category 121–122, 128; emerging
    alternative sexualities on TV 82–86;
    gay characters in movies 86–87; gay and
    lesbian magazines 208–210; gay
    lifestyles 131–132; history of sexuality
    115–133; homophobia 87–90; and the
    self 101, 121–133; queer theory
    134–151; *see also* intimate relationships
She magazine 185
Simonds, Wendy 245
Skeggs, Beverley 11–12
skinny women: myth of attractiveness 79;
    see also body image
Smallville (TV series) 61
Smith, Sharon 48
Smith, Tom W. 3, 249
social constructionism: definition 16; *see*
    gender roles
social learning theory 34
Some Like it Hot 46
Soutar, Mike 156–157, 162
Southwell, Tim 159, 171
Spears, Britney 61, 224–236, 252; attitude
    to gay dancers 226; on being a role
    model 226; career 224; criticised by
    Christians 225; fan responses 227–236
Speed 40
Spice Girls 216–219
Spicer, Andrew 17
Spin City (TV series) 85
Stacey, Jackie 40
Stald, Gitte 18
Star Trek: The Next Generation (TV series)
    26, 63–64
Star Trek: Voyager (TV series) 63–64
Star Wars 46, 110
Starr, Alexandra 190–191
Stevenson, Nick 159, 166–176
Stine, Jean Marie 239
Strange Days 40
Strinati, Dominic 55
strong women: in movies 39–40, 46–49,
    64–75; on TV 45; in magazines 53–54,
    187–193; in pop music 216–220,
    224–236; in self-help discourses 241; *see
    also* girl power

structuration theory 92–94
subversion and parody in queer theory 140–144
Sullivan, Andrew 166
Summerskill, Ben 171
Supergirl 46
Swordfish 21
symbolic annihilation of women (Tuchman) 43–44

Tales of the City (TV series) 84–85
Tasker, Yvonne 17, 40, 45
technologies of the self 125–129
television, passim, but *see* 43–45, 58–64, 82–86
ten things wrong with the media effects model 28–33
Terminator movies 40, 46, 65
testosterone 8
text: definition 16
The Advocate magazine 208
therapy *see* self-help
third way (Giddens) 92–93
Thirtysomething (TV series) 82
This Life (TV series) 84
Thompson, Emma 215
Three Men and a Baby 47
Thumim, Janet 45
Titanic 110
Tomb Raider see *Lara Croft*
toys and gender socialisation 10
tradition *see* post-traditional society
transformations 5, 13, 85, 106, 115–116, 129, 141, 145, 213, 240, 253, 256; *see also* gender roles; reflexive project of the self; self-help
transsexuals 82, 85–86; *see also* sexuality
Tuchman, Gaye 43–44, 51, 54
Tucker, Kenneth H. 114

Van Zoonen, Liesbet 17, 40
Vernon, Polly 61
violence *see* effects
Vogler, Christopher 109–110

Vogue magazine 185, 194, 199, 201

Walter, Natasha 78
website of this book 18
What Women Want 69–72
Whedon, Joss 61
Whelehan, Imelda 152–153
Whiteley, Sheila 218
Wickham, Gary 133
Wilke, Michael 82, 85
Will and Grace (TV series) 85
Williams, J. E. 35
Willis, Bruce 38
Wilson, Katherine 36
Winfrey, Oprah 6, 127, 186, 192, 237, 243
Winship, Janice 52–54, 153
women: in business 4; representation in parliaments 4; in media *see* as not one single category 136–139; representations of gender; *see also* femininity; gender roles; women's magazines
women's magazines 181–207; the academic debate (1970s–1990s) 182–183; and body image 191, 194–195; content and circulation 183–187; criticised by readers 202–204; heterosexual focus 189–190; ideal woman 200–202; men as sex objects 187–188; 'pick and mix' reading 196–198, 206; reader responses 193, 196–205; on relationships 190–191; on sex and sexuality 189–191; and thinking about identity 199–200
Woods, Tim 214
Woodward, Will 5

X-Men 73; as allegory for homophobia 87–90

Yell, Susan 153, 168
YM – Your Magazine 186–187, 188, 193

Ziglar, Zig 240